LITERATURE IN THE MODERN WORLD

# BLOCK 5
# END OF EMPIRE

*Prepared for the course team by Richard Allen, Angus Calder, Cicely Palser Havely, Graham Martin and Michael Rossington*

CW01597431

A319

Arts: a third level course

The Open University

### The course team

Richard Allen (author)
Jenny Bardwell (BBC producer)
Richard Bessel (author)
Dinah Birch (author)
Angus Calder (author)
Kate Clements (editor)
Tony Coe (BBC series producer and author)
Charles Cooper (BBC producer)
Tony Coulson (librarian)
Abigail Croydon (editor)
Roger Day (author)
Andrew Ferguson (course manager)
Margaret Harvey (block rapporteur)
Cicely Palser Havely (author)
Pam Higgins (graphic designer)
Barbara Humphreys (secretary)
G.D. Jayalakshmi (BBC producer)
Denis Johnson (tuition group chair)
Maggie Lawson (Project Control)
Beth Martin (BBC producer)
Graham Martin (course team chair, author)
Mags Noble (BBC producer)
W.R. Owens (editor of anthologies)
John Pettit (editor)
Michael Rossington (author)
Sue Staig (secretary)
Betty Talks (BBC producer)
Nora Tomlinson (tuition group)
Dennis Walder (author)
Keith Whitlock (author)
Amanda Willett (BBC producer)
Richard Wilson (block rapporteur)

**Consultants**

Dr Pamela Morris, member of the Open University's teaching and counselling staff (block assessor)
Professor Michael Wood, department of English literature at the University of Exeter (external assessor)

The Open University
Walton Hall, Milton Keynes MK7 6AA

First published 1991. Reprinted 1995, 1996, 1998



Typeset in 10 on 12 point Palatino.

Printed in the United Kingdom by Page Bros, Norwich

ISBN 0 7492 1039 7

This block is part of an Open University course. The complete list of blocks is given at the end of this binding.

If you have not enrolled on the course and would like to buy this or other Open University material, please write to Open University Educational Enterprises Limited, 12 Cofferidge Close, Stony Stratford, Milton Keynes, MK11 1BY, United Kingdom.

If you wish to enquire about enrolling as an Open University student, please write to: The Admissions Office, The Open University, PO Box 48, Walton Hall, Milton Keynes MK7 6AB, United Kingdom.

1.4

# Contents

*(Richard Allen wrote Sections 2 and 3; Cicely Palser Havely wrote Sections 5 and 6; Graham Martin wrote Section 1; Michael Rossington wrote Sections 4 and 7, except for the sub-section on Sorley MacLean which was written by Angus Calder)*

## Required reading

E.M. Forster (1989) *A Passage to India*, Penguin, first published in 1924 (set book)

John Arden, *Serjeant Musgrave's Dance* (in the Drama Anthology)

Poems by Philip Larkin, Ted Hughes, Geoffrey Hill, Donald Davie, Tony Harrison, Sorley MacLean and Kingsley Amis printed in the Poetry Anthology and the Broadcast and Cassette Notes.

*From the A319 Reader*

Edward Said, 'The discourse of the Orient'

Sara Suleri, 'The geography of *A Passage to India*'

Seamus Heaney, 'Englands of the mind'

(The A319 Reader is *Literature in the Modern World*, edited by Dennis Walder, 1990, Oxford University Press/The Open University.)

## Broadcasts/cassettes

TV 8 *Empire and Nation* (linked with Section 2)

TV9 *'Serjeant Musgrave' at the Court* (linked with Section 6)

Radio 8 *Indian views of Forster* (linked with Section 3)

Radio 9 *Poetry and the End of Empire: Larkin and Hughes* (linked with Section 7)

Radio 10 *Englands of the Mind*? (linked with Section 7)

Audio-cassette 3 Side 1, 'Sorley Maclean' (linked with Section 7)

Audio-cassettes 5 and 6, *'Serjeant Musgrave's Dance'* by John Arden (linked with Section 6)

(See also the Broadcast and Cassette Notes.)

## Aims and objectives

The principal aim of this block is to explore the reverberations within British literary culture of the dissolution of the British Empire, by detailed discussion of E.M. Forster's novel *A Passage to India* (1924), John Arden's play *Serjeant Musgrave's Dance* (1960), and a selection of British poetry, 1950–*c*.1980, by Philip Larkin, Ted Hughes, Geoffrey Hill, Tony Harrison and Sorley MacLean.

# 1 Introduction

*1.1* The block title, *End of Empire,* refers specifically to the British Empire, but when did it end? Was it in 1947, when Britain formally granted independence to India, long the centre-piece of the empire? Yet major African colonies – Kenya, Tanganyika, Nigeria and Northern Rhodesia – did not achieve political sovereignty until the early 1960s, nor did Fiji until 1970, the Bahamas until 1973. But it could also be argued that the key years were 1940–41 when, in exchange for American economic support in the war with Germany, Britain initiated the process whereby its imperial world-political role was eventually to be taken over by America. Our concern is with the effect of this extended history on British literary culture, influenced less by specific events than by how these were perceived, how they became an explicit element in the national consciousness. After the Suez débâcle of 1956, such consciousness had to register the inescapable fact that Britain could no longer sustain a world-political role independently of the United States. Together with France, Britain had invaded Egypt in order to maintain its imperial power in the Middle East, and when America refused support, that was the end of the affair. So, for the purposes of this block, 'end of empire' dates from the post-1956 years when it was clear that Britain could no longer act as if it were the centre of a world-wide empire.

*1.2* How did this recognition affect British literary culture? That Britain *was* an imperial power had certainly influenced writers since the 1890s. Rudyard Kipling's stories and poems expressed a passionate commitment to the imperial world-mission of Anglo-Saxondom. For Kipling, this was a lofty moral duty, the successful exercise of which would eventually bring the conquered 'backward' races, conceived as surly and undisciplined children, towards a civilized adulthood – a conviction responsible for much of his wide popularity in the first decades of the twentieth century. Other writers were more critical. In his novel *Howards End* (1910), E.M. Forster brooded over the question of whether the true spirit of his country was represented, not by its world-conquering imperialists, but rather by its poets and artists. By the time he completed *A Passage to India* in 1924 he was emphatically anti-imperialist. In the 1930s such liberal anti-imperialism became widespread. Auden (as we noticed in Block 3 Section 4) saw in the industrial stagnation of the post-Depression years unmistakable evidence that England's imperial history, together with that of the industrial and entrepreneurial middle class that had made it possible, was coming to an end. But the response of writers to that end, during and after the 1950s, was not uniform. The difficult question it posed engaged a writer's sense of the national identity: given the imperial history, and given that it had ended, what did it now mean to be an 'English' writer? For John Arden it meant attacking the military tradition (fostered by imperialism) on behalf of the industrial working class. For individual poets it meant a search for new conceptions of 'Englishness', and in literary culture generally it marked the emergence of writers previously ignored or marginalized.

*1.3* The study material for this block extends over five weeks, and falls into three parts. The first part, consisting of Sections 2–5 together with material printed in the Reader, discusses *A Passage to India* from a number of angles. This should be studied in the first two weeks. The second part, consisting of Section 6, together with the written text of *Serjeant Musgrave's Dance* and the performance of it recorded on Audio-cassettes 5 and 6, should be studied in the third week. The third part consists of Section 7, the relevant poems printed in the Poetry Anthology and the Broadcast and Cassette Notes and discussed on Audio-cassette 3 Side 1, and material printed in the Reader, and should be studied in the fourth and fifth weeks.

*1.4* Section 2 ('Empire, imperialism and literature') surveys aspects of the history of British rule in India underlining the fact that this had an important cultural strand and was not just confined to political and economic factors. It also discusses the meaning of the terms 'imperialism' and 'end of empire', issues directly relevant to the study of Forster's novel, but having a further relevance to texts studied later in the block. Section 3 considers Forster's novel in detail, and in relation to the issues set out in Section 2. Though published in 1924, *A Passage to India*, as a classic statement of English liberal anti-imperialism, was widely read and studied in the post-war years. The strengths and limitations of its critique of imperialism debated in this section are discussed further in Section 4 ('Orientalism'), which considers the novel in the light of European attitudes towards 'the East', attitudes that constructed an imaginary realm, and so prevented a true understanding of its historical reality. Section 5 carries forward the gender theme of the course in relation to the novel, and in discussing the issue of race points forward to Block 6. Section 6 discusses Arden's play, *Serjeant Musgrave's Dance*, in detail, both in relation to the block theme and to the question of its 'performance', developing the discussion of drama begun in Block 1 about *Endgame*. Section 7 considers poems by Larkin, Hughes, Hill and Harrison, exploring the degree to which the end of empire involved them in a fresh definition of their identity as English poets, and debating the argument proposed by the Irish poet Seamus Heaney, that their work draws upon different 'Englands of the mind'. The section concludes with a discussion of the Scottish Gaelic poet, Sorley MacLean, illustrating a hitherto marginalized and ignored British literary and cultural tradition.

2 EMPIRE, IMPERIALISM AND LITERATURE

# 2 *Empire, imperialism and literature*

*2.1* In this section I want you to think about the theme of the block and reflect on the word 'empire' and the related word 'imperialism'. I hope you will carry forward the ideas discussed in the previous block and remember the kinds of complex ideological relationships which we can trace between the texts examined there, the societies and cultures from which they originate, and those in which they are read.

*2.2* I should state openly that in this section I hope to provoke your thoughts by suggesting a specific way of thinking about empire and imperialism, and by putting forward a thesis about how we can think about twentieth-century literature in English in this context. I believe that it is very difficult to establish how literature is related to events which are, in simple terms, non-literary. On one hand there is the extreme position that literary texts *always* reflect events in the society in which they are produced. On the other hand it is argued that the boundary between fiction and reality is so blurred as to make mapping out a simple relation between them meaningless. What is certain is that literature is not separate from reality (or the non-literary). I find it comparatively straightforward to discover, for example, a parallel between a description of a character in James Joyce's novel *Ulysses* and a real person in Dublin described by his brother Stanislaus Joyce, and I am happy to assert with confidence that in *some* way *The Waste Land* is related to changes in twentieth-century society. But proving a direct and simple relationship in either case is hazardous, risking reducing the complexity of the historical moment, and the text, to absurdity.

*2.3* The British Empire was a worldwide phenomenon which was at the height of its power from around 1850. Its nature and the specific terms of its social and cultural organizations varied from place to place and I cannot explore these variations in the space available here. For this reason, and to allow this discussion to provide a context for your reading of *A Passage to India*, I shall concentrate my examples on the British Empire in India. India was, in any event, politically and economically at the heart of the British Empire, contributing huge amounts to both private and public purses from the early eighteenth century. The Indian Civil Service provided careers for the British middle class, and the Indian Army provided a force to police the empire. It is important to remember that, when we refer to the Indian Empire in the period 1876 to 1947, we mean not just the British Empire in India, but the Empire of India itself, wholly subordinate to London but ruling the modern states of India, Pakistan, Bangladesh, Burma and Sri Lanka.

## The nature of empire

*2.4* In the history of the western world the word 'empire' is used most commonly of the Ancient Roman Empire, the Spanish Empire, the Austro-Hungarian Empire and the British Empire. What kind of political, economic and cultural structures were characteristic of these empires? Each had its own special qualities, but in all of them, one state or nation controlled others, and I will now explore the nature of that control. Control can operate at some or all of a number of different levels in ways that are explored by Raymond Williams as follows:

> If imperialism, as normally defined in late nineteenth-century England, is primarily a political system in which colonies are governed from an imperial centre, for economic but also for other reasons held to be important, then the subsequent grant of independence or self-government to these colonies can be described ... as 'the end of imperialism'. On the other hand, if imperialism is understood primarily as an economic system of external investment and the penetration and control of markets and sources of raw materials, political changes in the status of colonies or former colonies will not greatly affect description of the continuing economic system as imperialist.
>
> (Williams, 1983, pp.159–60)

Within the British Empire this means that until independence (and sometimes after) a legal case initially brought to a court in Africa might end up being judged by the Privy Council in London. In the eighteenth and nineteenth centuries huge fortunes earned from cheap labour or cheap natural resources were transferred from Africa and Asia to support British aristocratic society, and control of the capital has remained in Britain.

*2.5* But, as Williams suggests, the relationship of imperial power and colony may not always be so directly visible. In India, for example, force was used to subdue the population and was the ultimate guarantor of British power. At the end of the eighteenth century Warren Hastings spoke of 'a dominion founded on the right of conquest' (Viswanathan, 1988, p.6), and after the first Indian War of Independence in 1867 the British reasserted their control with some ferocity. During the twentieth century too the British suppressed 'rebellion' vigorously. But for most of the last decades of the nineteenth century, and the beginning of the twentieth century, the white British garrison was comparatively modest in relation to the size of the Indian population, and its regiments depended heavily on Indian soldiers (who were, it need hardly be added, confined to the non-commissioned ranks). Imperial policy fostered the illusion of ruling by consent or in partnership with the Indians; for much of the nineteenth century, the British were dedicated to preserving 'an illusion of permanence'. In the nineteenth century

> A permanent *raj* seemed a practical possibility and to be confirmed by racial and political and religious theories as both sound and high-principled. In retrospect, the extent of the British dedication to this illusion of permanence seems to have been both regrettable and dangerous. The Empire, seemingly so stable, was in reality growing ever more fragile...
>
> (Hutchins, 1967, p.xii)

*2.6* In much of India the illusion that the empire would last forever was sustained by the way British power and presence infiltrated all of Indian life. The British controlled national and local government, but their efforts did not stop at such administrative actions. According to a plaque in the Red Fort at Agra, close to the Taj Mahal, it was to Sir John Stachey that 'India is mainly indebted for the rescued and preserved beauty of the Taj Mahal and other famous monuments'. Almost as an afterthought the plaque notes 'not forgetting the enlightened sympathy and timely care of others'; perhaps *some* of these were Indian! But for large parts of southern and central India – approximately two-fifths of the continent – a different pattern prevailed. In these parts the Indian princes appeared to be in control, governing in an Indian rather than a British way. However

> all of them [these Indian states], big and small, recognised the paramountcy of the British Government. In return the British guaranteed the Princes against any threat to their autocratic power, internal or external. Most of the princely States were run as unmitigated autocracies, with absolute power concentrated in the hands of the ruler, or his favourites.
>
> (Chandra *et al.*, 1989, p.356)

The state of Dewas Senior, where Forster worked in 1921, is an example of one of these Indian states, though perhaps not the most representative. The Maharajah was effectively installed, sustained and ultimately dismissed by the British. On the basis of his experience there Forster wrote, in 1922:

> History is full of ironies, and it is strange to reflect that those parts of India which the British deprived of independence are now the most independent ... the individual [Indian there] ... may hate the British and have good reason for doing so, but he would not exchange their yoke for an Indian Prince's...
>
> (*Abinger Harvest*, p.362)

To Forster's liberal mind the British sustained a more progressive ideology of citizenship where they ruled directly. The more cynical might say that they also sustained bastions of reaction in the Indian states precisely to sustain the illusion that British rule was benevolent.

*2.7* The idea of an Indian Empire was particularly emphasized after Victoria was proclaimed Empress of India in 1876 with a Viceroy heading an impressive government machine in India. But real executive authority continued to be dictated remotely by the Secretary of State for India who was a member of the Cabinet in London. Telegrams passed endlessly between Bengal and London. One might argue that throughout the British Empire the direct power relations between British political authority and the colonies were continually obscured by superficial measures to give the subservient states apparent autonomy. In other ways too the idea of one nation being clearly subordinate to another became apparently less clear as, especially in Africa and Australia, those who went out as foreigners to the colonies became settlers whose successors were apparently natives of the country.

*2.8* These political and economic processes are paralleled, as I have already implied, by cultural processes; colonial relationships and nationalist resistance were founded as much in cultural terms as in political structures, and then as now, education was a key vehicle for the transmission of culture. English literature played a key role in the process, particularly towards the end of the nineteenth century and at the beginning of the twentieth century. A specific example of the way the British controlled and banned Indian literature is described in TV8 *Empire and Nation*. At a first glance it might seem that British education and culture were simply imposed on India from an arrogant belief that they were superior and more advanced, but such a statement conceals the extent of the debates about the process which took place in Britain and in India.

*2.9* Education on British principles was initially introduced into India during the debates about the morality of those running the British East India Company. To Edmund Burke the immorality of these people had reached such a pitch that education was necessary to 'form a strong and solid security for the natives against the wrongs and oppressions of British subjects resident in Bengal' (Stokes, 1959, p.2); British virtues, apparently, were necessary to defend oneself against British vices. During the nineteenth century, as control of India passed from the private company to the British government and the foundations of the Indian Empire were laid and consolidated, there was a continuing debate between the British orientalists, who believed that one needed to understand the culture of Indians in order to govern them *and* that the accumulation of knowledge about Indian culture was to the good of mankind, and those one might describe as Anglicists, for whom the political skills necessary to equip someone to be a citizen of the Empire could only be learnt by an absorption of British education and traditions. Reforms in British education, particularly as symbolized by Thomas Arnold's work at Rugby, and later following principles developed by Matthew Arnold, were paralleled by developments in British cultural imperialism in India. This debate continued into the twentieth century and an interesting exchange took place in the years when Forster was writing *A Passage to India*. In 1917 a famous literary critic, William Archer, published *India and the Future* in which he came to the conclusion that 'the plain truth concerning the mass of the [Indian] population – and not the poorer classes alone – is that they are not civilised people' (Woodroffe, 1919, p.1). In particular Archer attacked Indian art and culture, claiming, for example, that it:

> tends to extravagance and excess ... There is more spirituality in ... the ideal head of Homer, seamed by suffering and furrowed by thought, than in the whole pantheon of Buddhist or Hindu sculpture.
>
> (Woodroffe, 1919, pp.159–60)

*2.10* Archer was in tune with the ideas of many of the British in India. A leader in *The Calcutta Daily*, for example, saw Indian Independence as unthinkable because it would put the British – who were to be in India for ever, you will remember – under the control of those 'who are not his peers in the sense of their having attained to the same plane of civilization and culture' (Woodroffe, 1919, p.146). A weighty response came from Sir John Woodroffe in a book titled ironically *Is India Civilised?* which lavished praise on a distinctly Indian culture. Woodroffe allows that India had achieved much in science and industry before the arrival of the British but his main emphasis is on the spirituality of Indian civilization. For him the future for India lay in the recovery of 'her urge towards the spiritual and the eternal [which] constitutes the distinct value of Her civilisation'. If this occurs not only will India be saved but also the world; 'either India will be rationalised and industrialised [by the British], or by her example ... She will spiritualise humanity' (Woodroffe, 1919, pp.39–40).

*2.11* Throughout the nineteenth and early twentieth centuries the imperial state viewed British religion with a scepticism which matched that shown by Woodroffe in his championing of Indian spirituality. Christian churches were built all over India for conqueror and conquered, but there was a fear that missionary zeal would inflame the subject race. English literature, which had already been invested with great significance in Britain as a way of teaching ethical living, was exported to provide a safer option avoiding both Christian fanaticism and oriental excess. For C.F. Trevelyan, writing in 1838, British education and English literature were clearly morally and spiritually uplifting:

> [the Indians] daily converse with the best and wisest Englishmen through the medium of their works, and form ideas, perhaps higher ideas of our nation than if their intercourse with it were of a more personal kind...
>
> (quoted in Viswanathan, 1988, p.23)

Viswanathan comments that, for these imperialists, 'the political significance of English literature rested on its inclining one's thoughts towards religion while maintaining its secular nature'.

*2.12* These developments in education and attitudes towards literature created in due course a long-standing market for English books in India which the British administration fuelled by suppressing Indian books; even among orientalists the impression was created that only a savage culture existed in India before 1800. In a continuing process the imperial state exerted its power culturally by flooding the empire with its own culture and values in its books and later in films. The educational system created in the colonies followed the British model and was directed towards that in Britain, so that the best scholars of the empire saw a natural destination in Britain and were rewarded with places at Oxford or Cambridge. The sons of the families who served the British attended British public schools, or copies of those schools in the colonies; E.M. Forster's close friend, Syed Ross Masood, was an example of the process. He was the grandson of Sir Syed Ahmed Khan who – with British encouragement – had founded the Muslim Anglo-Oriental College in 1875 at Aligarh, 'a sort of Muslim Eton' (Furbank, 1977, p.143). After attending this college Masood came to England, first to learn Latin (Forster became his tutor) and then to go to Oxford. In later life Masood returned to India to become an influential figure in education, and when Forster visited India in 1921, he was Director of Public Education in Hyderabad – a state particularly loyal to British rule – and involved in the founding of the Muslim Osmania University. British and Indian values were absolutely intermixed in his work and his character. Furbank describes him as remaining 'a blazing Muslim patriot, full of nostalgia for the splendour of the Mogul past' (p.143) and, thus, just as critical of the Hindus as were the British, and equally at home in western society, easily able to outface any English snobbery or racism with a forthright 'English' manliness.

## Empire and imperialism

*2.13* So far in this section I have not distinguished particularly between empire and imperialism. I now want to emphasize the difference between the two words and to suggest that for British culture and English literature during the period of the course, imperialism (and the adjective form, imperialist) is the key term. Dictionary definitions indicate that empire refers to a set of territories governed by an emperor, while imperialism describes the attitudes (and often enthusiasms) of the rulers. One might combine the terms in a sentence as follows: 'The empire is composed of states under the rule of the emperor who lives in the imperial palace supported by a government keen to pursue imperialist policies confident that their imperialism will be unchallenged.' You might have noticed that I am using the word 'empire' in a way that chimes with the first sentence of the quote from Raymond Williams in paragraph 2.4, and 'imperialism' to convey the process he described in the second sentence.

*2.14* British imperialism is then not limited within the time period that the British Empire existed, or was at its height, as a political structure (perhaps 1840–1965). Parts of the West Indies, for example, remain dependent on the British trade in sugar or bananas. Equally, more general links on the basis of a common language persist, as in the cases of Australia and South Africa. India provides an interesting example in this context. It is argued by some that English is the only language that can serve as a national language for India as a whole, and must be preserved as such to avoid the country falling into internal wrangling about which Indian language should be elevated to national status. As a national Indian language, it is argued, Indian English has already developed its own specific independent forms much as American or Australian English have. The imperial language remains but imperialism is downplayed. For others the use of English is regrettably more or less inevitable because it is the language of international high technology and trade; they resent its continuing presence precisely because it is a sign of lingering imperialism, and wish to raise further the standing of regional cultures. Britain itself retains a sense of imperialist importance as part of the developed world able to give charity and technological aid to ex-colonies. This apparently dependent relationship is given a kind of formal status through the continuing institution of the Commonwealth; no matter how isolated Britain may be in this group it seems, as I write, inconceivable that it should either leave or be expelled.

*2.15* In many now autonomous countries, previously part of the British Empire, British imposed educational systems have persisted. Pupils in what are regarded by many as the best schools in India are likely to wear British-style school uniforms (whatever the climate) and to work from books published by Longman on English literature, often without considering the works as written in a 'foreign' language. In a less direct way for Britain, the signs of cultural dominance remain in the world because English is the language of the economic empire of the USA.

*2.16* Imperialist thinking depends on assumptions of superiority based on nationality and race.

> Even in the rudest stages of civilisation, the European has exhibited a firmness, perseverance and enterprise, which strikingly contrast with the feeble, slow and irresolute character of the Hindoo. In the performance of ordinary labour … the labour of one Englishman is equal to that of three ordinary Indians.
>
> (quoted in Hutchins, 1967, p.68)

In *Is India Civilised?* Woodroffe summarizes tartly the thinking that underlies 'such falsities and hypocrisies': 'The cultural attack by Europe on the East is, in short, an effort to save its own psychic possessions by the assimilation of that which opposes them' (p.36). The idea of some higher cause or some principle of natural justice also covers up the naked fact of power and control. Around 1800 Warren Hastings wrote that:

> ...every accumulation of knowledge and especially such as is obtained by social communication with people over whom we exercise a dominion founded on the right of conquest, is useful to the state: *it is the gain of humanity*.
>
> (quoted in Viswanathan, 1988, p.6, my italics)

Despite all the shifts in imperial policy towards India after his fall from power, Hastings's words strike a key-note for what was to follow. Imperial ideology was intricately bound up with notions of 'humanity' – Indians were to be drawn from their Asiatic darkness into western enlightenment – and 'state' – Britain's role was to provide India with political institutions and citizens based on the British model. Even independence could eventually be drawn into this framework:

> We must apply ourselves to bring the natives into a state that will admit of their governing themselves in a manner that may be beneficial to our interests, as well as their own and that of the rest of the world.
>
> (quoted in Woodroffe, 1919, p.93)

*2.17* Indian culture – such as the *Rhadika Santwanam* that provides a focus for TV8 – and Indian civil society is suppressed, thus destroying

> ...the liberal ideas which had gained ground in Indian society in the previous period and which were ... ushering in a progressive life in India with a permanent rapprochement between the Hindus and Moslems and the eradication of decadent customs and institutions.
>
> (Mukherjee, 1974, p.316)

Imperialism sets the agenda and occupies all the ground of the argument, leaving for those like Woodroffe only spirituality as a counter force. For E.M. Forster even this seemed not to provide sure ground, as we shall see.

*2.18* The statements of British imperialist ideology are, in general, more important as a way of understanding British attitudes than as a way of understanding India. British colonial administrators of the kind caricatured by Forster in *A Passage to India* – and by those of a more liberal persuasion – saw themselves in paternal and patriarchal terms, and such ways of seeing have arguably characterized British attitudes to its ex-colonies beyond the 'end of empire'. The very phrase 'end of empire' preserves the imperialist perspective; from that perspective colonies are not seen as overthrowing an economically exploitative and repressive imperial yoke – thus revealing weakness in the imperial power – but as becoming 'independent'. The sense of defeat, whether in military or political terms, is concealed and the situation of the imperial state is confused by the use of, for example, the metaphor of the family. 'Independence' is construed among the enlightened imperialists as a sign of maturity in both the imperial 'parent' and the colonial 'child'; the troubles that occur when independence is sought are natural, as the child moves from the care of the parent to a perhaps disturbed adolescence.

*2.19* The strength of imperialist ideology is not only that it includes the idea of natural superiority but also that it can absorb almost any attack on its power. It can absorb the decline of empire while avoiding the notion that it is a defeat; it is this aspect that is important in the twentieth century and which I want to explore in the next section.

## The empire triumphant

*2.20* You have already encountered one example of the way the tensions between colonizer and colonized can be resolved in Kipling's story 'A Sahibs' War' (see Block 4 Section 2). Equally strong is the representation of imperial supremacy in Kipling's poem 'The White Man's Burden'. In this poem, often included in anthologies, the image of the so-called 'native' is of 'fluttered folk ... new caught ... half devil and half child'. The representation of the superiority of the white man is equally striking. The rule of the white man is for 'another's profit'; he stands 'guard' while they are 'brought ... *from* bondage' (my italics). The title of the poem is repeated in each verse to emphasize the process; power is a 'burden' for which one receives neither praise nor thanks, and little sign of triumph. Imperialism is a burden (that is, something from which one would gladly escape) but something which must necessarily be borne. The poem entirely obscures the fact that the burden rests on the colonized, in the form of taxes, unfair trade, and so on. This is concealed by the idea of duty and it is this that permits domination. Forster catches this process neatly in an exchange at the end of chapter V of *A Passage to India*:

> 'We're out here to do justice and keep the peace. Them's my sentiments...
> 'Your sentiments are those of a god,' she said quietly...
> Trying to recover his temper, he said, 'India likes gods.'
> 'And Englishmen like posing as gods' [she replied].
>
> (p.69)

*2.21* Superiority is seen as a permanent condition and this allowed the sense of crisis that continually arose to remain under control. The sense of permanence was buttressed by a comparison with other great empires; Kipling, for example, wrote a number of stories and poems which purported to be about Roman Britain but which actually bear more sharply on British India (see the story 'A Centurion of the Thirteenth', the poems 'A Pict Song' and 'A Song to Mithras'). A Victorian historian of India saw 1835 as a turning point in the British occupation of India because it was then that 'we deliberately recognised that a function had developed on us in Asia similar to that which Rome fulfilled in Europe' (Seeley, 1883, p.253).

*2.22* But anyone reflecting on the history of the Roman Empire or other great imperial civilizations could hardly fail to see that the history of previous empires is universally one of decline. Furthermore, the process of that decline has been arguably more fascinating than the triumph of the empire. In a wide-ranging discussion of Gibbon's famous work, *Decline and Fall of the Roman Empire*, and the context in which he wrote, Peter Burke shows that for more than 400 years the decline of Roman power fascinated historians who were often themselves subjects of new but more temporary sacred or secular empires: 'decline is seen as natural, more natural in fact than stability' (Burke, 1977, p.94). The Roman example thus epitomizes triumph and transforms a sense of decline into something fine.

*2.23* Throughout its history the British Empire resonated as much with crises as with confidence and triumph in a way that I can only touch on here. In the eighteenth century some saw the result of the American colonies as an indictment of declining values in Britain. In 1776 Richard Price wrote:

> From one end of North America to the other they are fasting and praying. But what are we doing? – shocking thought. – We are running wild after pleasure and forgetting everything serious and decent ...We are gambling in gaming houses: trafficking in boroughs: perjuring ourselves at elections: and selling ourselves for places – which side is Providence likely to favour?
>
> (quoted in Plumb, 1963, p.135)

If we educated the Indians on British lines, some argued, this would lead them to emulate the Americans. In the mid-nineteenth century the Sepoy Revolt of 1857 provoked a crisis in British attitudes. Before 1857 it had been accepted that Providence had decreed that Britain would inevitably reform 'the abominable depravity' of Indian culture (Hutchins, 1967, p.84), but the Revolt struck 'at the inner core of the English nation' (p.85) and especially at this belief in the providential nature of empire. The reaction was extreme, fuelling white racism and limiting Indian involvement in government. The continuing stability of the empire seemed equally threatened by the South African wars at the end of the century. David Thomson described the period 1895 to 1905 as one of aggression and jingoism in foreign policy, but ascribes this as much to a sense of threat as of confidence: 'it was another expression of ... [a] consciousness of decline ... It was the truculence that came from a great Power, recently so complacent in its greatness, finding itself ... suddenly ... on the defensive...' (Thomson, 1950, pp.203–4). In the twentieth century in India, nationalism and specific events such as the Amritsar Massacre provoked a further sense of crisis; in a Commons debate Edwin Montagu,

Secretary of State for India from 1917 to 1922, saw the reforms in India as 'fundamental to a continuance of the British Empire and vital to the continuation, permanent, I believe it can be, of the connection between this country and India' (quoted in Draper, 1981, p.229).

*2.24* The kind of contradiction that can be contained by imperialist ideology in the early twentieth century can be seen in the building of the huge imperial city of New Delhi, originally conceived in 1911 but not built until 1921–30. It was an extraordinary sign of imperial confidence, especially since it coincided with the continuing nationalist struggle which had taken on something of its final form with the return of Gandhi to India in 1915: 'from the latter part of 1927 ... the curve of the mass anti-imperialist upsurge began to take a marked upward turn' (Chandra *et al.*, 1989, p.260). From a different point of view Forster was, in 1924, already writing of the 'gathering tragedy' of British rule in India.

*2.25* The process I am suggesting exists takes a different form in the late twentieth century as colonies were granted independence, and the imperialist ideology had to adapt to accommodate a series of crises arising from the rapid contraction of the empire and redefinitions of Britain's strength and duty. The activities of nationalists in a succession of countries cast doubt on the ability of Britain to guarantee its power by military force or cultural supremacy. Some would say that the attack on imperial power and the stresses within the imperial ideology were too great, and that by the middle of the twentieth century imperialism had been relegated to a minor role. I believe that this is not the case and that the imperial ideology survived (even fed on) the apparently final crisis to be redefined in a new and powerful form in both cultural and commercial terms.

*2.26* It can, for instance, be argued as forming Britain's response to developing federalism within Europe. Britain preferred at first to continue as the leader of the world-wide network of the Commonwealth, and through language and history to claim a special relation with the new imperial power – the USA. These links acted to 'explain' a continuing reluctance to become part of Europe, but in turn they also prompted distrust of British attempts to become a member of the European Community. The imperialist ideology drives a final reluctance to abandon the national sense of importance that empire creates, and makes more unnerving the fear that the European Community will colonize Britain, placing it at the edge of a new kind of quasi-imperialist structure with Germany at its centre. Could imperialism absorb this apparently final crisis? If so, it would perhaps be because literature played a vital part, proclaiming Britain the land of Shakespeare, as Greece is the land of Homer.

## Reading the text

*2.27* The key elements in the argument I am advancing here are that:

(a) imperialism is a complex system of ideologies which is of great importance in understanding British culture in the nineteenth and early twentieth century;

(b) literature is inextricably intertwined with imperialism and its ideologies.

*2.28* *A Passage to India* is a particularly obvious example of a text marked by imperialism, but all of the texts of this block, we claim, are marked in their language and imaginings by the process we call 'end of empire'. As readers our aim must be to unpick the text – and our own readings – exploring the assumptions and 'truths' they express. We must be particularly attentive to what is repressed or smoothed over in a text, and to the social relations it represents. For example, in Kipling's poem 'The White Man's Burden' the phrase 'the white man's burden' suppresses the expression of white man's dominance and exploitation; one *should* say 'the white man *is* the burden'. Literature *can* express that truth more directly. In the novel *Heart of Darkness*, Conrad writes at one point:

> [a white man] got fever, and had to be carried in a hammock slung under a pole. As he weighed sixteen stone I had no end of rows with the carriers ... So, one evening, I made a speech in English with gestures, not one of which was lost to the sixty pairs of eyes before me, and the next morning I started the hammock off in front all right. An hour afterwards I came upon the whole concern wrecked in a bush – man, hammock, groans, blankets, horrors. The heavy pole had skinned his poor nose. He was very anxious for me to kill somebody, but there wasn't the shadow of a carrier near...
>
> (p.29)

This paragraph seems to me to confront far more directly the colonizing experience. The white man, 'with gestures, not one of which was lost to the sixty pair of eyes before me', can threaten and coerce. But Conrad uses illness and the alien landscape to emphasize the fine line between strength and vulnerability in the colonialist. The economic role of the colonizer is more sharply conveyed as the white man literally becomes a burden. The situation of the subject race – in this story they are Africans – is represented not through the confusing ideology of childhood but by them being reduced to the eyes which stare at the white man, mutely absorbing his commands but equally able – at their own will – to disappear from the relationship leaving the white man powerless and alone. Yet even here one must feel that the social and economic relationships are presented as mysteries which the text alone hardly permits us to decode and perhaps encourages us to pass over. The mystery lies partly in the use of the metaphor, but more importantly in the enigma of the white man's unrevealed words. The relationship is silent; we have no access either to the words used by the 'I' or to the point of view of the Africans whose mouths and minds are suppressed by their identification only as 'pairs of eyes'. In the next section we shall look at how directly Forster confronts the colonial experience.

*2.29* The investigation however should not stop with those texts which in some visible way, like the Conrad story, refer to imperialism. If a feature of imperial ideology is that it obscures the source of the power from which it derives, and through the use of ideas of duty, and so on, even attempts to conceal the power itself, then the logical conclusion is that we should extend the investigation to encompass all texts written within the period of British imperialism. The point is put sharply by the Indian critic, Aijaz Ahmad:

> There has ... been a considerable rereading of Kipling and Conrad, Orwell and Forster, Melville and Malraux, Joyce Carey and even Doris Lessing. Gradually, it dawned upon some that no reading of English and French Literatures was possible without taking into account the constitutive presence of the colonial experience in those literatures: Shakespeare and Jane Austen, Samuel Johnson and George Eliot, Shelley and Tennyson, André Gide and St John Perse were all implicated in it, and the vocabulary of colonial racism was there even in texts that were ostensibly not about colonialism at all – *Wuthering Heights*, for example.
>
> (Ahmad, 1989, p.124)

*2.30* In our discussion of texts in this block we do not pursue this ambitious argument so widely. However, I think Ahmad's claim is important in voicing the idea that in examining texts and the ideologies they contain, we need to have in mind questions of imperialism and nationalism as well as questions about gender, class and race relations – and need to think about how these different areas interact.

# 3 *A study guide to 'A Passage to India'*



*ACTIVITY*

The first text for study in this block is E.M. Forster's novel *A Passage to India*. If you have not already done so, please read the novel right through now.

*3.1* When *A Passage to India* was published in 1924 it was greeted with considerable interest. Forster was well known as a novelist but he had written no full-length novel since 1910. Moreover, as we shall see, his subject matter was extremely topical. *A Passage to India* came to be his most popular book: in 1936 it became one of the first Penguin paperbacks, and was reprinted no less than fifty times between 1936 and 1989; after 1945 it appeared more and more regularly on school and university syllabuses. But all along Forster has had his critics, and has particularly been accused of writing in a superficial way for a narrow clique of readers. Comments in letters written by D.H. Lawrence – with whom Forster has often been contrasted – and which were written at the time of the novel's publication are symptomatic of what was to follow:

> Life is more interesting in its undercurrents than in its obvious; and E.M. does see people, people and nothing but people ad nauseam…
>
> All races have one root, once one gets there. Many stems from one root: the stems never to comingle or 'understand' one another. I agree Forster doesn't 'understand' his Hindu. And India to him is just negative: because he doesn't go down to the root to meet it. But the *Passage to India* interested me very much. At least the repudiation of our white bunk is genuine, sincere, and pretty thorough…
>
> (quoted in Bradbury, 1970, p.47)

## End of empire? (chapter I)

*3.2* How then should we begin to relate this novel to the theme of the block? We could perhaps look for evidence in the letters and articles Forster wrote while working on the book. For example:

> When I began the book I thought of it as a little bridge of sympathy between East and West, but this conception has had to go, my sense of truth forbids anything so comfortable. I think that most Indians, like most English people, are shits, and I am not interested whether they sympathise with one another or not. Not interested as an artist; of course the journalistic side of me gets roused over these questions.
>
> (quoted in Furbank, 1978, p.106)

Or we might look at contemporary reviews, such as this review in the *Boston Evening Transcript*, 3 September 1924:

> *A Passage to India* … goes deeper into the problems of Anglo-India, while at the same time it offers us as clear and as accurate a picture of the conditions under which English and Indians live as any we have read.
>
> (quoted in Gardner, 1973, p.261)

## *ACTIVITY*

But we need also to look in the novel itself for evidence of 'the constitutive presence of the colonial experience' (see paragraph 2.29). It would be unrealistic to expect you at this stage to be able to formulate conclusions about the book as a whole so let us look at the first two chapters in this context, focusing on two questions:

(a) How far is imperialism evident as a political system? (See paragraphs 2.4–2.9 if you are unsure about how to define 'political' here.)

(b) How far is cultural imperialism present? (Again, see paragraphs 2.4–2.9 if you are unsure of this term.)

(Note: In the opening sections of this study guide I shall ask you to work at some length on relatively small parts of the book. I hope you will find this rewarding and not become impatient. Forster's language has been read as relatively straightforward and unproblematic; you will see that I think this is not the case and that *A Passage to India* deserves the same kind of concentrated attention as *The Waste Land* or a short story by James Joyce.)

## *DISCUSSION*

(a) The use of India as a setting immediately constitutes *A Passage to India* as in some degree about colonialism – or to use the British term – imperialism. In the first paragraph the point is obliquely reinforced by the interpolation of 'then imperial' with its implied question 'what is it now?' posed for the reader to answer. In the second paragraph imperialism becomes more explicitly present with the reference to the Civil Station and the creation of a geographically and politically stratified setting. At the lowest level is the river with the old town, inhabited by Indians, on its banks; on the boundary is the maidan – an open area where people from all races can meet without the formality of doors, chairs and so on. Beyond this open area and on higher ground are the houses of the people of mixed race and the railway. Then the land sinks to form a valley – a kind of moat perhaps – before rising steeply to a second rise on which stands the British Civil Station. All this shows a world marked by apartheid.

On the rise the British residential area, which in India was often called the cantonment to emphasize its isolation and exclusion, is laid out in typically neat fashion. In these two paragraphs Forster has decisively placed the novel in an imperial setting.

(b) Cultural imperialism is perhaps more difficult to pick out at this point. The worlds of ruler and ruled appear separate, with the area of the ruled being 'sensibly planned' while the Indian areas are described as mean and dirty, but there is no mention of the one influencing the other. However, the chapter does refer to the differences of view characteristic of cultural imperialism. From the height of the Civil Station the view is of the tops of the trees which 'screen what passes below'; newcomers have to be 'driven down to acquire disillusionment'. Conventional western ideas of nature and the exotic interpose a screen between European eyes and India.

Something of the concentration of Forster's language can be seen already in the phrase just quoted which telescopes the idea that one must drive down to see the reality of the Indian world and the idea that this can only bring disillusion to the idealistic imperialist. The pushing together of these ideas also suggests that the imperialist is naturally a weary and disillusioned person. The general point of view here seems British rather than Indian – like many of those British who were sympathetic to Indian life Forster seems to present the glory as being firmly in the past. Forster's fascination with India can be felt in the third and fourth paragraphs which present a dazzling evocation of Indian nature:

> By day the blue will pale down into white where it touches the white of the land, after sunset it has a new circumference – orange, melting upward into tenderest purple. But the core of blue persists, and so it is by night. Then the stars hang like lamps from the immense vault ... when the sky chooses, glory can rain into the Chandrapore bazaars, or a benediction pass from horizon to horizon. The sky can do this because it is so strong and so enormous.
>
> (p.32)

When Forster went for a second time to India in 1921, his love of the country was obvious to his friends. Virginia Woolf wrote:

> Morgan goes to India and I think forever ... He will become a mystic, sit by the roadside and forget Europe ... we shan't see him again.
>
> (quoted in Furbank, 1978, p.67)

When he was in India he was happy to try to absorb himself into Indian life; in later years many testify to the warm friendship and help he gave to Indians visiting Britain. In personal terms, then, it seems quite inappropriate to see cultural imperialism here in terms of crude cultural domination. Yet Forster was an Englishman with strong links with the British establishment formed by family ties, by his school days and his time at Cambridge. Indirectly he could also trace links with the creation of British India in the nineteenth century; his father's family was part of the Evangelical group known as the Clapham Sect, which included several of the men who laid down the principles of government and education for India between 1810 and 1850. For all of the length of Forster's stays in India (seven months in 1912–13 and nine months in 1921–22) he remained ultimately (and for him frustratingly) a British tourist. Photographs of him in 1921 in India show him wearing local dress and sitting crosslegged among Indian friends, but they only highlight the paradox of his love of the country and his own westernness.

## Modernism (chapter I)

*3.3* From chapter I it seems clear that imperialism will be a context for *A Passage to India*. The date of publication of the novel – 1924 – might have already suggested another framework into which the novel might fit, namely Modernism, which you studied in Block 2. In chronological terms Forster's novel fits easily into the range of texts considered in Block 2: *The Waste Land* was published in the same year as *A Passage to India, Mrs Dalloway* a year after, and most of the Yeats poems you have worked on date from 1919 to 1926. Modernism is a stylistic movement, as you will remember. In Block 2 Graham Martin noted:

> This concern for 'style' was widely shared by 'Modernist' novelists: James himself, Conrad, Joyce, Woolf and many others ... [They aimed to use] ... a prose that deliberately incorporates features more usually associated with poetry, in the precision and evocative power of its imagery, and in the deployment of a more or less explicit symbolism, both as carrier of the novel's deeper significance and one source of its aesthetic unity.
>
> (Block 2 paragraph 1.30–31)

*3.4* But the distinctive style of Modernism has also a complex relation to political issues:

> Modernism ... is the one art that responds to the scenario of our chaos. It is the art ... of the destruction of civilization and reason in the First World War, of the world changed and interpretated by Marx, Freud and Darwin ... Modernism is then the art of modernization – however stark the separation of the artist from society may have been, however oblique the artistic gesture he has made...
>
> (Bradbury and McFarlane, 1976, quoted in Block 2 paragraph 1.9)

### *ACTIVITY*

How does chapter I of *A Passage to India* relate to these comments about Modernism?

### *DISCUSSION*

Graham Martin's description of Modernist prose could hardly be bettered as a description of Forster's prose in chapter I, especially when he writes about nature. The final two sentences

> Only in the south, where a group of fists and fingers are thrust up through the soil, is the endless expanse interrupted. These fists and fingers are the Marabar Hills, containing the extraordinary caves.
>
> (pp.32–3)

seem to contain 'a more or less explicit symbolism' and, as you will know from your reading of the novel as a whole, the hills and caves are indeed carriers of the novel's 'deeper significance and one source of its aesthetic unity'.

The point of view also shifts from paragraph to paragraph in chapter I, suggesting that, in the words of Bradbury and McFarlane, Forster will live, like a Modernist, 'amidst the tools of modern relativism, scepticism', but we cannot be sure yet of the 'hope for secular change'. Finally, although the first chapter does not directly describe the 'scenario of our chaos', one can sense a response to such a state in the emphatic opening of the final paragraph, 'The sky settles everything...'. In adopting what we can see as a Modernist style in the opening of the book Forster perhaps gives us a signal that he is presenting imperialism in crisis rather than at the height of its power and confidence.

## A change of direction? (chapter II)

*3.5* The language of chapter I seems resonant, demanding close attention. But there is an abrupt gap between the final words, 'the Marabar Hills, containing the extraordinary caves', and the opening of chapter II, 'Abandoning his bicycle...'. Have we moved to a different kind of novel?

### *ACTIVITY*

Please read chapter II and ask yourself if imperialism (political or cultural) is still on the agenda. If it is, how is it presented now?

### *DISCUSSION*

I think you will have concluded that imperialism in the political sense continues to be present. The geographical structure of the settlements, mimicking the divisions between the races, is again visible, as is the extent to which the separate worlds are alien to each other. For example, as Aziz enters the order of the British Civil Lines, Forster describes how his whole frame of mind changes, 'depression suddenly seized him ... He felt caught in their meshes...' (p.39). The conflict of the races also appears in the anecdote:

> There had been a 'case' last year – an Indian gentleman had driven up to an official's house and been turned back by the servants and told to approach more suitably ... its fame spread wide.
>
> (p.39)

and is emphasized in a number of other details, for example:

> '...He has found out our dinner-hour, that's all, and chooses to interrupt us every time, in order to show his power.'
>
> (p.38)
>
> So it had come, the usual thing – just as Mahmoud Ali said. The inevitable snub – his bow ignored, his carriage taken.
>
> (p.39)

But there is a clear difference in the style of presentation. Now that Forster has embarked on an account of events the comments are embedded in the presentation of character and incident and are much less foregrounded for our attention.

Apart from the events and the setting you might have registered an act of imperialism in the way Forster confidently depicts the minds of Indian characters here, as Kipling had entered into the mind of the Indian soldier in *A Sahibs' War*. As with the Kipling story the explicit aim may appear laudable; the English are to be presented as 'shits' (Forster's word). Second thoughts may leave one feeling there is an act of appropriation here. But to me Forster's work differs from that of Kipling because his Indians are presented as very much Anglicized, and less exotic than the soldier depicted by Kipling. Forster still uses quaintness of speech to mark the Indians ('hookah is so jolly now') but overall they are allowed to be easily fluent in the language of their 'masters', aware of the faults of its culture, and apparently able to make a world of their own in the gap between India and Britain.

## Getting started (chapter II)

*3.6* Detective work on the manuscripts of *A Passage to India* shows that Forster almost certainly began writing the novel in 1913 at what is now chapter II, and continued on to chapter VII before returning to write the first chapter and revise what he had written. Certainly there is a sense, in conventional terms, that in chapter II things are getting started as characters are introduced to fill the setting he has created. We are pitched into the middle of a scene and must work out the prevailing tone as we go along.

Chapter I seems little help to our reading, for now we seem to be in a social comedy, where serious things are only to be mocked:

> '...Mr Mahmoud Ali, how are you?'
> 'Thank you, Dr Aziz, I am dying.'
> 'Dying before your dinner? Oh, poor Mahmoud Ali!'
> 'Hamidullah here is actually dead. He passed away just as you rode up on your bike.'
>
> (p.33)

*3.7* Whatever expectations may have been created at the end of chapter I by the references to the sky, the hills and the caves, for the following five pages we are confined within the shifting surface of the conversation which 'unrolled and expanded interminably' (p.36). The arrival of the servant with a note is used as a means of changing the pace and the tone and the focus begins to sharpen. Increasingly we feel confident that, among the Indian characters, Aziz will be the most important as the narrating voice provides us with more and more detail about his character. Forster's plan requires that we centre our interest on Aziz and adopt, or become involved in, his point of view, but instead of a long exposition telling us about his character, his past and so on, the process is achieved through incident. Messages are passed to us through trivial details, as when the bicycle and the puncture are introduced not only to dramatize Aziz's character, but to depict the gap between Indian life and the 'arid tidiness' of the Civil Lines where servants attend to all the small inconveniences of life. The incident with the tonga is introduced to dramatize even more sharply that even an educated and Anglicized Indian such as Aziz had no status in British eyes.

## *ACTIVITY*

Did you notice other points at which innocent details are embedded in the narrative conveying important messages?

## *DISCUSSION*

My eye was caught by the way Forster dresses Aziz in 'pumps' (slipper-like shoes often worn with formal evening dress or for dancing). This detail seems to occur entirely naturally, and it has a role to play in the plot – were he not wearing pumps he would not need to turn into the mosque to rest and would not meet Mrs Moore. But the detail also symbolizes Aziz's situation. Pumps, 'a poor preparation for any country' (p.40), are appropriate to an English life style in which one can always get a tonga to go dancing at the Club. But they are entirely unsuited to the Indian world of mean streets and crowded bazaars described in chapter I. The detail thus conveys the problems that beset those who, like Aziz, try to live on the border between the racial groups, and a major theme of the novel is rapidly touched on and drawn to our attention.

*3.8* If you have in mind the analysis of the way narrative operates which you worked through in Block 2 (pp.39–42) you will see, perhaps, that I am arguing that in chapters I and II, Forster's narrative is insistently, but ambiguously, *proleptic*. He creates a mass of expectations of what might follow, but refuses to give us much in the way of *analepsis*, or anchoring of events, by providing any past. Our attention is held in the present, first because we have no way of resolving the enigmas of chapter I, and secondly because we have no clear way of foreseeing what may arise from the story at the beginning of chapter II. The possibilities in the narrative only begin to narrow, to my mind, as Aziz is allowed to be alone and centre-stage on page 41. As 'he turned into a mosque to rest' so our minds settle into paying more sustained attention to him. The heightened language suggests he will have a role in something more than a social comedy:

> Here was Islam, his own country, more than a Faith, more than a battle-cry, more, much more ... Islam, an attitude towards life both exquisite and durable, where his body and his thoughts found their home.
>
> (p.41)

## *ACTIVITY*

Read the second paragraph on page 41 and ask yourself what hints are given of the attitude we should have towards this character. If you are not sure of how to proceed you might find it helpful to compare this paragraph with the introduction of the two British women on page 39.

## *DISCUSSION*

One can have little doubt that Forster intends us to be critical of the British women; whatever one's ideas about appropriate behaviour the text coerces the reader by the use of phrases like 'full of their own affairs' and particularly through the use of 'screeched' (p.39). Furthermore one has only the most external view of these characters, whereas in the paragraph describing Aziz on page 41 we are given a much more extended view of his thoughts and feelings. We are drawn into imagining a character from the inside rather than simply observing a caricature from the outside. An attack on the prejudiced attitudes of the British is at the heart of the depiction of the women. By contrast, while the prejudice Muslims may feel against Hindus is expressed in the character of Aziz, it is heavily cushioned and only indirectly seen, as in the phrase 'the rhythm was uncongenial to him'. We may equally pass by the innocent detail that Aziz wants to 'build a mosque ... so that *all* who passed by should experience the happiness he felt' (my italics), forgetting the divisions between Hindus and Muslims and that the Muslim occupation of India was characterized by the destruction of Hindu temples and the building of mosques in their place. In the rest of this chapter the Hindu world remains unspoken and absent; the possibility that divisions may exist is only glimpsed when Professor Godbole is introduced in chapter VII, but even then Forster seems intent on keeping the issue far from the centre of the story.

*3.9* Finally in chapter II the character of Mrs Moore is introduced. In retrospect we can see that until this has happened the novel cannot properly be said to have begun, but Forster's introduction of the character is typically casual: 'Another pillar moved, a third, and then an Englishwoman stepped out into the moonlight. Suddenly he was furiously angry...' (p.42). The conversation that follows has at first a fractured quality, with the reader's own uncertainty about what is going on being dramatized in the feelings ascribed to Aziz:

> 'May I know your name?'
> She was now in the shadow of the gateway, so that he could not see her face, but she saw his, and she said with a change of voice, 'Mrs Moore.'
> 'Mrs –' Advancing, he found that she was old. A fabric bigger than the mosque fell to pieces, and he did not know whether he was glad or sorry.
>
> (pp.42–3)

Thereafter details are introduced that suggest that the characters will come to be linked. The conversation between Aziz and Mrs Moore about their children places them 'in the same box'. But Forster signals this moment for the readers' attention by adding 'he said cryptically' (p.44) which draws our attention to the fact that Aziz has been far from being in the same box – or rather tonga – as Mesdames Callendar and Lesley. The togetherness of the characters is further emphasized by narrative comment: Aziz 'was excited partly by his wrongs, but much more by the knowledge that someone sympathized with them' (p.45). With that unity comes a kind of excitement in Aziz, which we share because of our closeness to his character. 'The flame that not even beauty can nourish was springing up, and though his words were querulous his heart began to glow secretly' (p.45).

## *ACTIVITY*

Where has chapter II left us? Do you feel that the imperial issues have been established and are likely to dominate the book? Or has Forster merely borrowed the Indian scene to provide an exotic (or even mystic) backdrop to a tale which could be set elsewhere.

## *DISCUSSION*

It is more likely that you found it a little difficult to choose between the options I have offered you here, and you may have wanted to place the novel, on your reading so far, somewhere between these categories. If you opted firmly for one of the possibilities it may be that this reflects your own ideas about the book, about Forster, or about India. Clearly the context of the course may be influencing your reading. On the other hand, Forster is not known as a political novelist and his earlier novels seem often to steer clear of direct references to political issues. Recently *A Passage to India* has been identified with a group of so-called 'Raj novels', including Paul Scott's *The Raj Quartet* and M.M. Kaye's *The Far Pavilions*; this has been encouraged by the film of *A Passage to India* directed by David Lean in 1984. In the Raj novels the real political tensions of India are dissolved into stories of personal relationships, and are usually focused on British experiences so that these appear to be the most significant events in the end of empire. The key mood is one of nostalgia. In an article on the popularity (and the falseness) of these fictions, Salman Rushdie refers to the way Forster's novel has been pressed into this company, and particularly to the way it has been revised for the film. Rushdie is able to use Lean's words to make the point. In an interview Lean said:

> Forster was a bit anti-English, anti-Raj and so on. I suppose it's a tricky thing to say, but I'm not so much. I intend to keep the balance more. I don't believe all the English were a lot of idiots. Forster rather made them so. He came down hard against them.
>
> (in Rushdie, 1984, p.128)

Referring to the final paragraphs of the book Lean also claims the novel is not really political: 'I thought that bit rather tacked on. Anyway, I see it as a personal not a political story' (in Rushdie, 1984, p.129). Without going as far as Lean, one might say that, despite the imperial setting and the references to discrimination, Forster does not put true Indian political life on the agenda in this early part of the book but remains within a British context. In this light, perhaps, imperialism – or one might prefer here the word colonialism – in a *full* sense is a strongly significant absence in the novel. In Macherey's words:

> ...the book is not self-sufficient; it is necessarily accompanied by a *certain absence*, without which it would not exist. A knowledge of the book must include a consideration of this absence.
>
> This is why it seems useful and legitimate to ask of every production what it tacitly implies, what it does not say.
>
> (Reader, p.217, see also Block 4 Section 3)

Round objects Minister.

The text itself certainly seems to leave scope for doubt. If one looks at the last paragraph of chapter II, for example, the elements of division and discrimination which are at the heart of imperialism are all present in the references to the exclusion of Indians from the Club and the contrast of 'lovely mosque' and 'flabby Hindus', but we are urged firmly to see these things as not mattering; the state of 'being happy' can drive out these concerns.

---

*3.10* Forster himself was not easily prepared to accept that he had written only a political novel. He saw the best literature as necessarily having a serious purpose but was reluctant to equate that seriousness with political life, which seemed too narrow, dry and partisan. He claimed that political questions puzzled him, even though after the First World War he was drawn to the Labour Party. He was asked to use his experiences in Egypt during the war to write a pamphlet about that country for the Fabian Society, and for a time he became Literary Editor of the *Daily Herald* (spurning the opportunity to work in the Foreign Office around the same time). But in a letter he said that the pamphlet was written less from motives connected to the ideas of the Fabian Society than 'for the sake of Mohammed and his sufferings' (Lago and Furbank, 1983, p.318). (Mohammed el Adl was the tram-conductor with whom Forster had fallen in love in Egypt, and with whom he had his first full sexual experiences. He died soon after Forster returned from India in 1921.) In two other letters written around this time Forster wrote that 'the trouble is that I am not sure what the Common People want. My past has ... been uniformly refined', and after meeting a group of miners, that 'sentimentally I am on their side, but my intellect argues that clerks, university teachers etc., are really the oppressed class today' (Lago and Furbank, 1983, pp.300, 319).

*3.11* Later, in the 1950s, Forster wrote of *A Passage to India* that:

> ...the book is not really about politics, though it is the political aspect of it that caught the general public and made it sell. It's about something wider than politics, about the search of the human race for a more lasting home, about the universe as embodied in the Indian earth and the Indian sky, about the horror lurking in the Marabar Caves and the release symbolized by the birth of Krishna. It is – or rather desires to be – philosophic and poetic...
>
> (quoted in the introduction to the Penguin edition, p.25)

In a perceptive article on his work published in 1927, Virginia Woolf had seized upon Forster's desire to present some wider reality as fundamental to an understanding of his work. She wrote that in his novels he wanted always to include a sense of 'a burning core' which lay beneath the concern people feel for 'the bicycle and the duster'. She defined this core as 'the soul ... reality ... truth ... poetry ... love' (Woolf, 1966, p.343). It was this desire that prompted him always to push together 'the paraphernalia of reality' and a 'moment of illumination' (p.346), and to shift, even in his most realistic scenes, 'from realism to symbolism' (p.346).

ie What is ultimate reality??

*ACTIVITY*

Arguably the greatest shift from realism to symbolism takes place later in the novel at the Marabar caves, but a briefer instance of the process occurs at the end of chapter III. Please read the paragraphs on page 55, from 'The note of anxiety...' to the end of the chapter. How is there a change from realism to symbolism here?

*DISCUSSION*

The first of these paragraphs explores that most common element of the realistic novel – character. Here too we are plainly concerned with issues of value. For example, how should we estimate Aziz's character? Must we be bound by conventional prejudice? But then the language shifts. Character and reader are carried beyond the detail of Anglo-Indian relations to a 'moment of illumination', to use Woolf's phrase. Mrs Moore's sudden absorption in the wasp rather than the larger question of India, or Adela's marriage, suggest that the reader should also allow his or her attention to go beyond the simple surface of character and event, but the consequences of such a move are not clear. We may see the significance of the wasp as closely linked with Mrs Moore rather than having any intrinsic meaning itself: its purpose is to direct us towards 'He did not wake, but *her* voice floated out to swell to the night's uneasiness' (my italics). Because of this we are yet more certain that Mrs Moore has some kind of privileged status in the novel. If we look for an intrinsic significance in the wasp it may lie in the difference between this Indian wasp and English wasps which, we are told, never sleep in this way. The Indian wasp has no 'sense of the interior'; to it 'inside a house' is just 'a normal growth of the eternal jungle'. Furthermore it can easily sleep 'while jackals in the plain bayed their desire and mingled with the percussion of the drums'. By implication the wasp represents all of the alien strangeness which the British find in India. The British exclude the Indians from their world, but through the detail of the wasp Forster is able to comment on the narrowness of British life in India.

## The bridge party (chapter V)

*3.12* Elsewhere in her article on Forster Woolf coins another perceptive analogy to describe the mixing in Forster's work of everyday detail and something wider. It is worth quoting in full because it also sums up a set of values that Woolf and Forster both despised. For Forster, Woolf writes:

> It is the soul that matters; and the soul, we have seen, is caged in a solid villa of red brick somewhere in the suburbs of London. It seems, then, that if his books are to succeed in their mission his reality must at certain points become irradiated; his brick must be lit up; we must see the whole building saturated with light. We have at once to believe in the complete reality of the suburb and in the complete reality of the soul.
>
> (Woolf, 1966, p.346)

In a letter of 1919 Forster wrote, 'isn't it awful how all the outward nonsense of England has been absolutely untouched by the war – still this unbroken front of dress-shirts and golf' (Lago and Furbank, 1983, p.300). These comments may remind you of the description of the Civil Station in chapter I with its 'sensibly planned' layout and its 'grocer's ... cemetery, and ... bungalows ... disposed along roads that intersect at right angles' (p.32). Forster's critique of British imperialism is inextricably bound up with his critique of suburban values. There is a gender bias here, moreover, to which Woolf does not refer, for in Forster's presentation, suburban and imperial men can achieve a kind of practical dignity through work (this is particularly the case with Ronny in *A Passage to India*), whereas 'screeching' women are beyond redemption. In this context the characters of Adela Quested and Mrs Moore take on a special significance: their presence demonstrates that the restrictions can be overcome. Moreover, in the scene in the mosque, we begin to see intimations of the 'complete reality of the soul', potentially the most positive element in the book. At this stage of the novel it seems Forster paradoxically identifies both the most negative and the most positive elements as linked with the female.

## *ACTIVITY*

Chapter V seems to show a number of examples of both the suburban life of the British in India and of those points when reality is irradiated. Please read the chapter now and make notes of points when each of these elements seems to predominate.

## *DISCUSSION*

Through the characters Forster presents a clearly satirical picture of an attempt to bridge the racial divide by the British. I would pick out the way Forster uses the exchange of Mrs Moore and Mrs Bhattacharya (pp.63–4) to dramatize the impossibility of communication even at a most basic and trivial level. Narrative commentary is used to press the point home:

> The Englishmen had intended to play up better, but had been prevented from doing so by their womenfolk, whom they had to attend, provide with tea, advise about dogs, etc...
>
> [Adela] and Ronny would look into the Club like this every evening ... while the true India slid by unnoticed.
>
> (p.66)

Forster again uses apparently innocent details to drive the point home – here with comedy. What society can be healthy and open minded when its diet is

> Julienne soup full of bullety bottled peas, pseudo-cottage bread, fish full of branching bones, pretending to be plaice, more bottled peas with the cutlets, trifle, sardines on toast: the menu of Anglo-India ... the food of exiles, cooked by servants who did not understand it.
>
> (p.67)

I noted two moments when something deeper seemed to strike through this surface triviality. The first is on page 59 when amid the description of the gathering, the perspective and focus seemed suddenly to shift:

> He pointed to the dusky line beyond the court, and here and there it flashed a pince-nez or shuffled a shoe, as if aware that he was despising it. European costume had lighted like a leprosy. Few had yielded entirely, but none were untouched.

The reference to leprosy is brief and in passing, but there could hardly be a more violent attack on Anglicized Indian life. Immediately afterwards a different kind of shift occurs and another deeper reality seems present, now echoing the language of chapter I:

> Some kites hovered overhead, impartial, over the kites passed the mass of a vulture, and, with an impartiality exceeding all, the sky, not deeply coloured but translucent, poured light from its whole circumference. It

> seemed unlikely that the series stopped here. Beyond the sky must there not be something that overarches all the skies...
>
> (pp.59–60)

This moment is echoed at the end of the chapter when Mrs Moore thinks about religion. Unlike Ronny who 'approved of religion as long as it endorsed the National Anthem, but ... objected when it attempted to influence his life', Mrs Moore seeks a more transcendent being. But in India, western religion seems inadequate; unable to measure up to the feeling that 'outside the arch there seemed always an arch, beyond the remotest echo a silence' (p.71).

---

## The terms of the argument (chapter VII)

*3.13* It is safe to say now, perhaps, that what is at issue is not whether there is a relationship between *A Passage to India* and imperialism, but how that relationship is constructed and how the terms are defined. Imperialism is presented, first, from a largely European viewpoint; we hear Indian voices but all are Anglicized. The emphasis is not on fitting events in India into a political framework but in contrasting them with some kind of wider or more fundamental reality. Finally, the investigation of imperialism is built into a novel which shares the paradoxes of Modernism, turning inward on itself at the same time as it turns out to depict a world in crisis; all this while producing at times an intensely poetic effect.

### *ACTIVITY*

Please now read chapter VII with these issues in mind. How does the wider or more overarching reality that Forster plainly wants to include in the book appear here, and is there some kind of link between this kind of reality and the poetic element in the book?

### *DISCUSSION*

Forster is often rather vague and allusive in his references to a wider reality but in chapter VII you might have noticed signs that it can take on a human face. Your reading of the novel as a whole will tell you that this chapter is particularly important because it provides a meeting between Fielding and Aziz. From the beginning Forster creates a 'fundamental goodwill' between them (p.84); a quality that here can overarch the individual idiosyncrasies and racial differences. This quality will increasingly come to be tested as the story progresses, up to and including the final paragraph. The only other relationship given anything like this status so far is that of Aziz and Mrs Moore, and it is noticeably absent from the conventional married couples.

The most striking moment of illumination, when the wider reality is made visible, occurs at the end of chapter VII, first as Godbole sings, and then in the moment of silence that follows.

> It was the song of an unknown bird. Only the servants understood it. They began to whisper to one another. The man who was gathering water-chestnut came naked out of the tank, his lips parted with delight, disclosing his scarlet tongue. The sounds continued and ceased after a few moments as casually as they had begun – apparently halfway through a bar, and upon the subdominant ... Ronny's steps had died away, and there was a moment of absolute silence. No ripple disturbed the water, no leaf stirred.
>
> (pp.95–6)

---

*3.14* There are links with other parts of the book to reinforce our sense of the significance of this moment. The silence reminds us of the silence at the end of chapter V. The anonymous Indian character, half naked and suspended in some special kind of movement links with the references to the punkah-wallah in the trial scene. Nature is also a constant source of reference. But amid these elements the description of the ending of the music seems to stand out rather oddly. The music is Indian, and the deeper reality apparently something only Indian life can give one access to. The narrating voice struggles to define the music but it will not fit into western conventions; satisfaction and completeness for a westerner cannot be provided by an ending on the subdominant. The narrating voice can give us no further help with the song and Mrs Moore's questioning takes us no further. Godbole explains that Krishna does not come to the milkmaid in the song despite her pleading.

> 'But He comes in some other song, I hope?' said Mrs Moore gently.
>
> 'Oh no, He refuses to come,' repeated Godbole, perhaps not understanding her question. 'I say to Him, Come, come, come, come, come, come. He neglects to come.'
>
> (p.96)

The sense that the narrator is caught within the conventions of western music is enhanced for me by the way the chapter as a whole seems to flow in a way akin to a sequence of movements in an opera (the finale of an act in a Mozart opera, for example). It is as if Forster is setting what might be regarded as one of the higher realities of western culture against the Indian experience here, but by the end of the chapter even these western values seem inadequate. The chapter opens with a prelude showing Fielding alone; Forster then begins a duet as Aziz enters (pp.81–5), and expands this to a quartet with the arrival of Adela and Mrs Moore (pp.85–9). Godbole's arrival makes it a quintet (pp.89–92), although for a time only a trio of voices is heard. With Ronny's arrival we move to a full sextet, but it is rather a fractious ensemble that unites only in the sequence of goodbyes on page 95. The whole sequence, which began with an English solo, is rounded off by Godbole's mysterious coda. This musical analogy may strike you as fanciful, but it seems to me that one needs something of this sort to respond to the fluidity of the scene and the way the voices move easily together and apart. The structure seems to be hinted at within the scene too by the comment, put into Fielding's mind, that what we see is: 'A scene from a play, thought Fielding, who now saw them from the distance across the garden, grouped among the blue pillars of his beautiful hall' (p.94).

*3.15* Forster uses analogies with music in his discussion of how novels should be constructed in *Aspects of the Novel.* He refers, discussing Proust, to the way particular phrases can tie a novel together in a way that seems to me excellently to describe the way our understanding of *A Passage to India* is carried forward by repeated ideas and phrases.

> There are times when the little phrase … means everything to the reader. There are times when it means nothing and is forgotten, and this seems to me the function of rhythm in fiction; not to be there all the time like a pattern, but by its lovely waxing and waning to fill us with surprise and freshness and hope.
>
> (Forster, 1962, p.168)

In chapter VII, I wonder if you noticed how music-like motifs link the situation of different characters. On page 84 we read Aziz 'grappled beneath the shifting tides of emotion'; this metaphor is echoed in the comment on page 92 that 'Adela had no conception of its underdrift'. Repeated metaphors form motifs within a single character: on page 89 when Aziz is confident 'wings bore him up' and on page 93 as his confidence falls 'His wings were failing'.

*3.16* How does one balance this kind of formality of organization against the enquiry into imperialism? Does it enhance it, or is it an example of Forster preferring to be a fine writer rather than – in Lawrence's phrase – going down to the root of things? One might say that the style – and the comedy – distract us from the events of India after 1918. But one might also argue that Forster is pursuing a more complex course. Western cultural forms, particularly those of the nineteenth century like the novel or the symphonies of Beethoven, tend to end with a sense of completion and resolution and our sense that this completion will arrive is bolstered by the organization of the piece – the repetition of a word or phrase, the use of conventional imagery, a pattern or rhythm of words or sounds. Your work on *A Passage to India* so far should have shown that it is very much a work built on these principles using small details – like the collar stud (pp.83,97) – to create an intricate web of meaning, a higher reality overarching the individual details as they occur. In this way, perhaps, the structure of the novel itself is a part of its central question – must there not be something that overarches all? Is it not the duty of the novelist to provide answers?

## *ACTIVITY*

Let us turn back now to the analysis of imperialism. How is that presented in chapter VII?

## *DISCUSSION*

It might be helpful to begin by saying how it is *not* defined. In general terms imperialism is marked by divisions between those who have power and those who are subordinate, and the division is based on race. Gender also plays an important role; the relation of the male imperialist to the colonized man is different from that of the female imperialist. This might lead one to conclude that 'imperialism' and, for that matter, 'political' implies a treatment based on groups and classes of people – as is the case in sections of the bridge party. To my mind such a way of thinking is inappropriate for chapter VII, or in fact for large sections of the novel. In chapter VII characters are seen as individuals throughout, for example, in the summary sentence on pages 93–4: 'A strange quartet – he fluttering to the ground, she puzzled by the sudden ugliness, Ronny fuming, the Brahman observing all three'. Part of the force of what I have described as the musical organization of the chapter is perhaps that within such a structure each character has its own voice – there is no chorus and even the parts played by incidental characters are carefully separated out.

In creating the meeting of Fielding and Aziz Forster emphasizes the individuality and almost randomness of utterance rather than creating formed dialogue, for example, in Fielding's oddly colloquial ,'I hae ma doots' (p.83), and Aziz's explanation of why one wears a collar, 'We wear them to pass the police' (p.83).

The individuality evident in the narrative technique inevitably spills over into the arguments Forster enters into. It is plain from the earlier chapters that Forster is antagonistic to a particular kind of colonial behaviour and this is presented often in general terms; in chapter VII he refers to 'his brother civilians ... the pinko grey male ... Most Englishmen prefer their own kinswomen' (p.80). But the individual characters who are described in chapter VII are consistently defined outside this kind of generality; they are, as it were, eccentrics rather than exemplars.

Thus Fielding is not a typical Englishman any more than Aziz is a typical Indian; both are caught between the cultures. Mrs Moore and Adela are also set up as very different from typical Englishwomen. Even when characters come close to being exemplars Forster is careful to add details which not only humanize them but actually contradict the main drift of the character. Thus Godbole, who seems cast as a fount of genuine knowledge about India, is dressed by Forster in a faintly ludicrous way in 'waistcoat, dhoti, socks with clocks ... as if he had reconciled the products of East and West' (p.89). When he sings there is at times, for all the Indianness, 'the illusion of a western melody' (p.95). At this point in the story Ronny Heaslop is perhaps the least complex and the most 'exemplar' character but, as the novel progresses, his stereotypical image begins to fracture.

The insistence on individuality leads to a somewhat paradoxical situation whereby the narrative consistently works on what one might call a political level, depicting racial discrimination and the stereotyping of racial and gender identity within colonial society, while at another level creating characters in an extremely individualistic mode. The consequences of this are perhaps clearest at this stage of the novel in relation to Fielding and Aziz. Fielding is defined against the model of the typical narrow-minded imperial administrator: 'He had discovered that it is possible to keep in with Indians and Englishmen, but that he who would also keep in with Englishwomen must drop the Indians' (p.80).

Forster does not suggest that Fielding is in any general way in sympathy with the Indian nationalist movement, preferring to show him 'happiest in the give and take of private conversation' (p.80) and culturally rooted in Italy. In terms of the argument of the novel one might argue that to make Fielding involved in Indian nationalism would have seemed too much a schematic 'pattern' (to use Forster's own term, see paragraph 3.15). However, it would not necessarily have been so extraordinary in 'realistic' terms since Annie Besant was involved with the Indian National Congress from 1914 and became its President for a time in 1918. In 1924 *A Passage to India* was related by some to this world.

> [Forster's] picture of an Indian mofussil station [rural station as distinct from chief station] is a caricature and not even a clever caricature. One is led to speculate as to what Mr Forster's Indian experience may have been. Was he taken round the country by the gifted lady president of the Theosophical Society [i.e. Annie Besant]?
>
> (unsigned review in the Calcutta *Statesman*, 1924, quoted in Gardner, 1973, p.244)

Aziz is constructed as poised between two cultures, both of which are carefully identified by Forster – the official British world of the hospital, and the predominantly Muslim Indian world. In chapter VII the specific Muslimness of his world is exemplified by the references to Moghul Emperors (p.88). Here Forster is not placing Aziz within the generality of the political context of the development of the Muslim League and the struggle within it between conservatives loyal to the British and the radical nationalists, or the Lucknow Pact of 1916 which united the Hindu and Muslim nationalists. (The latter is alluded to later in the novel but again within the precise context of the novel, and without mention of the general situation.)

---

*3.17* One must avoid thinking that it would have been somehow 'better' for Forster to have written a different kind of novel, in which, perhaps, Mrs Moore became a heroine of the nationalist movement. It is also far from easy to recover the truth about why the novel was written as it was. For example, did Forster avoid the example of Mrs Besant so as to avoid the particular kind of mysticism her view of India contained? Did he also avoid referring to Muslim nationalism so as to avoid the Muslim religion's fundamentalism which many in the League encouraged? The point to register is that the construction of characters and incidents involves choices which have ideological implications of a quite subtle and often paradoxical kind. For all its explicit avoidance of the representation of political groups, *A Passage to India* was related to the current struggles.

## The expedition to the caves (chapters XII–XVI)

### *ACTIVITY*

Please now look again at these chapters.

*3.18* The expedition to the caves was to be a display of Indian hospitality – a replacement for the visit promised by Mrs Bhattacharya in chapter V and a parallel to the hospitality offered by Fielding in chapter VII. It is a further example of attempts to build bridges and thus contributes to one of the major strands of the novel – an exploration of whether, and if so how, individuals in all their separateness can form links and bonds with other individuals. To explore this issue Forster has chosen the most hostile and testing terrain in which barriers of race, gender and power are added to normal obstacles. In the exchanges between Adela and Aziz on pages 156–7, the issue is raised when Adela recommends 'the universal brotherhood' which Aziz admires, but this possible unity is deflected by mention of the planned marriage and by the emphasis in the narrative that Adela will 'become what is known as an Anglo-Indian' (p.157). The gap is indicated more indirectly through the introduction of Mrs Moore's letter: 'She took out her writing-pad and began, "Dear Stella, Dear Ralph," then stopped, and looked at the queer valley and their feeble invasion of it' (p.160). It is also there at the end of the chapter XV in the juxtaposition of the adjectives 'honest, decent, inquisitive' with the question 'Have you one wife or more than one?'

*3.19* Earlier in the novel Aziz and Fielding are constructed as 'friends, brothers' (p.133), and Fielding is associated with those who can make a true bridge party when Adela and Mrs Moore meet Aziz and Professor Godbole. But the 'stupendous replica of the tea party' (p.140) is fractured from the start when Fielding and Godbole miss the train and for most of the excursion are missing from the narrative. When Fielding is reintroduced we read 'all [is] so pleasant and jolly' (p.166) and it seems as if the atmosphere may be recovered. Forster uses Fielding to allow an interpretation of the events which sees the Indian as wronged – Adela's rapid departure is 'impolite' (p.169) and it is this interpretation that holds sway on the return journey culminating in the final ironic comment by Aziz, 'This picnic is nothing to do with English or Indians; it is an expedition of friends' (p.170). Such an interpretation is promptly cast aside with Aziz's arrest. The English point of view, characterized by the 'perforated doors of zinc' and the presence of Turton 'like a god in a shrine' (p.172), comes to dominate.

## A turning point in the novel?

*3.20* Despite the presence of these familiar elements the expedition to the caves represents a turning point in the book for many critics. How might this be? You might have noticed, first, a change in the setting Forster creates. The novel appears to move to a different kind of India. The initial 'passage to India' taken by Adela and Mrs Moore leads only to another version of England; the possibilities of the mosque are frustrated by the inanity of *Cousin Kate*. But Aziz's outing seems likely to redeem the promise of a real 'passage to India'. Will the novel now become a story of foreign parts, or should we remember that it was written entirely in England? In pondering the question we might remember that Forster had, in his earlier novels, used a foreign country (Italy, for example, in *A Room with a View*) simply as a means of criticizing English narrow-mindedness. India might present simply an opportunity to depict the English at their most narrow-minded, and a country which was very different from the home counties.

*3.21* There are passages in chapters XII–XVI that directly depict the Indian scene. At the beginning Forster's narrating voice moves between a neutral descriptive tone (as in the paragraph beginning 'The night was still dark...', p.142) and an absorption in Aziz's point of view. English male characters – the symbols of authority – are excluded from the scene and the two Englishwomen are described as having 'no race consciousness' (p.142).

*3.22* As the narrative focuses more and more on the caves, so our sense of the foreignness of India becomes more dominant. Imperialism – the sense that the British point of view is automatically superior to the native one – appears only in a small and rather comic way. Adela mistakes 'the withered and twisted stump of a toddy-palm' (p.152) for a snake, and this prompts the villagers and Aziz to exclamations that match the European sense of the exotic danger in India. Even when Adela sees that she has made a mistake, the Indians refuse to abandon the word of an English woman: 'She had put the word into their minds, and they refused to abandon it.' But this small symbol of subservience is here almost swallowed up by the larger descriptions of the landscape and the foreigners: 'Nothing was explained, and yet there was no romance ... A patch of field would jump as if it was being fried, and then lie quiet' (p.153). This foreignness culminates in the description of the caves themselves.

> They skirted the puddle of water, and then climbed up over some unattractive stone, the sun crashing on their backs. Bending their heads, they disappeared one by one into the interior of the hills. The small black hole gaped where their varied forms and colours had momentarily functioned. They were sucked in like water down a drain. Bland and bold rose the precipices; bland and glutinous the sky that connected the precipices; solid and white, a Brahmany Kite flapped between the rocks with a clumsiness that seemed intentional. Before man, with his itch for the seemly, had been born, the planet must have looked thus. The kite flapped away ... Before birds, perhaps ... And then the hole belched, and humanity returned.
>
> (p.158)

There have been hints of this strange world in chapter I, but the descriptions here, which avoid all gentle or picturesque connotations and emphasize a primitive quality, are now directly linked with the story.

*3.23* This quotation from page 158 also indicates a further turning point in the novel, a shift from a kind of Anglo-Indian social comedy (which has perhaps defused our sense of the political) to a more sardonic and intense mood. Forster uses semi-ridiculous imagery (for example, a drain) not to mock social conventions but to highlight (and perhaps make more manageable) a kind of pre-human reality.

*3.24* The episode is also a turning point in precipitating striking changes in the characters of Aziz, Mrs Moore and Adela. It allows a shift to a consideration of deeper levels of personality and the confronting of hitherto only implicit feelings.

## A turning point in the writing of the novel

*3.25* It was fairly common knowledge among Forster's circle that he had begun a novel about India in 1913, which was put aside in 1914 and not taken up again until 1922. From comments in the letters we can tell that a sense that the world was suddenly changing was a principal reason for putting the novel to one side, but to know precisely where the break in composition occurred we need evidence from Forster's working papers. Fortunately large amounts of these have been preserved and edited with great skill by Oliver Stallybrass. Research into the manuscripts of a text is a key aspect of literary scholarship. It can help date a work's composition (as distinct from the date of publication) by finding out when paper was bought or even by comparing the ink used with that used in letters. It can also establish a 'correct' text by discovering, for example, errors introduced by printers. Assembling the rough drafts can help us to see the writer's skill in action as he or she rejects one word or metaphor in favour of another. The manuscript also helps us to see what the author did *not* write – ideas, words and phrases that were rejected. This, in turn, can help us refine our sense of what is there. Incidents, metaphors, and so on, may be introduced to give sharper emphasis to something, but equally they may be excluded so as to leave matters more open.

*3.26* The history of Forster's novel is described briefly by Stallybrass in the introduction to the Penguin edition. In his introduction to the complete edition of the manuscripts he writes of his working methods:

> The writing of *A Passage to India* was a long, painful and complicated process ... Forster did not ... write his way steadily through a first draft, revise this systematically, produce a second draft ... and so on. The exact sequence of events can never be known since ... much of the evidence is missing ... Speculatively, but without undue extravagance, one might hazard a guess that, as Forster completed his first draft of the final page of the novel, other pages were in anything from the first to their tenth avatar [or version]...
>
> (Stallybrass, 1978, p.xi)

*3.27* The manuscripts show that an incident in the caves was always a part of Forster's plan. But they also show that this was the point at which he stopped writing in 1914; comparison of different versions of chapter XV should then be especially helpful in fixing our sense of the final published text. Working on manuscript changes can be very time consuming, requiring very slow and detailed reading, so I have picked out two sections for discussion. The following extract is the published version:

> There were real difficulties here – Ronny's limitations and her own – but she enjoyed facing difficulties, and decided that if she could control her peevishness (always her weak point), and neither rail against Anglo-India nor succumb to it, their married life ought to be happy and profitable. She mustn't be too theoretical; she would deal with each problem as it came up, and trust to Ronny's common sense and her own. Luckily, each had abundance of commcn sense and goodwill.
>
> But, as she toiled over a rock that resembled an inverted saucer she thought, 'What about love?' The rock was nicked by a double row of footholds, and somehow the question was suggested by them. Where had she seen footholds before? Oh yes, they were the pattern traced in the dust by the wheels of the Nawab Bahadur's car. She and Ronny – no, they did not love each other.
>
> (p.162)

*3.28* Oliver Stallybrass's presentation of this passage is not easy to follow if you are not familiar with his methods so, at risk of falsifying the complicated crossings out of Forster's handwritten manuscript, I have created a version of the text that shows both the final version and Forster's earlier workings, and which is easier to read. In the version below, the published text is printed in italics. Words enclosed by arrow brackets, that is <...> or <<...>>, are ones that Forster wrote and then deleted. Occasionally he inserted a word or phrase at a later stage into the emerging text – these are indicated by oblique lines, \.../.

## *ACTIVITY*

After you have read the version below pick out two or three points where Forster has changed the text and make notes on the effects of the changes. Decide, for example, whether Forster was simply trying to make the text read more smoothly or whether he was adjusting the meaning of what he was writing more substantially.

> *There were* <difficulties \over that/ – she knew Ronnie's limitations and tried to know her own> *real difficulties here – Ronnie's limitations and her own – but she* <always faced her> *enjoyed facing difficulties, and* <tried to think them out, and it seemed to her> *decided that if she could* <keep her temper> *control her peevishness (\always/ her weak point), and neither rail against Anglo-India nor succumb to it, their* <lives might> *married life ought to be happy and profitable. She* <must not be theoretical: Mr Fielding was a good model here> *mustn't be too theoretical; she would deal with each problem as it came up, and trust to Ronny's common sense and her own. \Luckily, each had abundance of common sense and goodwill./*
>
> *But as she toiled over a rock that resembled an inverted* <bowl> *saucer she* <suddenly thought> *thought,* <do I love him> <do I love the man I'm going to marry> <do I love> *'What about love?' The rock was nicked by a double row of* <footholds which ran up like a pattern traced by a wheel> *footholds, and somehow* <her> *the question was suggested by them. Where had she seen* <them> *footholds before? Oh* <yes! \ the hyena/> *yes, they were* <like the track of the Khan Bahadur's car which she and Ronny had <<tracked the>> <<examined>> \seen/ in the dust after colliding with the hyena.>*the pattern traced in the dust by the wheel of the Nawab Bahadur's car.* <No, she did not love <<Ronny>>, didn't love anyone.> *She and Ronny – no, they did not love each other.* <She was incapable of passion.>

## *DISCUSSION*

I have picked out three points which seem to me to show a range of changes.

(a) In the rather complicated shuffling of the details of the pattern of the car tracks we can see Forster apparently knowing he wants to introduce a cross-reference to the earlier incident and searching for the smoothest way of doing this.

(b) The rock is first compared to a bowl and then to a saucer. Here Forster seems to be aiming to make the analogy sharper; a rock may look like an upturned bowl but the flattened image of the saucer corresponds more to 'toiled'.

(c) The manuscripts show Forster struggling with what became Adela's question, 'What about love?' There is a shift from a very specific question about two individuals to the more open-ended question. This may suggest a broader question of whether the English are capable of emotion, or perhaps it focuses our attention more directly on Adela. A similar reworking at the end of the extract shows how Forster struggled to get Adela's character right here, and how difficult that was.

*3.29* The next extract I would like you to look at is one that Stallybrass found which has no direct equivalent in the published text and which provides an alternative ending for events in the caves. It began on a torn piece of paper which he was able to match to one on which Forster had worked on the words 'thinking "Damn the English even at their best" he plunged into one of them to recover his balance' (p.164). This time I have reproduced the text as Stallybrass gives it; it may seem rather confusing at first, but I think you will soon become familiar with the style. The editorial marks are broadly as before:

(a) single or double oblique lines around a word or phrase (\ / or \\ //) indicate where Forster has inserted something into an existing sentence;

(b) arrow marks (< >) are used to indicate a word Forster has deleted;

(c) square brackets indicate a comment by the editor, perhaps indicating a word difficult to decipher or misspelt.

The references to B48, B49, B50 and A186v refer to the manuscripts Stallybrass is deciphering, that is, the passage is mostly on pages 48, 49 and 50 of a manuscript he is referring to as B, but a passage is also quoted which is found on the back (v for verso) of page 186 of a manuscript referred to as A.

## *ACTIVITY*

Please read the following extract now and make notes on how it differs from the published text.

> Adela followed at her leisure. She <was insensitive to her minor blunders, and> thought he had run on to prospect. The huge <rock> bowl-shaped rock came to an end and she <found herself on a lean> \reached a vague/ outer shoulder of the Kawa Dol with a view of the plain. <The place was> \It was a place/ full of curves and twists and spattered with broken boulders \and ending in a precipice/– a place not easy to describe nor indeed remarkable except for the black holes which were lavishly punched in it. Original spawning <of the> ground of the caves! Fifteen or twenty were assembled here, their mouths \turned/ in every direction<, some[?]>. The guide did not go to them but ran to the further edge and <appeared to be> looking down at something\\<. He> \he/ <shout[ed]> called out a word that sounded like "motor" but she took no notice//. <She, aimlessly enough,> \Aimlessly enought, she/ followed the tracks in the granite, cut she supposed for the convenience of visitors, and they led her \past the main grupe [*sic*]/ to a cave that rose like a prompter's box. Because it was covered with a thin skin of granite \rock/, and not embedded in the precipice, she thought it might not [*B48:*] be equally dark inside<, and went in to see>. It was of course quite as dark.
>
> [*B48 evidently replaced the deleted A186v, which opens with the same first four words. A186v:*]
>
> be equally dark inside. It was equally dark. She removed her sun-helmet and stood for a moment in the cool \of the circular chamber/, thinking of her future and rubbing her hand along the invisible wall <of the circular chamber>. <Perhaps Ronny didn't> Probably Ronny didn't "love" her either. And perhaps the reason was that neither of them had beautiful bodies – a humiliating reason, but like all things it must be faced. <Common sense> \Intelligence education/ and good-will pull us through – she had no doubt of <them> that. "Yes we all have our limitations" she thought, withdrew her <hand> {palm} \fingers/ from the wall and laid it [*sic*] on her forehead.
>
> [*B48, continued:*] She stood for a moment in the cool, thinking of her plans and rubbing her finger along the invisible wall. \\She thought <what a pity it was> \again/ that she was not in love [with] Ronny. Perhaps he didn't love her. And perhaps the reason was that they neither of them had beautiful bodies. It didn't matter how <beautiful> ardent their souls were,

the <realm> \coldness/ of Matter intervened[?].// An extra darkness showed that someone was following her down the entrance tunnel. "Doctor Aziz –" she began, glad to continue the conversation.

At first she thought that <she was being robbed,> he was <holding> \taking/ her hand \as before/ to help her <out>, then she realised, and shrieked at the top of her voice. "Boum" <went> \shrieked [?]/ the echo. She struck out and he got hold of her other hand and forced her against the wall, he got both her hands in one of his, and then felt at her <dress> \breasts/. "Mrs Moore" she yelled. "Ronny – don't let him, save me." The strap of her Field Glasses, tugged suddenly, was drawn across her throat. She understood – it was to be passed once round her neck, <it was to> she was to be throttled as far as necessary and then ... [*Forster's suspension points*] Silent, though the echo still raged up and down, she waited and when the breath was on her wrenched a hand free, got hold of the glasses and pushed them at \into/ her assailant's mouth. She could not push hard, but it was enough to <free her> hurt him. He let go, and then with both hands \on her weapon/ she smashed <him to pieces> \at him again/. She was strong and had horrible joy in revenge. "Not this time" she cried, and he answered – or <perhaps it was> the cave \did/. She gained the entrance <and> of the tunnel, screamed like a maniac lest he pulled her in when she stooped, and <regained> \then [*sic*]/ the open air, her topi smashed, her fingers bleeding.

"No I mustn't faint, there's not the time, he'll come after me" she thought, and threw herself down a ravine, bumping twenty feet into a water course, [*B49:*] and began to run. Once she looked up and saw the bright green tree \jeering at her over the precipice/. <"Not this time"> she sobbed. "Oh I'm safe, oh I wish I were dead." She kept on falling, hurting herself further on the boulders, she pitched on her face and fell among thorns. She was saved, but what was the use of it. Dim through her tears rose the yellowish levels of the plain.

"Miss Quested!" she heard a voice. A woman was hurrying up the water course – Miss Derek.

"Oh be kind to me" sobbed Adela falling \again/. "I'm no one, I'm done for."

"Whatever is it?" Miss Derek knelt, her face trembling.

"Doctor Aziz ... [*Forster's suspension points*] Oh can you keep him away."

"I think we shall manage that" said the other with a short laugh. "The first thing is to get <me to you \down/ to my car."

"Your car?"

"I drove Mr Fielding out. Don't worry. \Can you walk?/"

"Is Mr Fielding with you? I couldn't –"

"He's gone out to find your camp. I'm going to take you straight back to Chandrapore. Do you see?"

"How good you are."

"We'll see about <that> \my goodness/ later" said Miss Derek white with rage. "Shall I send off my chauffeur and drive you myself."

"Oh thank you – oh you know what I want – Miss Derek, I have been lacking in sympathy myself all my life, I feel."

[*B50:*] "Can you walk is the chief point?"

"I can walk quite well now I have found you" said Adela, more calmly. "You see I escaped, I am <safe> \quite all right/."

"I see. Take my arm."

"I hit him with Ronny's Field Glasses."

Miss Derek paid no more attention to her, except to point out that Mr Fielding could <return with> \escort/ Mrs Moore. She shouted to the chauffeur to go <there too> \after him/ – she would bring on the car herself \in a minute/, she said. The coast now being clear, she helped Adela in, and made her as comfortable as possible. To return at once to Chandrapore seemed to her the <better> \sounder/ course, though Miss Quested complained of thirst and head-ache. She turned the car, laughed at the <agitate[d]> distant protests of the driver, and drove slowly as far as the railway station. Crossing the line, they came to the main road, and there she went full [speed?] reaching the <McBrydes'> \Police Officer's/ bungalow at eleven. Mrs McBryde was in. She would not allow Adela to go any further and put her into her own bed\\ – it was she who had once been a nurse in a native state. Adela <was not injured> \seemed uninjured/, but \there was danger of sun stroke/ her ancle [*sic*] and wrist were covered with minute cactus spines which unless removed at once might work into her blood//. <Meanwhile> \Leaving them together/ Miss Derek rang up Major Callander, and after him Mr McBryde, <the Collector> \Mr Turton/, and Ronny.

(Stallybrass, 1978, pp.241–5)

## *DISCUSSION*

I expect you found the manuscript version rather startling. Stallybrass comments that it is 'of the utmost interest, answering as it does, *for this stage of the novel's genesis*, the question which in the final version Forster leaves so scrupulously unanswered' (p.241, my italics). You must be careful not to conclude, 'Ah, so he did do it; the British were right', remembering that this extract has – in truth – no place in the final text.

The final version is considerably shorter, and you will have noticed that a good deal of the interaction of Adela and Aziz and the detail of Adela's reactions are removed. Looking forward, then, the changes make Aziz's reactions on page 168 more plausible and the reader more sympathetic to this:

> 'We were having an interesting talk with our guide, then the car was seen, so she decided to go down to her friend.' Incurably inaccurate, he already thought that this was what had occurred. He was inaccurate because he was sensitive. He did not like to remember Miss Quested's remark about polygamy, because it was unworthy of a guest...

The changes are crucial as the plot develops towards the trial scene. The revised version allows the reader to define the situation much more for his or herself. In the earlier versions the reader is in no doubt that Adela is at least indecently assaulted. Forster's adoption of the popular convention of three dots (referred to by Stallybrass as 'suspension points') – 'She was to be throttled as far as necessary and then...' and 'Dr Aziz...' – leaves the nature of the assault vague, but the reader is sure something has occurred and that Aziz is responsible. Moreover, in the earlier versions Forster introduced a more or less reliable companion, Miss Derek, to testify to Adela's credibility. Had the earlier version been followed, the chapter might have ended not with uncertainty but with the realistic paraphernalia of escape, telephone calls, and so on. Finally, the language has a strongly melodramatic tone. For example:

> She was strong and had a horrible joy in revenge...
>
> She looked up and saw the bright green tree jeering at her over the precipice...

In contrast the tone of the final version is utterly matter of fact,

> She followed at her leisure, quite unconscious that she had said the wrong thing, and not seeing him she also went into a cave...
>
> (p.164)

Remember that the manuscripts are not a kind of footnote giving information hidden in the final text. What they show is how Forster reworked the episode over a period of ten years and changed the text so as to prevent the reader forming an easy reaction to the events. The changes move our attention away from the detail of the assault in chapter XV to the surrounding pages, to Mrs Moore's disillusion which precedes the incident and to Aziz's feelings which follow.

Finally, in the earlier drafts Forster risks directly evoking the long-standing myth of the sexual potency and aggressiveness of the black slave or brown native subject which both fascinate and terrify the white woman and man, even though he does so only to question the truth of the myth. By making the events secret in the final version, he poses a more subtle question for the reader, namely, does it lie within your nature to believe that this myth is true?

---

## A symbolic reading of the novel

*3.30* In recent years the dominant strands of criticism of *A Passage to India* seem to have favoured a view of the novel as organized much more in terms of symbols. Often such interpretations emphasize the three-part structure of the novel. In his own 'symbolic' interpretation of the novel Wilfred Stone praises G.O. Allen's article 'Structure, symbol and theme in *A Passage to India*' as:

> ...perceptive and just in seeing that the three sections emphasize certain qualities of mind and soul – to the Moslem belongs the emotional nature ['Mosque'], to the Anglo-Indian the intellect ['Caves'], and to the Hindu the capacity for love ['Temple'].
>
> (Stone, 1966, p.311)

*3.31* The journey to the caves remains a turning point in the narrative but in a different way. Stone uses the episode as the title for his study of the whole of Forster's work – *The Cave and the Mountain*. In the chapter on *A Passage to India* he writes:

> But most important are the hollowness and roundness of the caves, and all the mythological evocations of these forms. The novel is one great echo chamber, one great round, but in so constructing it Forster is not simply creating a private fictional universe; he is recreating the world of the Indian religious consciousness ... The adept in Indian art and religion ... would recognize the snakes and flames, the 'bou-oum' and the caves themselves as ancient symbols far transcending any one artist's private myth...
>
> (Stone, 1966, p.307)

*3.32* The chief meaning of the caves – interpreted symbolically in this way – is a representation of some kind of transcendent amoral world. Adela's response is one of terror which she can only counter by allowing the intellect to take over and convert the threatening mystery into the attack. Mrs Moore's response to this experience, which negates all the conventional values of Christianity, is to retreat from it but also from all her previous life. The crucial passage in the novel is:

> Hope, politeness, the blowing of a nose, the squeak of a boot, all produce 'boum'. Even the striking of a match starts a little worm coiling, which is too small to complete a circle, but is eternally watchful. And if several people talk at once an overlapping howling noise begins, echoes generate echoes, and the cave is stuffed with a snake composed of small snakes, which writhe independently.
>
> (p.159)

For G.O. Allen the snake here and elsewhere in the novel represents 'the universal will':

> In the cave, the echo spoke out to her of the oneness of all things; it revealed itself to her as a serpent, the universal will, composed ... of a manifold of wills, writhing independently, struggling against each other.
>
> (Allen, 1955, pp.136–7)

The shock that Adela feels is the result of her perception that she is cut off from this kind of transcendent oneness.

*3.33* An interpretation of the novel based on the symbolic structure produces a meaning for the novel beyond local character and incident. Support for this kind of interpretation can be found in the language of the episode which seems to insist that the story is to be understood on a non-realistic level, as on page 159, or as in the following quotes:

> The elephant walked straight at the Kawa Dol as if she would knock for admission with her forehead, then swerved, and followed a path round its base. The stones plunged straight into the earth ... The sky dominated as usual, but seemed unhealthily near ... It was as if the contents of the corridor had never been changed.
>
> (p.153)

> The small black hole gaped where their varied forms and colours had momentarily functioned. They were sucked in like water down a drain ... the hole belched, and humanity returned.
>
> (p.158)

Mrs Moore is a character fatigued in a realistic way by the oppressive heat of the cave, but she is also a vehicle for a confrontation between the West and the East, and this confrontation is not productive but rather threatens 'to undermine her hold on life' (p.160).

> But suddenly, at the edge of her mind, Religion appeared, poor little talkative Christianity, and she knew that all its divine words from 'Let there be light' to 'It is finished' only amounted to 'boum'. Then she was terrified over an area larger than usual; the universe, never comprehensible to her intellect, offered no repose to her soul...
>
> (p.161)

*3.34* The chapter ends 'She lost all interest, even in Aziz, and the affectionate and sincere words that she had spoken to him seemed no longer hers but the air's.' After the heightened symbolism of the caves, it has been argued, Forster's representation of Mrs Moore's shifts. From here, it seems, she does not act as a realistic guide to the uniting of English and Indian values. In realistic terms her character becomes less coherent and symbolic meanings come to dominate.

*3.35* Lionel Trilling's essay on *A Passage to India*, written in 1943, is not as wholeheartedly symbolic an interpretation as that of Allen or of Stone, but it does put considerable weight on symbolic structure in the book. For example:

> The presence of the wasp, first in Mrs Moore's consciousness, then in Godbole's, Mrs Moore's acceptance of the wasp, Godbole's acceptance of Mrs Moore – in some symbolic fashion, this is the thread of the story of the novel as distinguished from its plot. For the story is essentially concerned with Mrs Moore's discovery that Christianity is not adequate.
>
> (Trilling, 1970, p.86)

Trilling also places great weight on the caves episode, seeing it within 'a web of reverberation [which] ... gives ... [the] book a cohesion and intricacy usually found in music' (p.87). In the essay he then quotes the two paragraphs beginning 'A Marabar cave' (p.158), but his response is not to hold them within the narrative structure of *A Passage to India* but to see them as part of a web spanning Forster's work as a whole.

> Panic and emptiness – Mrs Moore's panic has been at the emptiness of the universe. And one goes back beyond Helen Schlegel's experience of the Fifth Symphony in *Howards End*: the negating mess of the cave reminds us of and utterly denies the mess of that room in which Caroline Abbott saw Gino with his child [in *Where Angels Fear to Tread*] ... then the mess had been the source of life and hope...
>
> (Trilling, 1970, p.88)

*3.36* Trilling does return to the novel to comment on the influence the barely present Mrs Moore has on the remainder of the novel, but the effect of the emphasis on the caves as symbolic is overall to take the book away from the presentation of India.

> The book simply involves the question in ultimates ... the question, after it has been involved in the moods and visions of the story, turns out to be the most enormous question that has ever been asked, requiring an answer of enormous magnitude. Great as the problem of India is, Forster's book is not about India alone; it is about all of human life.
>
> (p.91)

*3.37* Glen Allen and Wilfred Stone link their symbolic readings of the novel with Jungian ideas whereas Trilling adopts a looser and more general philosophical framework. But it is also possible to produce a symbolic reading of the novel which is more linked with Freudian psychoanalytical ideas and which again sees the caves episode as a turning point in the novel. A Freudian approach might lead one to decode the 'true' meaning which is embedded in the text. A brief resumé of such a reading risks caricature but might be usefully set against the reading of Stone and Allen and the interpretation of Trilling. It might draw directly on Freud's *Interpretation of Dreams*, freely admitting that there is no evidence that Forster read a word of Freud, but arguing that such ideas had a general currency in the circle in which he moved. The importance of the narrowness of the entrance to the cave, described on page 158 as a 'small black hole' and as 'the entrance tunnel', is that, in Freud's words, 'Anyone ... who has had a little experience in translating dreams will at once reflect that penetrating into narrow spaces and opening closed doors are among the commonest sexual symbols' (Freud, 1976, p.521). Elsewhere Freud comments that snakes are 'those most important symbols of the male organ' (p.474). In this context the movement of characters that Forster describes may be seen as symbolic of sexual intercourse. This kind of symbolic interpretation may lead one to see Forster as presenting not just the cold unemotional nature of the English which is contrasted with the emotional nature of the Indian, but a positive fear in Adela of male sexuality and sexual intercourse, the supposed encounter with Aziz then standing as surrogate for the potential future encounter with Ronny.

## Noble imperialism?

*3.38* After the caves episode Forster moves the narrative from an isolated and symbolic landscape back into a social and political context. The next crucial scene in the novel is the trial scene in chapter XXIV. Before moving on to that I would like you to look briefly at some of the intervening scenes, particularly where the narrative draws on our memory of earlier scenes. The scene in the English Club in chapter XX parallels that in the opening chapters of the novel; the settings used by Forster are comparatively limited and the return to the changed and symbolic world of the Club creates a visible structure in the novel. In both cases the Club crystallizes a particularly English life which forms a contrast with the Indian scene.

### *ACTIVITY*

In the earlier scene Forster presents racial differences but these are pitched at an individual level – particularly in relation to the characters of Mrs Moore and Ronny Heaslop – and wrapped in everyday conversation. How is racial difference presented in the later scene in the Club (pp.188–97)?

### *DISCUSSION*

The emphasis here is on tension and on ominous confrontation. In the opening paragraph on page 188 the calculated 'studious calm' is set against the native drums. The drums express threat not only because they traditionally represent the possibility of direct attack on the English, but also because they represent a separate Indian culture, conveyed by the reference to Mohurram (p.189). The imperialist attitude is caught here in the use of 'merely' to describe the Indian festival and the detail of separating the women from the men. This is, on one level, a sign of the seriousness of the situation but it is also a sign of fragmentation – Forster presents the English male response to racial divisions as not to try to restore unity but to intensify divisions, much as on a larger canvas the British constantly worked to increase Hindu and Muslim divisions and Muslim fundamentalism.

The presentation of the character of Turton is crucial to the novel's representation of power. At the moment of Aziz's arrest on page 172 he is seen as 'a god in a shrine', but in the later scene Forster puts confused feelings into the character, setting 'the old weary business of compromise and moderation' against the 'good old days when an Englishman could satisfy his honour and no questions asked' (p.190). Forster glosses the contrast, urging the reader away from 'the good old days' by introducing the 'stray subaltern'. Through this character old habits and old responses to India are felt by the reader to be crude and violent, and it is significant that Turton shares in this turning away. The narrative seems to me to push the reader away from the 'good old days' in a more positive way through the character of Fielding.

### *ACTIVITY*

Look now particularly at page 193 and try to work out how Forster organizes a response or sets out a debate here.

### *DISCUSSION*

For me the narrating voice begins to signal a preferred option with the comments, 'Fielding took his pipe from his mouth and looked at it thoughtfully', followed by 'The Collector ... kept silent ... the official in him still hoped that Fielding would toe the line', and finally: 'Fielding rose to his feet, supported by murmurs and exclamations, for no one yet suspected his integrity.'

The narrative increasingly defines Fielding against the crowd, and simultaneously defines being in the crowd as toeing the line. In the final comment the reader is drawn by the irony of 'no one yet suspected his integrity' to a position close to Fielding's and apart from the others. These smaller details prepare for the major moment in the scene when Forster uses the device of the general rising of the gathering when Heaslop enters. Rising to one's feet indicates the arrival of a social superior or someone defined as having special qualities (a woman, perhaps). It is also a sign of respect for the dead. Forster draws on both the former two conventions to create Fielding as unpatriotic and conventionally unchivalrous, refusing respect to Heaslop's special situation. The scene is cast in weighty language:

> He always showed deference to his superiors, but now it came straight from his heart. He seemed to appeal for their protection in the insult that had befallen him, and they, in instinctive homage, rose to their feet.
>
> (pp.194–5)

---

*3.39* The narrative seems to transfer Adela's pain to Ronny, and to construct him as the noble warrior who has to be avenged and whose suffering sanctifies and justifies the imperial ideology of dominance. But there is an immediate retreat from this language in the next sentence with the narrative commentary that everything is 'tainted with officialism'. The grounds of the critique implied in these words are spelled out with the words 'they condemned Aziz and India'; the rhetoric is brought up against a human individual and against India. But the references to India are made only in passing; the emphasis falls on 'ungracious … caddish … perhaps … unsound' and thus on human sympathy. Later the situation is reversed.

*3.40* The scene in the Club may be seen in the structure of the novel as a kind of trial or accusation of Fielding which parallels that of Aziz earlier, and that of Miss Quested which is to follow. Fielding has been established as an informal liberal foil to the serious public English world. Here – in contrast to the earlier scenes in the mosque or at Fielding's house, where it seems possible to create links between the races – Forster pushes different positions to extremes rather than experimenting with unity. In a sense Adela's injury is transferred to Ronny; the sexual nature of the attack and the consequent 'femininism' of Ronny make the supposed attack particularly dangerous to the imperial (patriarchal) power. Conversely Fielding's private liberal sympathies are pressed to a more public stance. 'I am waiting for the verdict of the courts. If he is guilty I resign from my service, and leave India. I resign from the Club now' (p.196).

*3.41* The final version of this passage represents a crystallization of a potentially longer version which can be constructed from the manuscripts, that is:

> 'I am waiting for the verdict of the courts. The evidence against him will fall to pieces under cross-examination. If it doesn't and he is guilty then I shall resign from my service and leave India. That is all I have to say.'
>
> 'Hear, hear. That's all right,' said one or two of the men, who liked the tone of the speech and had not grasped its implication.
>
> 'I am resigning from the Club now,' Fielding added. 'If my friend is innocent and you care for me to come back, I shall resume my membership with pleasure.'
>
> 'Yes, to pick up more information,' muttered Callander. 'Now we know why everything leaks out.'
>
> (Stallybrass, 1978, pp.330–1)

## *ACTIVITY*

What is Forster emphasizing in the final version?

## *DISCUSSION*

There is an emphasis on the desire for truth; a man is innocent until proved guilty. The truth is also imagined as something supported by institutions, that is, the courts. The second sentence of the final version does not allow of political chicanery in the court; such a possibility might be allowed if the text read 'If he is *found* guilty'. The emphasis is in this way shifted to the loss of faith in India. The reader's position here can hardly be detached. Forster has hitherto used our sympathy for Mrs Moore and Fielding to set up India as a place of meaning; if Aziz is guilty then our world too will be turned upside down.

---

*3.42* In this scene in the Club Forster seems to be addressing directly the nature and value of individual and personal responses to imperial politics and values. By implication Forster is also addressing here the issue of Indian nationalist violence. For Turton and the others at the Club the situation is simpler; the 'savagery' displayed by the Indians justifies their holding aloof, the British sense of superiority, and their right to rule. The situation is more difficult for the liberals; for their views centre on the notion of a basic fellow feeling and shared sense of values in Indian and English alike; the anguish of the position is conveyed in the official view of Turton as he damns Fielding: 'You are weak, weak, that is what is wrong with you' (p.196).

*3.43* But it is possible to see him also addressing more directly the political events of the time in the build up to the trial scene. These sentences are embedded within the narrative, but I hope you will have picked up a reference in the paragraph on page 188 to the 'air of the Residency at Lucknow' evoking the events of the Sepoy uprising of 1857. A further extension of the frame of the novel, carrying it momentarily beyond the individual, occurs on page 190, when Forster puts into the Collector's thoughts 'but the Government of India itself also watches – and behind it is that caucus of cranks and cravens, the British Parliament'.

*3.44* Readers in the 1920s could well have seen here an allusion to the debates between those, including many in the imperial government in India, who clung to an 'old' imperialist desire, particularly in Britain, to hold together the empire, and those with a desire to recreate it in a more modern form. From London it was crucial that in the 1914–18 war India had apparently consented to be part of the empire. Those seeking independence had not taken advantage of the absence of British garrisons as troops were moved to the European war; Indian soldiers had again made common cause with the British. Edwin Montagu wished to build upon this. His statement to the House of Commons in 1917 began:

> The policy of His Majesty's Government, with which the Government of India are in complete accord, is that of the increasing association of Indians in every branch of the administration and the gradual development of self-governing institutions with a view to the progressive realization of responsible government in India as an integral part of the British Empire...

However, even he added

> ...progress in this policy can only be achieved by successive stages ... guided by the cooperation received from those upon whom new opportunities of services will thus be conferred and by the extent to which it is found that confidence can be reposed in their sense of responsibility.
>
> (quoted in Rumbold, 1979, p.89)

After 1921, and after the time of the novel's publication, the reforming faction lost ground, squeezed between the demands of the radical Indian nationalists and the more trenchant imperialists in Britain. Tensions also arose between the nationalists in India. Signs of these shifts are perhaps to be found in the words Forster gives to Turton, which I have quoted above.

## The trial scene

### *ACTIVITY*

Please look again at pages 217–33 and try to identify one or two key moments or elements in the scene which you feel are particularly significant.

### *DISCUSSION*

The most obvious key moment in the scene is Adela's willingness to give damning evidence against Aziz. Up to this point the evidence has been ambiguous. On one hand the narrative of events at the caves includes gaps, and our sense of Aziz's behaviour largely exonerates him. On the other hand the narrative later articulates the accusations against Aziz with some conviction, for Adela is constructed as a reliable witness. Even her eventual direct testimony contradicts earlier certainties. It is worth noting that the reader is confined within the narrative and there seems to be no other possible perpetrator of the deed than Aziz; the guide simply and neutrally disappears from the story. Because of the lack of other suspects and our closeness to Aziz, the text scarcely allows us to ask 'who did it?' and pushes us instead towards 'what happened?' Even after the trial the narrative remains open. The most that can be said is that the withdrawal of the accusation creates a consistency between Adela's point of view and the events of chapter XV. The trial thus seems to confirm a sense that knowledge is possible, but that it is negative and limited.

Other key moments which you might have picked out are when the English are first elevated to and then dethroned from the platform. These moments dramatize the fact that imperialist and official values dominate but then, equally importantly, we see that they may be reduced to apparent subservience to a higher set of values.

You might see the reappearance of Mrs Moore – at least in spirit – as the Hindu goddess 'Esmiss Esmoor' as a key moment, showing Forster perhaps optimistically presenting a victory for the racial harmony she represents (the 'just official' is Indian). A less optimistic view might arise from the condescension which lies behind the delegation of power to the Indian magistrate (p.223), and the fact that the truth is delivered by a white witness rather than an Indian one, or that the whole mechanism for discovering truth is merely a 'flimsy framework' (p.232) subject to wider forces in the narrative.

---

*3.45* Many critics, however, have preferred even in this scene to move away from the realistic surface to emphasize a deeper set of meanings – perhaps in part promised by the openness Forster leaves in his account of what happened at the caves. Lionel Trilling, for example, first comments that the scene 'brings to spectacular virulence the latent antagonisms between rulers and ruled' (1970, p.83), yet later in the essay he writes:

> Although Mrs Moore abandons everything, even moral duty, she dominates the subsequent action. As 'Esmiss Esmoor' she becomes to the crowd around the courthouse, a Hindu goddess who was to save Aziz. And, we are given vaguely to understand, it is her influence that brings Adela to her senses and the truth.
>
> (pp.89–90)

*3.46* Wilfred Stone in *The Cave and the Mountain* sees the same kind of fractured society represented in the trial scene but focuses on the figure of the punkah wallah, quoting extensively from the paragraph on pages 200–1 and commenting:

> One of the most moving portraits in the novel is that of the Sudra, the untouchable, who pulls the punkah ... The swirls of air carried on the rhythms of that passage become part of the common respiration of all the races in that courtroom, but they do not remind them that they are one. Even Godbole ... is separated from his god.
>
> (Stone, 1966, p.319)

Later Stone draws on the uncertainties Forster leaves in the narrative referring to Godbole's words on pages 185–6:

> that action was performed by Dr Aziz ... It was performed by the guide ... It was performed by you ... It was performed by me ... And by my students. It was even performed by the lady herself.

Stone comments:

> What exactly did happen to Adela in the caves? Nothing happened to her, in two senses of the word. In a literal, legal sense no event occurred ... But nothing also occurred in a psychic sense: she had a glimpse into the everlasting no, the pit of nada, the ultimate negation lying at the bottom of the unconscious. She had seen what can be explained mythologically as the archetypal emptiness preceding existence itself.
>
> (pp.334–5)

Given such a reading it is not surprising that Stone treats the trial scene and the search for truth only briefly.

## Another real India: the Amritsar Massacre

*3.47* I want now to set beside these readings one based more on political events that occurred at the time when Forster was writing the novel. I do not want to suggest that Forster intentionally modelled the novel on the events I describe below; it was alien to Forster's idea of novel writing to attempt any kind of dramatized documentary or historical novel, and *A Passage to India* does not provide a literal depiction of the events to which I refer. Yet there are parallels between what happened at Amritsar and in the novel, and the events at Amritsar caused such a sensation that one must at least see them as forming a context for the novel. My own instinct is to go beyond this and see Forster as intervening – albeit at a suitably allusive tangent – into the controversies raised by the massacre. Forster was extremely well placed to know of the events not only from his visit to India but because his close friend, Malcolm Darling, was serving near Amritsar at the time of the massacre. Darling was an Imperial Civil Servant but he held liberal views; he seems to have supplied some of the seeds of the character of Fielding and the events of the novel. In the rash of accusation and counter accusation after the massacre, Darling was 'accused of dereliction of duty – that is to say, of refusing to help a colleague in time of emergency. The gossip in the Club was that he had shown cowardice' (Furbank, 1978, p.60). He later wrote to Forster:

> But what of India you say ... What's the Statesman's panacea? Dyarchy or Democracy. For India, with her 300 million illiterates – God's truth, we must be possessed ... Yet I almost believe it's the only way out of the mess Montagu and his gang have got us into. Home Rule is so much in the air,

> that now the only way is to let them have it. Let 'em taste the poison they long for ... It can't last, any more than a sandcastle before a rising tide.
>
> (quoted in Furbank, 1978, pp.60–1)



*3.48* The introduction to the Penguin edition of *A Passage to India* refers to the massacre that took place at Amritsar in 1919 (see p.13). The massacre came in the wake of nationalist resistance to a series of Acts, called the Rowlatt Acts, which gave the imperial police stringent powers of arrest and search 'severely curtailing the civil liberties of Indians in the name of curbing terrorist violence' (Chandra *et al.*, 1989, p.181). Mridula Mukherjee describes the response as:

> Constitutional protest having failed, Gandhiji stepped in and suggested that a *Satyagraha* [an act of passive resistance or civil disobedience, particularly advocated by Gandhi in the Indian nationalist struggle] be launched. The sixth of April was fixed as the date on which the *Satyagraha* would be launched. The movement that emerged was very different from the one that had been anticipated or planned. Delhi observed the *hartal* [a day of national mourning when business is suspended, used as a form of boycott in the nationalist struggle] on March 30 because of some confusion about dates, and there was considerable violence in the streets ... Punjab, which was suffering from the after effects of severe war-time repression, forcible recruitment, and the ravages of disease, reacted particularly strongly and both in Amritsar and Lahore the situation became very dangerous for the Government. Gandhiji tried to go to Punjab to help quieten the people, but the Government deported him to Bombay.
>
> ...In Amritsar, the arrest of two local leaders on 10 April led to an attack on the town hall and the post office; telegraph wires were cut and Europeans including women were attacked. The army was called in and the city handed over to General Dyer, who issued an order prohibiting public meetings and assemblies. On 13 April, *Baisakhi* day, a large crowd of people, many of whom were visitors from neighbouring villages who had come to the town to attend the *Baisakhi* celebrations, collected in the Jallianwala Bagh to attend a public meeting. General Dyer, incensed that his orders were disobeyed, ordered his troops to fire upon the unarmed crowd. The shooting continued for ten minutes. General Dyer had not thought it necessary to issue any warning to the people nor was he deterred by the fact that the ground was totally hemmed in from all sides by high walls which left little chance for escape. The Government estimate was 379 dead, other estimates were considerably higher.
>
> (in Chandra *et al.*, 1989, pp.181–2)

A British historian of India commented on the actions of General Dyer as follows:

> Dyer had been placed in a position of much difficulty. It was of great importance to regain control over the city quickly, because it was a focus for rebellion. But the force under his command was very small for that purpose. His communications were cut and his information uncertain. The civil authorities had abdicated and he was without their guidance. He was entitled to the view that a warning of his intention to fire would have been inaudible and a futile formality. But, after everything possible is said in Dyer's justification, the conclusion must be that, as the crowd made no attempt to attack, he should have tried to give warning of his intention; that in continuing to fire for so long he used a degree of force which was palpably excessive; and that he behaved with callous inhumanity. Dyer's upbringing in the domiciled European community at Simla gave him a race consciousness which prejudiced his power to handle calmly his dilemma. As Churchill later said, it was 'a terrible, a monstrous deed'.
>
> (Rumbold, 1979, p.143)

*3.49* Several elements of the event relate quite directly to *A Passage to India*. Firstly, the incident sprang from a religious occasion; the interest in Indian religion shown in the novel could, as with Mrs Besant, be seen as a politically charged stance. Secondly there is what Rumbold calls the 'race consciousness' which influenced Dyer's actions and which Forster describes in the Club scenes. This indirectly violent behaviour must in the novel stand for the British violence in the massacre itself to which, like Indian nationalism, Forster makes no reference. He does, however, seem to refer to incidents in the rioting which briefly followed the massacre in which British civilians – not implicated in the military massacre – were attacked. Malcolm Darling was sickened by the massacre itself but also horrified by the way the Indians turned indiscriminately on the British:

> Enter infuriated general – 'I took 30 seconds to make up my mind', said he to Watkin – and then – 1500 rounds. God it makes me sick to think of it...
>
> On the other side you can guess the effect of the Amritsar murders [that is, the revenge attacks on the British by Indians]. They were awful Morgan. Two of the men I knew slightly. But it was the way they tried to batter the women to death. One [Miss Marcia Sherwood], a friend of Josie's, who had ridden into the City to save *Indian* girls (Christian) was set upon and knocked down half a dozen times before she was left for dead. Mon Dieu, it's a bad world...
>
> (in Furbank, 1978, p.61)

In the ensuing events the fact that Miss Sherwood had been taken in and nursed by an Indian family at some risk to themselves was forgotten.

*3.50* General Dyer's response was more direct than Darling's:

> On 19 April Dyer saw the bandage-swathed figure of Miss Sherwood ... He was so outraged that he decided a special punishment would have to be devised for the cowardly attack on the woman who had done so much for the local people. As he held all white women to be sacred he ordered that the Kucha Tawarian, the narrow lane in which the attack had taken place, should become hallowed ground. He went to the scene and ordered a tiktiki, or whipping triangle, to be erected in the middle, posted pickets at each end and issued instructions that any Indian who wished to pass along the lane would have to do so on all fours. It was not a rash decision for he had 'searched his brain for a suitable punishment' that would bring home to everyone the enormity of the crime. No one was exempt from the order...
>
> Although Dyer preferred to describe his order as 'going on all fours', it in fact meant that people had to squirm along on their stomachs because soldiers stood over them and prodded them with rifle butts and bayonets if they lifted their legs or arms...
>
> As the days passed and conditions worsened, the Kucha Tawarian became almost uninhabitable. In normal times it was a squalid, insanitary street, but during the seven days the order was in existence it became a foul-smelling, refuse-strewn sewer ... The sick remained unattended because doctors had no wish to visit patients and arrive covered in filth and smelling like a dung heap...
>
> Dyer had erected the whipping triangle in the middle of the lane for the express purpose of publicly chastizing the people responsible for the attack on Miss Sherwood, and when six youths were arrested on suspicion of having been involved he did not wait for them to be tried. He became a self-appointed judge and jury, reached his verdict and ordered them to be taken to the 'Crawling Lane', tied to the tiktiki and given thirty strokes each. It did not matter to him that they might have been punished unfairly...
>
> Dyer's action was ... condoned by the Adjutant-General, Lieutenant-General Sir Havelock Hudson, during a debate in the Viceroy's Council:
>
> 'I feel sure that the Council will agree that it is not surprising that the officer in command took the view that some unusual measures were necessary to bring home to the mob that such acts of violence directed

> against innocent women could not be tolerated. Something was required to strike the imagination and impress on all the determination of the military authorities to protect European women.'
>
> The 'Crawling Order' remained in effect until 24 April when [the Provincial Lieutenant Governor] Sir Michael O'Dwyer heard about it and asked the Viceroy to order its withdrawal.
>
> (Draper, 1981, pp.111–3)

*3.51* Dyer's action was thus largely supported by the more local British government in India, but not at the national level. The India Office in London was horrified by Dyer's measures. A Committee of Inquiry was set up in India which met in October 1919 (the Hunter Committee), and at this point reports and discussion of the incidents previously suppressed under martial law again began to appear in the British press. On 13 December the *Daily Express* carried a report of the inquiry proceedings which balanced the horror of the event – '2,000 Indians shot down' – against a certain respect for the situation of General Dyer who had had a 'horrible duty' to perform. The final report of the Hunter Committee which appeared in May 1920 was inconclusive; it split on racial lines with the Indian minority report being especially condemnatory of Dyer. As in Forster's novel, judicial inquiries did not lead to truth and solutions but only to further racial divisions, but Dyer was relieved of his command and fell into a measure of disgrace.

*3.52* The controversy over the events continued in Britain. When the report was discussed in Parliament in July 1920 the Conservatives used the occasion to attack the liberal policies of Montagu and to defend Dyer. Montagu was a Jew and the Conservatives, led by Sir Edward Carson, played on this; a contemporary described the attack as 'a very astonishing exhibition of anti-Jewish feeling' (quoted in Rumbold, 1979, p.202). In Britain the massacre also had wider significance, particularly in relation to Ireland. Judgements on the conduct of Britain as an occupying and civilizing power in India also reflected on its conduct and policies in Ireland and vice-versa. Carson had been instrumental in safeguarding Protestant rights in Ulster. In 1922, for example, 'the collapse of the British policy in Ireland ... prompted fears of a similar misfortune in India' (Rumbold, 1979, p.316).

*3.53* Officially the story might have ended there, but in 1922, as Forster returned from India, the Amritsar Massacre again returned to the news. Sir Sankaran Nair published *Ghandi and Anarchy* in Delhi. Nair was a nationalist but moderate and pro-British. His book attacked the civil disobedience policies of Gandhi but it was also highly critical of O'Dwyer, who had imposed martial law and backed General Dyer in 1919. O'Dwyer mounted an action for libel against Nair in 1924, and the events of the massacre itself and the subsequent events were again reviewed in court and in the press. Astonishingly, despite all the evidence of the massacre collected by the Hunter Committee, Dyer and O'Dwyer were successful in their case. O'Dwyer claimed the verdict 'vindicated ... British rule in India' (Draper, 1981, p.261).

*3.54* But it was more a tribute perhaps to the partisanship of the judge, who peppered his comments with pro-British remarks and said in his summing up to the jury, 'General Dyer, in the grave and exceptional circumstances, acted rightly, and in my opinion he was wrongly punished by the Secretary of State for India' (Furbank, 1978, p.123). The sole dissenting juror was Harold Laski, who by chance was called to the jury and who was already an expert on the affair. His exchanges with the judge enlivened the trial. Again Forster had a privileged access to information since he knew Laski slightly. Forster's fury at the verdict is expressed in a letter to Darling in India in June 1924. The language is different from that employed in the novel, but it is worth pausing to reflect on whether the letter and novel share the same political feelings, or whether, for Forster, events had already overtaken the feelings expressed in the novel.

> Thus: – Sir S. Nair, a shit, writes a book against Ghandhi, which incidentally contains a sentence libelling O'D. Besides being a shit, he is a Moderate so O'D takes the opportunity of discrediting that party by bringing an action, and wrecking our best hopes of coming to terms with India. – Is this correct? It is impossible to suppose O'D minded the attack personally, moreover only three copies of N's book ever came to this country. God, I have been enraged. A dirty political manoeuvre.
>
> (quoted in Furbank, 1978, p.123)

## 'Life returned to its complexities...'

*3.55* Interest in the libel action and in Indian politics made *A Passage to India* Forster's most popular novel and in 1924 it could hardly escape its political and racial context. Most readers could only construe Forster as being pro-Indian in the novel and anti-imperialist. At times, too, the narrative seems very definitely to be making an intervention into a political discourse. For example, at the end of the trial scene in the last paragraph of chapter XXIV there is a powerful emphasis in the sentence 'Victory on this side, defeat on that – complete for one moment was the antithesis' (p.233). But the emphasis and political certainty is immediately partly withdrawn in the next sentence which begins 'Then life returned to its complexities...'. The chapter ends:

> ...no one remained on the scene of the fantasy but the beautiful naked god. Unaware that anything unusual had occurred, he continued to pull the cord of his punkah, to gaze at the empty dais and the overturned special chairs, and rhythmically to agitate the clouds of descending dust.
>
> (p.233)

### *ACTIVITY*

Does anything in this strike you as unusual?

### *DISCUSSION*

There is still a sense that this is the end of a scene, but the use of the word 'fantasy' and the phrase 'Unaware that anything unusual had occurred' should catch our attention. These few words attributable to the narrator appear to undercut the weight of the previous scene. To assert that 'life returned to its complexities' from the stark polarization of the English and Indian worlds would count as a subversive comment to those readers who believed that the rights of the dominant race should be reasserted. But the comment disappears in the final sentence; and one is led into seeing the events dissolve, rather than echoing in other wider polarities. This tactic, whereby one feels simultaneously that things are being drawn to a conclusion and that things are incomplete, is common in the novel (see, for example, chapters III and VIII). The puzzle that this generates leads some critics to emphasize the symbolic and non-realistic elements in the novel.

### *ACTIVITY*

Chapters XXV–XXXII share overall something of this rather ambiguous sense of conclusion and closure. Look briefly at the beginning of chapter XXVI (pp.239–42).

## *DISCUSSION*

The sense of closure here takes the form of a lingering reprise of the discovery of the truth. The language of Fielding is constructed from language akin to that of an examiner or inquisitor. For example, 'it's an important piece of evidence ... Let us go back ... My belief – and of course I was listening carefully ... Let me conclude my analysis' (pp.240–2). The reader follows Fielding here, still interested in knowing what 'really' happened at the cave, but the narrative again undercuts this. This is perhaps most obviously the case in the narrator's intervention on page 241: 'There was a moment's silence, such as often follows the triumph of *rationalisation*' (my italics), but you might also detect this in the descriptions of Adela that are built into the narrative rather than dramatized. For example, 'the vision disappeared whenever she wished to interpret it ... the question had lost interest for her suddenly' (pp.241–2).

*3.56* The importance of knowledge is again downgraded in relation to Aziz. The events of the trial might be thought to bring him relief but Forster makes this unimportant. In the prominent opening sentence of chapter XXXI the narrative proclaims 'Aziz had no sense of evidence' (p.268). Neither does the assertion of truth lead to inspiration, and in this context we read, 'science was merely an acquisition, which he laid aside when unobserved, like his European dress' (p.265). Finally, in the Indian society described in chapter XXX the knowledge that arises from the trial does not resolve anything but leads to a worsening of racial tensions; in this respect the outcome is parallel to the aftermath of the Hunter Inquiry. In the novel Aziz becomes more anti-British – the change in relations is signalled by the way he ceases to be a paid employee of the Raj and instead pursues it for damages. There is a Hindu–Muslim accord and Indian nationalism is strengthened. By comparison, with the exception of Fielding and Adela, Forster reduces the English characters to silence and stereotypical actions and attitudes. You will remember that earlier in the novel the relationship of Mrs Moore and Aziz was presented as a realistic image of possible unity between the races. Mrs Moore is removed from the novel on page 214 but retains a presence during the trial (for example, pp.228, 254) and after.

## *ACTIVITY*

What do you make of the references to Mrs Moore after the trial (for example, pp.252, 259, 261)?

## *DISCUSSION*

Firstly there remains a sense that as a character Mrs Moore has importance and value. The querulous language and the actions that Forster had introduced into the character after the expedition to the caves are downplayed, and instead we read of Aziz's view that Mrs Moore 'will solve everything' (p.252). Fielding and Aziz evoke her as a repository of fine feeling (p.259). Once Mrs Moore leaves India Forster can use her character more freely, like the events in the caves.

This seems to me in keeping with the way the narrative after the trial adopts a more fractured style. The endings of chapters XXV, XXIX, XXXI and XXXII all seem to share the inconclusiveness of chapter XXVI. The openings of the chapters also seem abrupt and disconcerting.

*3.57* The novel becomes more self-refential but the allusions made by characters do not always coincide with the reader's perceptions. For example, when Fielding looks back to 'the evening after the catastrophe' (p.249) the direct reference is to the ending of chapter XX. This was a very important passage, containing some of the most striking language.

> ...the Marabar Hills ... leapt into beauty; there were Montsalvat, Valhalla, the towers of a cathedral, peopled with saints and heroes, and covered with flowers ... the Marabar Hills ... seemed to move graciously towards him like a queen, and their charm became the sky's.
>
> (p.197)

But at the end of chapter XXVI the language, 'the fists and fingers of the Marabar swell until they included the whole night sky' (p.249), surely also takes the reader more immediately back to the opening chapter where the echo of 'fists and fingers' is more precise. This referring back to the beginning of the novel becomes more common in the 'Temple' section.

*3.58* There are further occasions when the language seems to pull away from the realistic discourse which dominates the novel. Look, for example, at the paragraph on page 262 beginning, 'A friendliness...'. This is ostensibly about Adela and Fielding, but meaning is surely troubled rather than expanded by the initial references to the friendliness being like 'dwarfs shaking hands'. The repetition of this image troubles the reader further; the sense of sudden detachment from the present situation they experience is in realistic terms relatively straightforward, but what about the comparison to 'dwarfs talking, shaking hands and assuring each other that they stood on the same footing of insight'?

*3.59* Similar perplexities arise as first Adela and then Fielding experience the passage *from* India. In the case of Adela, there is the sudden gratuitous introduction of the American missionary who, seeing the Lesseps statue which marks the gateway to the East at Port Said, can only comment on 'the cute position of his hands, one of which holds a string of sausages' (p.263). Fielding's passage to Europe is marked first by a rather striking and novel image as Egypt is seen as 'a green strip of carpet' (p.277), but the language then shifts to a bland travel-writing style mixed with a rhetoric which the rest of the novel urges us to view with suspicion.

## Temple

*3.60* The final part of *A Passage to India* begins with a shift in the setting of the novel; Chandrapore ceases to be an appropriate place for the Indian-dominated society that is now presented (see page 18). The representation of Indian culture also changes as the imperial frame disappears. During the build up to the trial, the main, exclusively Indian event mentioned – the primarily Muslim Mohurram celebration – existed only as a series of interruptions into the narrative, for example, as a threat to British life or a sign of disorder (pp.188, 198) and as a sign of the supremacy of the British.

> The last day of the festival, the great procession left its official route, and tried to enter the Civil Station, and a telephone had been cut because it interrupted the advance of one of the larger paper towers. McBryde and his police had pulled the thing straight – a fine piece of work.
>
> (p.201)

*3.61* In contrast in chapter XXX the Hindu ceremony fills the narrative. In the earlier part of the novel and in the trial scene (apart from the punkah-wallah) the Indian lower class is seen only as a crowd and a mass (for example, p.233) which threatens the English. Yet on page 281, with only a small qualification, the narrative sees the village Hindus as 'the toiling ryot, whom some call the real India'. It seems that the 'real India' is no longer the cave or the echo or even the oppressive relations of British and Indians, but a crowd which the narrator defines as existing 'in a tender, happy state unknown to an English crowd' (p.281). There is still strangeness, but here it lies in the rather paradoxical sense that meaning lies in 'a silver image the size of a teaspoon' (p.281) and 'a red silk napkin' (p.285) rather than the 'terrifying echo' (p.158) of the caves which causes Mrs Moore to sit 'motionless with horror' (p.161). The world of Godbole, placed earlier in the novel always as an alien presence amid something familiar (for example, p.95), is now at the centre of the narrative.

*3.62* For all the newness in chapter XXXIII, however, I expect you noticed a number of ways in which the last section is more congruently linked with what has gone before. On page 283 there is the reference to Mrs Moore:

> Godbole, though she was not important to him, remembered an old woman he had met in Chandrapore days. Chance brought her into his mind while it was in this heated state, he did not select her ... he remembered a wasp seen he forgot where...

One might argue that Forster is playing games in the narrative here; the text tells us that Godbole is moved by 'chance'. Yet the reader must feel the pressure of pattern. He or she knows more than Godbole in being able to supply the name of the old woman and to find precisely where the wasp exists in the story. The memory of Mrs Moore also arises on page 286 when the narrator comments on Christianity. Doubts are raised in the caves episode, where Christianity is seen as trivial in contrast to the endless echo in the caves. The problem is now reformulated:

> There is fun in heaven. God can play practical jokes upon Himself, draw chairs away from beneath His own posteriors ... By sacrificing good taste, this worship achieved what Christianity has shirked: the inclusion of merriment. All spirit as well as all matter must participate in salvation, and if practical jokes are banned the circle is incomplete.
>
> (p.286)

*3.63* You may have noticed other links. One might even argue (if one wished to pursue the symbolic interpretations of the novel) that there is a pattern in the way the flask-like roundness of the caves has been converted into the circles represented by the ritual games described on page 286.

*3.64* The character of Aziz might also be seen as establishing links with what has gone before. He represents still the outsider caught between two cultures – the situation is neatly caught in a geographical metaphor when Forster describes him at work 'in a room accessible to Western science by an outer staircase' (p.286). Through Aziz there are links with other characters and other strands in the story. On page 289 the Fielding story is picked up in the cards and letters and the report of marriage. But this strand is picked up only to be thrown aside like the letters Aziz 'destroyed unopened ... the end of a foolish experiment' (p.289). There are also hints of a return to earlier political themes, although the Indian native state is different from Chandrapore. The English political agent, Colonel Maggs, is firmly located as a figure lacking the ultimate power of Turton, although seen equally forcefully as representative of an imperious culture urgently desiring to fulfil demands which are trivial:

> ...the note turned into the sort of note that always did arrive from the State Guest House. Wanting something. No eggs. Mosquito nets torn. When could they pay their respects to His Highness?
>
> (p.291)

Perhaps, then, Colonel Maggs seems not a new character but an extension or remixing of earlier qualities Forster puts into the scenes at the Club.

*3.65* Chapter XXXVI consolidates the sense of racial separateness and, for most readers, the sense that in its own way Forster's almost multiracial India is preferable to the narrow Englishness in the novel. The sympathy for Aziz that develops in the earlier sections is confirmed because the narrative is confined within the pain and puzzle of his point of view in chapter XXXIV. Equally, the flowing language of the narrative in chapter XXXIII has also swept us into sympathy with an Indian point of view. If one had to pick out a phrase to push this point home one might select, from page 282, 'the approaching triumph of India was a muddle (as we call it), a frustration of reason and form'. The bracketed phrase presses us into reading 'muddle' as westerners but also into seeing it as a word local to our culture. The flow of the narrative pushes us into rejecting the English judgements on native India embodied in the novel in favour of, for example, 'completeness' (p.283). The phrase 'a frustration of reason and form' chimes in with the way in which evidence and the search for truth have been seen as only a partial view (see paragraphs 3.44, 3.55–6). It is not surprising then that when truth does break out at the end of chapter XXXV the result is represented as far from simple:

> Cyril followed him through the mud, apologizing, laughing a little, wanting to argue and reconstruct, pointing out with irrefragable logic that he had married, not Heaslop's betrothed, but Heaslop's sister. What difference did it make at this hour of the day? He [Aziz] had built his life on a mistake, but he had built it. Speaking in Urdu, that the children might understand, he said: 'Please do not follow us, whomever you marry. I wish no Englishman or Englishwoman to be my friend.'
>
> (p.298)

*3.66* Truth seems less important than the sense of cultural belonging. The detail 'speaking in Urdu' is given a realistic justification but symbolically it might count as a reclaiming of language and consciousness by the Indian and a rejection of the imposed English speech. The meaning of Englishness has shifted away from questions about who may invite whom to the Club (as in chapter III) and who may sit in judgement upon whom, and has become something much wider.

## *ACTIVITY*

Please read again the final two chapters of the novel. How far can the case I have advanced for *A Passage to India* being read as a political and pro-Indian novel be sustained here? How does Forster represent the two races in these chapters?

## *DISCUSSION*

Plainly Hindu India exerts a powerful force, and descriptions continue to be supported by the interventions of the narrating voice. For example:

> The festival flowed on, wild and sincere, and all men loved each other, and avoided by instinct whatever could cause inconvenience or pain.
>
> Aziz could not understand this, any more than the average Christian could.
>
> (p.299)

Implicitly here a distinction is made between the westernized Muslim Indian and the Asian Hindu Indian, and implicitly the passage contains anti-imperial, pro-Indian sentiments. Yet crucially this representation of something quintessentially Indian is not advanced into any more coherent overall image. Something is claimed for Godbole in chapter XXXIII and in chapter XXXVI (for example, 'Aziz always felt like a baby in that strange presence', p.300), but Forster constructs Godbole as almost entirely obsessively religious, prone to old-fashioned imperial fantasies (the 'King Emperor George Fifth High School') and incapable of operating within the plot. The narrator tells the reader that Godbole 'had never been known to tell anyone anything' (p.300); because of this the reader and Aziz pursue quite the wrong track for almost two chapters. This surely prevents the reader feeling he can offer any key to the problems Forster describes.

Equally the individual British characters have mostly only a small presence and are isolated. Forster now presents Ronny as having declined into the conventional British state:

> 'You are lucky to be out of British India at the present moment. Incident after incident, all due to propaganda, but we can't lay our hands on the connecting thread. The longer one lives here, the more certain one gets that everything hangs together. My personal opinion is, it's the Jews.'
>
> (p.303)

The inference in these chapters is that, without an Indian cause to pursue, outside India and within British society, Fielding's liberal values also wither. This is emphasized in Ronny's letter and the way the narrative asserts firmly at the beginning of chapter XXXVII that Aziz and Fielding are 'Friends again, yet aware that they would meet no more'.

---

*3.67* One might feel that it is this pessimism that is dramatized in the Anglo-Indian expedition which takes place in the final chapters as the British, almost accidently accompanied by Aziz, take to boats to see the Indian ceremony from the 'grandstand' view of the lake. Throughout this introduction to *A Passage to India* I have asked you to see the novel as having what one might call broad structure sustained by overall patterns and rich local detail. Meaning emerges from both. The final expedition on the lake may be compared to the journey to the caves, and to other special events in the book which create 'set piece' sections in the narrative. The parallels seem clear. In each case an event is designed to achieve unity and to allow sight of something that the British regard as the *real* India, and in each case something happens which disrupts the surface of life releasing other meanings. In the final scene the Rajah dies and the boats collide intruding into the ceremony. In the bridge party at the beginning of the novel the events come close to farce when the Nawab Bahadur arrives and runs into the flower beds (p.61), releasing rather than removing racist feelings in the British. On a much larger scale, of course, the visit to the caves comes to grief. Registering the parallels in these scenes presses one into a sense of the structure of the narrative but one also registers differences. At the end of the novel the attempts at a 'bridge' in Chandrapore have been abandoned in favour of a kind of tourist visit to the native state; the austere religious sense of the cave has become the humane and highly populated Hindu ceremony.

### *ACTIVITY*

What other differences are there between this final event on the lake and the journey to the caves?

*DISCUSSION*

To me the shift from the over-ordered train to elephant journey (p.151) and the confusion of the night-time boat trip are most striking.

> The strange temporary life of the August flood-water bore them up and seemed as though it would last for ever.
> The boat was a rudderless dinghy. Huddled up in the stern, with the spare pair of oars in his arms, the guest asked no questions about details. There was presently a flash of lightning, followed by a second flash – little red scratches on the ponderous sky.
> (p.307)

The temporariness and flux of the water contrasts with the ageless fixity of the Marabar Hills. The contrasts here and elsewhere seem to create a very ordered and planned novel, but drawing the pattern together into a decisive statement about values is more difficult. Forster seems to have constructed instead an evenly balanced image. In the case of the westerners, for example, both Adela and Fielding seem to require both sympathy and irony. More significantly neither is allowed any kind of prominence at the end of the novel. Aziz, too, seems held in a sort of stasis. In this respect the presence of a new character almost free of previous narrative events and relatively uninvolved in the pattern is significant.

> What a strange-looking youth, tall, prematurely aged, the big blue eyes faded with anxiety, the hair impoverished and tousled! Not a type that is often exported imperially. The doctor in Aziz thought, 'Born of too old a mother,' the poet found him rather beautiful.
> (pp.303–4)

Were one seeing a sign of Forster's own presence in the novel one might see it here rather than in the larger, more involved, and more British figure of Fielding. Forster's novel, in 1924, arrived late on the imperial scene, yet with a point of view which is 'prematurely aged' by knowledge and particularly 'tousled with anxiety'.

## The end

*3.68* Finally, I should like you to think about the last section of the novel from page 314, 'They did' to the end. This is an extremely dense section which we cannot cover fully here, so I should like you to concentrate on exploring the ways Forster represents something beyond a simply defined political solution through the friendship between the individuals Aziz and Fielding which, it is promised, can exist after the Indians have driven 'every blasted Englishman into the sea' (p.316). The force of the paradox expressed here will vary, I think, in different readings and will be conditioned by the emphases given to earlier elements in the novel. One may value the promise of unity between individuals or register the violence of the metaphor which describes the progress to unity.

*3.69* The setting Forster creates for the image of unity is important. You will, I think, have noted already the use of particularly resounding language which I have described as creating a sense of closure or ending. For example:

> He paused, and the scenery, though it smiled, fell like a gravestone on any human hope. They cantered past a temple to Hanuman – God so loved the world that he took monkey's flesh upon him – and past a Saivite temple,

> which invited to lust, but under the semblance of eternity, its obscenities bearing no relation to those of our flesh and blood. They splashed through butterflies and frogs; great trees with leaves like plates rose among the brushwood. The divisions of daily life were returning, the shrine had almost shut.
>
> (p.315)

The most striking effect perhaps is the scale of the natural world which dwarfs the people; 'the great trees' fit with 'the semblance of eternity' to create something that seems to transcend human life. Forster draws on the extremes of religion, parodying Christianity in the references to Hanuman and linking both with the sensuality of the cult of Shriva in the Saivite temple. This construction of a grand scale occurs again in the final paragraph. Taken on their own, the final words 'No, not yet ... No, not there' seem sharply pessimistic. The inclusion of the sky, which in chapter I 'settles everything', in Forster's final listing of the things that bar the friendship of Fielding and Aziz, contributes to an overall pessimism about the scheme of things. The reference to 'the earth ... sending up rocks through which riders must pass single-file', reminding one perhaps of the 'groups of fists and fingers' of the Marabar caves 'thrusting up through the soil' (p.82), has a similar effect.

*3.70* It seems to me entirely in keeping with the sophisticated nature of the narrative that, in these final pages, Forster displaces the racial and political fractures which lie in the novel into natural images and individual relations, but portrays those images and relations as broken and in conflict. The narrative does not 'escape' into personal relations but rather allows the political pessimism and alienation of imperialism to flow over the final human pairing. The promise of a transcendent unity in nature seen in chapter I is in part fulfilled in the resounding final images but also frustrated.

*3.71* Yet it is hard to ignore the way the Temple section does move the narrative away from the discourse of a political narrative of India. The political imperialism of the British, shifting increasingly in the 1920s to something based on trade and 'influence' rather than direct colonial diktat, and the growing vigour of the nationalist movement are put to one side, and the structure of feeling that Forster expresses in the final section describes the tension between the exoticism of India felt by the sympathetic liberal traveller and the pessimism of the liberal. The prevailing perspective is of distance – an impression that lingers on from the description of Ralph Moore, 'faded with anxiety'.

# 4 Orientalism

## Why *Orientialism*?

*4.1* In this section we shall look at two extracts from Edward Said's book *Orientalism* (1978) which are reprinted in the Reader. By way of introducing the author, here is a brief profile:

> He is a Palestinian, born in Jerusalem in 1935, and is a member of the Palestine National Council (the Palestinian parliament-in-exile). As well as being a literary critic, he is well known in the United States as a writer, spokesperson and activist for the Palestinian cause and has written several books on Palestine, Islam, and the treatment of these subjects in the Western media. Said came to the United States in the late 1950s, and was educated at Princeton and Harvard. He is now Parr Professor of English and Comparative Literature at Columbia University...
>
> (Salusinszky, 1987, pp.123–4)

*4.2* Why are you being asked to read from *Orientalism* at this point in Block 5, or indeed in the course? There are three reasons: first, Said's book provides us with a way of addressing the block theme by considering the legacy of European imperialism and questioning how far it can be said to have ended; secondly, *Orientalism* builds on a discussion of the imperial ideology with which you are familiar from your work on Kipling and Camus in Block 4; thirdly, and most importantly for your present purposes, your study of *Orientalism* will, I hope, suggest alternative, deconstructive ways of reading *A Passage to India.*

*4.3* What follows is a brief study guide to the extracts from *Orientalism*, including a summary of the main points of Said's argument. In the first extract, from the introduction, Said defines his use of the term 'Orientalism'. Obviously reading extracts is no substitute for reading the whole of the book, but the introduction forms the basis of the book's argument and by studying it you will have access to its main objective. The other extract is characteristic of the greater part of the book in which Said examines the work of western writers about the Orient since the late eighteenth century; here Said discusses Kipling and T.E. Lawrence. *A Passage to India* is not discussed in detail in *Orientalism*, because Said's book deals mainly with the Middle East, but his critique of western representations of the East has an important bearing on how we read the novel. Finally, because of the influence of Said's book on recent literary studies you will, I hope, be able to see how his argument relates to the issues of race and gender discussed in Blocks 6 and 7.

*4.4* You might be puzzled by the use of the word 'Orientalism' in the title of Said's book. Why does he use this word and why does he refer to 'the Orient' rather than to 'the East'? To answer this, let's look at one dictionary definition of the noun 'Orient', the etymological source of which is the Latin *oriens, orient-em* (rising sun, east):

> That part of the earth's surface situated to the east of some recognized point of reference; eastern countries, or the eastern part of a country; the East; usually, those countries immediately east of the Mediterranean or of Southern Europe, which to the Romans were 'the East', the countries of South-western Asia or of Asia generally ... Now *poetic* or *literary*.
>
> (*Oxford English Dictionary*)

The Orient describes, then, what is situated 'to the east of some recognized point of reference', that is, it has a relative rather than an absolute geographical frame of reference. It also denotes those countries 'which to the

Romans were "the East"'; in other words its compass is defined by an ancient European empire. Note, finally, that the word is described as now having only a *poetic* or *literary* usage; so we can say that it describes a geography of the imagination rather than of actuality. Now look briefly at the dictionary definitions of Orientalism, but remember that Said's use of the word is distinctive and has its own resonances:

> (a) Oriental character, style, or quality; the characteristics, modes of thought or expression, fashions, etc. of Eastern nations; with *pl.* an Oriental trait or idiom.
>
> (b) Oriental scholarship; knowledge of Eastern languages.
>
> (*Oxford English Dictionary*)

The Orient and Orientalism are both words, as the dictionary definitions reveal, that suggest how the Orient has been defined by the West, as a projection of the western imagination.

## A study guide to Said's *Orientalism*

### *ACTIVITY*

Please now read the extract from the introduction to *Orientalism* reprinted in the Reader, page 234 to the top of page 237. Make brief notes in answer to the following three questions:

(a) What are the three meanings of Orientalism discussed on pages 235–6?

(b) In what sense is the Orient defined as 'the Other'?

(c) When does Orientalism begin historically, according to Said, and how does it relate to empire?

### *DISCUSSION*

(a) The first meaning of Orientalism, given in the second paragraph on page 235, describes the academic study of the Orient: 'Anyone who teaches, writes about, or researches the Orient … is an Orientalist, and what he or she does is Orientalism'. This pervasive idea of Orientalism as a way of studying the Orient is a crucial dimension of Said's third definition, as he suggests in his conclusion to this paragraph: 'Orientalism lives on academically through its doctrines and theses about the Orient and the Oriental'.

The second meaning of Orientalism, put forward in the following paragraph, describes the imaginative conception of the Orient: 'Orientalism is a style of thought based upon an ontological and epistemological distinction made between "the Orient" and (most of the time) "the Occident"'. 'Ontology' is a 'branch of metaphysics dealing with the nature of being' and 'epistemology' is 'a theory of the method or ground of knowledge' (*Oxford English Dictionary*). Said claims, then, that Orientalism is a way of thinking, manifest in all kinds of writing, which as its very basis seeks to contrast the Orient and the Occident (from the Latin, *occident–em*, setting, sunset), East and West. Orientalism is founded on this absolute difference, inscribed in western culture from Aeschylus's play *Persae* to Marx's concept of the Asiatic Mode of Production and beyond.

The third meaning of Orientalism, the one with which Said's book is concerned, is set out on pages 235–6, and it both synthesizes and moves beyond the other two. He describes it as 'more historically and materially defined' than either the academic or imaginative meanings of Orientalism. Here is the central part of the definition:

> Orientalism can be discussed and analyzed as the corporate institution for dealing with the Orient – dealing with it by making statements about it, authorizing views of it, describing it, by teaching it, settling it, ruling over it: in short, Orientalism is a Western style for dominating, restructuring, and having authority over the Orient.
>
> (Reader, p.235)

The thread that runs through this sentence is the issue of power. Orientalism, in Said's definition, is a means by which the West exerts authority over the Orient, not just politically and economically but through the way it represents the Orient, therefore through imagination and language. Said combines an essentially political and cultural theory of domination with an analysis of the authority of the language of academic study and of literary imagination. You will have noticed that he acknowledges the notion of 'discourse' employed by Michel Foucault (1926–84), the French philosopher and historian of ideas, now a commonplace in literary theory. 'Discourse' for theoreticians is a way of describing language so as to demonstrate how it is implicated in ideology:

> Discourses, sign-systems and signifying practices of all kinds, from film and television to fiction and the languages of natural science, produce effects, shape forms of consciousness and unconsciousness, which are closely related to the maintenance or transformation of our existing systems of power. They are thus closely related to what it means to be a person. Indeed 'ideology' can be taken to indicate no more than this connection – the link or nexus between discourses and power.
>
> (Eagleton, 1983, p.210)

This sense of Orientalism as a discourse that is linked with power is, it seems to me, at the heart of Said's third definition. The structuralist view of language, to which Graham Martin introduced you in Block 2 in his discussion of the theories of Saussure and Jakobson, is that language does not simply reflect the world as a transparent medium but that it moulds, and in a sense, constitutes what it describes. Hence Said's claim that 'without examining Orientalism as a discourse one cannot possibly understand the enormously systematic discipline by which European culture was able to manage – and even produce – the Orient' (pp.235–6). Said's third definition describes Orientalism, then, as a discourse that 'produces' the Orient, such that 'the Orient was not (and is not) a free subject of thought or action'. The idea is that it is produced for the consumption of the western viewer, reader or scholar.

(b) The Orient is defined as 'the Other' in the sense that it is *different* from, or other than, the West. What the third definition, discussed above, helps us to understand is that in order to explain Orientalism, we have to concentrate on the consciousness that produces the Orient, that is the West (Europe and America). While the second meaning of Orientalism emphasized the importance to the western literary imagination of the *difference* between East and West, it also emphasized that the two terms, Orient and Occident, are in fact locked in a mutually dependent bind. Paradoxically, they reinforce one another in the very difference and alienation which they emphasize. The idea of the Orient and the Occident being locked in this dialectical bind that is full of conflict but also, in a sense, mutually supporting is, of course, founded not simply on geographical proximity but on the political fact of European imperialism, a point to which we shall return in a moment. The important point to address here is the inseparability of Europe and its Other:

> The Orient is not only adjacent to Europe; it is also the place of Europe's greatest and richest and oldest colonies, the source of its civilizations and languages, its cultural contestant, and one of its deepest and most recurring images of the Other. In addition, the Orient has helped to define Europe (or the West) as its contrasting image, idea, personality, experience.
>
> (Reader, p.234)

Not only is Europe dependent on the Orient economically, but Europe has used the Orient to define its own identity. Europe is not totally self-defining but is constituted in contrast to the East, in the same way that the Orient is dependent for its existence on the West. The notion of the Other as that which is alien suggests both something that threatens a being or a consciousness as well as, ironically, that which produces the cohesion of that being or consciousness, and therefore defines its own identity. This dialectical relationship works also to privilege the Orient as a site of fantasy, beauty, imaginative freedom and, frequently, the feminine. This combination of fear and fantasy of the Other informs Said's aim 'to show that European culture gained in strength and identity by setting itself off against the Orient as a sort of surrogate and even underground self' (p.236). The Orient as Other comes to represent what is repressed, and is figured in terms of Freudian psychoanalysis (though Said never pursues this in detail).

(c) According to Said, Orientalism begins in the late eighteenth century with the establishment of empires in the East, and is primarily 'a British and French cultural enterprise' (p.236). From the beginning of the nineteenth century until the end of the Second World War, France and Britain dominated the Orient and were the main agents in the practice of Orientalism, through imperial influence and commercial exploitation, to be replaced since then by the United States. Orientalism thus coincides with colonization of the East and the high point of nineteenth-century imperialism, the vestiges of which Forster anatomizes in *A Passage to India*. Certainly the description of the Civil Station in the second paragraph of chapter I (pp.31–2) endorses Said's point that:

> ...none of this Orient is merely imaginative. The Orient is an integral part of European *material* civilization and culture. Orientalism expresses and represents that part culturally and even ideologically as a mode of discourse with supporting institutions, vocabulary, scholarship, imagery, doctrines, even colonial bureaucracies and colonial styles.
>
> (Reader, p.234)

## *ACTIVITY*

Now read pages 237–40 of the Reader, which reiterate most of the points made above.

---

*4.5* By way of summary, I have divided the main points of this extract into two central issues: (a) Orientalism as representation rather than reality, and (b) Orientalism as the empowering of the cultural hegemony of the West.

### Representation

*4.6* The Orient 'is not merely *there*, just as the Occident itself is not just *there* either' (p.237). The Orient does not exist as an independent geographical fact but rather as 'an idea that has a history and a tradition of thought, imagery, and vocabulary that have given it reality and presence in and for the West' (p.237). One of the epigraphs to *Orientalism* is from Marx's *Eighteenth Brumaire of Louis Bonaparte*: 'They cannot represent themselves; they must be represented.'

*4.7* Said's concern is with 'the internal consistency of Orientalism and its ideas about the Orient' (p.237) rather than with the correspondence, or lack of it, between the idea of the Orient projected by Orientalism and the 'reality' of it, were such a thing possible to define. This is not to deny that 'the Orient was *essentially* an idea, or a creation with no corresponding reality' (p.237) but merely to emphasize that it is the representation of the Orient, not the reality, that is the issue of the book.

*4.8* 'One ought never to assume that the structure of Orientalism is nothing more than a structure of lies or of myths which, were the truth about them to be told, would simply blow away' (p.238). Orientalism is neither simply a fantasy nor a deception. Said emphasizes that it is a legacy that still determines our perceptions, 'a created body of theory and practice in which ... there has been a considerable material investment' (p.238) (the adjective 'material' being used here in the Marxist sense of the actuality of lived human life and its history).

**Power**

*4.9* 'The Orient was Orientalized not only because it was discovered to be 'Oriental' in all those ways considered commonplace by an average nineteenth-century European, but also because it *could be* – that is, submitted to being – *made* Oriental' (pp.237–8). The Orient is frequently represented as the silenced and passive Other incapable of representing itself. The case of Flaubert's 'Oriental woman', Kuchuk Hanem, is an example of this.

*4.10* After describing the Gramscian definition of hegemony as what gives Orientalism its durability (pp.238–9), Said remarks that 'Orientalism depends for its strategy on this flexible *positional* superiority, which puts the Westerner in a whole series of possible relationships with the Orient without ever losing him the relative upper hand' (p.239). Whereas we are used to thinking of knowledge as a neutral domain and of imagination as autonomous and transcendent, they are shown in the discourse of Orientalism to be embedded in the relations of power: 'The scientist, the scholar, the missionary, the trader, or the soldier was in, or thought about, the Orient because he *could be there*, or could think about it, with very little resistance on the Orient's part' (p.239). The idea of a colonialism of the imagination is one to which we shall return in this block when you read Seamus Heaney's essay 'Englands of the mind', reprinted in the Reader.

## *ACTIVITY*

Please now read the extract from *Orientalism* entitled 'Orientalism now' reprinted in the Reader on pages 240–4, in which Said discusses Kipling and T.E. Lawrence.

*4.11* From Cicely Havely's discussion of 'A Sahibs' War' in Block 4 and Graham Martin's introduction to this block, you will know that Kipling's view of empire is quite different from Forster's. Indeed the 'culturally sanctioned habit of deploying large generalizations' (p.242) about race and mentality is something that Forster often criticizes in his characters (for example, Heaslop and Aziz). *A Passage to India* could also be said to try to overcome those statements which convey 'the irreducible distance separating white from colored, or Occidental from Oriental' (p.242) – remember Forster's comment, 'When I began the book I thought of it as a little bridge of sympathy between East and West' (but also refer back to the rest of the comment quoted by Richard Allen on p.17). So Forster manifestly does not fit simply into Said's critique of Kipling's view of empire or T.E. Lawrence's description of the Arab mentality. But, while I wish to discourage you from unhelpful generalizations about *A Passage to India* in terms of Said's *Orientalism*, there are ways in which the twin issues of representation and power in the discourse of Orientalism can contribute to a reading of Forster's novel.

## *Orientalism* and *A Passage to India*

### *ACTIVITY*

Please now re-read the following extracts from *A Passage to India*: chapter I (pp.31–3); chapter XII (pp.137–9); chapter XXXII (pp.277–8 ); chapter XXXIII, from page 281 to the end of the first paragraph on page 284. Write brief notes on the following question:

In the light of Said's *Orientalism*, how does the language of each of the passages inform the perspective of India that is presented?

### *DISCUSSION*

All four passages are chosen because they mark out the structure of the novel, a structure to which Forster devoted a lot of attention, as Richard Allen has shown.

The language of the first passage is generalizing and evaluative; it makes us think critically about conventional images of the beauty of the Orient in which the Anglo-Indian has an investment – the trees and vegetation around the Civil Station 'glorify the city to the English people who inhabit the rise, so that newcomers cannot believe it to be as meagre as it is described, and have to be driven down to acquire disillusionment' (p.32).

Rather than ask whether it is a legitimate representation of the fictional Chandrapore or not (remember that *Orientalism* teaches us to be concerned with the representation itself rather than whether it corresponds to the 'real' Orient), what I want you to think about here is the structure of the opening chapter of the novel and the way that the language shifts in tone as it progresses. It begins with the river Ganges, moves to the illusory elevation of the Civil Station and, in the final two paragraphs, to the overarching sky. As Richard Allen has pointed out to you in relation to other parts of the novel, Forster repeatedly deflects attention away from the earthly and the human aspects of India, dissolving political and imperial problems into a universal drama which transcends them. This movement away from the material problems of Anglo-Indian rule is an intrinsic part of the discourse of Orientalism; the Orient is perceived and, to an extent, utilized as a means to higher self-awareness for the western consciousness. This is true in a very general sense for characters such as Adela and Fielding for whom India functions primarily as a means to greater self-knowledge.

The opening chapter of the caves section establishes a further manoeuvre in the discourse of Orientalism by which the primeval identity of the mountains of India, 'older than anything in the world' (p.137), is deemed to have a special significance. The location of the Marabar caves is conceived of in terms of an Otherness that defies reason:

> There is something unspeakable in these outposts. They are like nothing else in the world, and a glimpse of them makes the breath catch. They rise abruptly, insanely, without the proportion that is kept by the wildest hills elsewhere, they bear no relation to anything dreamt or seen. To call them 'uncanny' suggests ghosts, and they are older than all spirit. Hinduism has scratched and plastered a few rocks, but the shrines are unfrequented, as if pilgrims, who generally seek the extraordinary, had here found too much of it.
>
> (pp.137–8)

Such an emptiness of value is clearly troubling, given the major event of the novel which the description heralds:

> Nothing is inside them, they were sealed up before the creation of pestilence or treasure; if mankind grew curious and excavated, nothing, nothing would be added to the sum of good or evil.
>
> (p.139)

This 'nothing' makes India an example of a specific aspect of the colonial era when, according to Said, 'The Orient was ... not Europe's interlocutor, but its silent Other' (Said, 1985, p.17). This silence, which enwraps the episode in the caves and defies rational explanation and judicial inquiry, and which undermines all stable values, is something that Mrs Moore seems to understand and accept, and when Adela's echo disappears, she too recovers. The Orient is not spoken for in the novel but rather its silence demands to be recognized, and violently so.

The language that describes the caves in this chapter suggests a primal, unconscious realm which pre-dates the human race and all attempts, including religion, to explain the meaning of human existence – an issue with which the novel is preoccupied. Graham Martin has commented that the caves do not represent the Otherness of India to the West, but a primeval force at odds with both the English characters' attempts to define India and the Indian characters' sense of their own culture and history. For him, the caves represent the indifference of the material universe to all human constructions of value. But my own view is that here Forster is using a typical nineteenth-century formulation of world history in which the Orient had been a paradigm of antiquity and origins. As Said puts it with reference to the great nineteenth-century philosophers of history, Hegel, Marx, Burckhardt, Nietzsche and Spengler:

> Oriental history ... was useful in portraying a region of great age, and what had to be left behind ... As primitivity, as the age-old antetype of Europe, as a fecund night out of which European rationality developed, the Orient's actuality receded inexorably into a kind of paradigmatic fossilization.
>
> (Said, 1985, p.17)

Equally, one could interpret the caves in terms of Freud's theory of the repressed nature of the unconscious; remember Said's comment that 'European culture gained in strength and identity by setting itself off against the Orient as a sort of surrogate and even underground self' (p.236).

In chapter XXXII, Fielding's journey back to England is represented in terms of the white, male liberal consciousness recovering its identity:

> The buildings of Venice, like the mountains of Crete and the fields of Egypt, stood in the right place, whereas in poor India everything was placed wrong.
>
> (pp.277–8)

> ...but something more precious than mosaics and marbles was offered to him now; the harmony between the works of man and the earth that upholds them, the civilization that has escaped muddle, the spirit in reasonable form, with flesh and blood subsisting.
>
> (p.278)

While this recovery of equilibrium at the end of the caves section is mediated through the character of Fielding, the narrative voice is insinuated into an impersonal, authorial set of statements, despite the fact that elsewhere in the novel the narrative voice notes his faults and limitations:

> The Mediterranean is the human norm. When men leave that exquisite lake, whether through the Bosphorus or the Pillars of Hercules, they approach the monstrous and extraordinary; and the southern exit leads to the strangest experience of all. Turning his back on it yet again, he took the train northward, and tender romantic fancies that he thought were dead for ever flowered when he saw the buttercups and daisies of June.
>
> (p.278)

The presentation of the crowded Hindu festival and of the final scene of the novel suggests that Forster prefers an amused detachment from, rather than a resolution of, the impenetrable mystery of India symbolized by the caves: 'they did not one thing which the non-Hindu would feel dramatically correct; this approaching triumph of India was a muddle (as we call it), a frustration of reason and form' (p.282). It is here, in Said's terms, that Orientalism enacts what cannot be understood, and Fredric Jameson has commented that this seems part of the deliberate structure of the novel: 'the Hindus being specifically designated as that Other, inaccessible to Western representation' (Jameson, 1988, p.17n).

## *ACTIVITY*

As a way of thinking about the kinds of Orientalism which are present in *A Passage to India* as a whole, please now read the article by Sara Suleri, 'The geography of *A Passage to India*', reprinted in the Reader, pages 245–50. How does Suleri suggest that the issues of imperial domination and female sexuality are linked in the novel?

## *DISCUSSION*

Suleri's reading of the novel is informed both by Said's argument in *Orientalism* but also by psychoanalysis and deconstruction. The landscape in *A Passage to India* is a defensive male representation of an impenetrable sexuality, according to Suleri. Thus Forster is engaged in a metaphorical exercise whereby the caves and the event that occurs in them are linked:

> ...India is ultimately reprehensible because it denies the fixity of an object that the narrative subject can pursue and penetrate ... Forster manipulates the image of landscape as metaphoric of that possible fulfillment which is continually on the verge of emptying into disappointment.
>
> (Reader, p.248)

She goes on to emphasize that Forster's homosexuality plays a key part in the portrayal of three of the characters in the novel:

> In considering Adela Quested, it is difficult to ignore the complicated defences that cause Forster to represent her as a cipher almost as arid as the Marabar caves. For rather than a woman abused or abusive, Adela essentially plays the part of a conduit or a passageway for the aborted eroticism between the European Fielding and the Indian Aziz.
>
> (Reader, p.249)

Suleri shows that *A Passage to India* goes beyond the conventional fictional encounter with an Orient represented as beautiful, fertile and feminine (a fantasy that signals repressed guilt about the imperial dream) by representing a brutality in its Otherness. In its gendered treatment of India, the novel realizes the masculine dimension of imperialism.

## Conclusion

*4.12* Orientalism provokes several questions which you might like to pursue in relation to *A Passage to India*. These are:

(a) Does the theory of Orientalism pay sufficient attention to historical changes in attitudes and perceptions towards the East? Although Said is commendably concerned with the detail of specific texts throughout his book, he appears to maintain a supra-historical status for Orientalism, and some critics have attacked him for not giving sufficient attention to those western writings that show a self-awareness in relation to the East, and have been critical of the hegemony of that discourse which, Said argues, conditions all writing about the Orient. However, it could be argued that Forster's novel supports Said's point, since although it is a critique of empire, it can also be seen to endorse the imperialist legacy.

(b) Is there any western literary or academic representation of the East which is not implicated in a hegemonic discourse? Even Mrs Moore and Adela in *A Passage to India*, who question the conventional understanding of India, are themselves shown to be incapable of surmounting the barriers of Orientalism.

(c) What is the place of 'the feminine' in Orientalism? Said's *Orientalism* shows an awareness of the issues of gender stereotyping and of sexuality in relation to the Orient. The implication of Suleri's article is that imperial domination and the repression of female sexuality are connected in *A Passage to India*. In the following section, Cicely Havely takes up the wider issues of race and gender in the novel.

# 5 *Race and gender in 'A Passage to India'*

*5.1* During the farcical trial – in which comedy all but hides Aziz's point of view – Mr McBryde

> ...remarked that the darker races are physically attracted by the fairer, but not vice versa – not a matter for bitterness this, not a matter for abuse, but just a fact which any scientific observer will confirm.
>
> (p.222)

He voices one of the great lies of empire. Something nearer the truth was politely swept under the Indian carpet: the embarrassing Eurasians who were very, very seldom the children of white mothers. One of these unfortunate scraps of imperial flotsam makes a token appearance as Nawab Bahadur's comic chauffeur, Mr Harris (pp.87–9).

*5.2* What Mr McBryde likes to call 'just a fact' was perhaps closer to the expression of a great fear, and that fear was the inversion of a truth. Like *A*

*Passage to India*, Paul Scott's *Raj Quartet* has as its crux the putative sexual assault of an English woman by Indians. (And as with Forster's novel, many who read it or saw the television version persisted in thinking that it was about India, instead of about the British in India; or they thought that the two were the same.) This atavistic fear may have its source in guilt – not so much guilt for the commonplace liaisons between the ruling males and women of the subject race, as guilt for the greater subjugation of which such liaisons were merely symptoms. It was the body of India itself that white men desired, and that body is presented at the crisis of the narrative in terms of an ambivalent and for the most part repugnant sexuality.

*5.3* With this theme at the centre, it was essential for Forster to ascribe to his Oriental a sexual identity – and, indeed, Aziz is the only sexed character in the novel. But he constructs this sexuality in a manner consistent with his creation of the whole character: he gives with one hand and takes away with the other. Aziz's marriage is surely well done. The photograph of his late wife which he shows to Fielding and which is then abused by the prosecution is a powerful – and economically used – sign of a great cultural divide.

*5.4* More problematic is Aziz's plan to visit a Calcutta bordello (see chapter IX). Fielding, we are told (p.115), would sympathize; and this in the value scheme of the novel is an exoneration. Fielding is the keeper of Forster's seal of approval. McBryde hypocritically interprets Aziz's letter as evidence of his improper urges. But why did Forster choose to strike this particular note?

*5.5* His ostensible wish, as with all other aspects of Aziz's character, is to establish *difference* or *otherness*: 'the vague jollity that would culminate in voluptuousness' (p.115) doesn't sound very British. He may have wished to suggest a healthy, more open and self-aware attitude. We have to remember when the novel was written: *Lady Chatterley's Lover*, which tried to make the British – who banned it – face the realities of sex, was only four years in the future. Lawrence wrote of Forster's novel:

> [he] doesn't understand his [*sic*] Hindu. And India is to him just negative: because he doesn't go down to the root to meet it. But the *Passage to India* interested me very much. At least the repudiation of our white bunk is genuine, sincere, and pretty thorough...
>
> (letter to J.M. Murray, 3 October 1924, in Aldington, 1950, p.149)

*5.6* As a homosexual, Forster had his own reasons to loathe what might be called the British hole-in-the-corner attitude to sex. So perhaps the brothel is an attempt to make Aziz more 'manly' for his readers, and counteract the love of poetry which, as he points out, is quite sufficient to differentiate him from most British males in matters of the heart. But it seems a trifle lurid and a little inept: an aesthete's rather amateurish notion of sexuality. Perhaps Forster's fastidious distaste is revealed when he writes severely of the 'type of lie he should tell to get away' (p.116).

*5.7* Is there an incongruity between prostitution and purdah? The double standard is part of an ideology that had certainly not been brought to the full light when Forster was writing. It could be that for some male readers Aziz is thus made rather enviable – either as a fantasy of Orientalism (like Eliot's 'silken girls bringing sherbert' from *The Journey of the Magi*) or by his candid enactment of what in British society is generally surreptitious.

*5.8* Thus far Forster is non-judgemental or ambivalent. But the Fielding seal of disapproval is brought down bang on another aspect of Aziz's sexuality: his coarse but surely understandable attitude to Adela after the trial. Look at the dialogue beginning on page 252: 'Dear Dr Aziz, I wish you had come into the cave; I am an awful old hag, and it is my last chance'. Fielding shuts him up: 'Oh, I wish you wouldn't make that kind of remark ... It is the one thing in you I can't put up with.' Does Fielding object because the remark is so ungentlemanly? (Earlier he had 'found a touch of bad taste in [Aziz's] reference to a lady's breasts', p.131.) Or because he cannot allow a white woman to be insulted by a native? Either way, Aziz is put in the wrong, and the source and standard of right behaviour is the white man's. Not the commonplace white man's – *he* might see eye to eye with Aziz on this point; but a lofty, ascetic standard that smacks of another form of the snobbery that Fielding finds so reprehensible in Aziz:

> ...sexually, he [Aziz] was a snob. This had puzzled and worried Fielding. Sensuality, as long as it is straightforward, did not repel him, but this derived sensuality – the sort that classes a mistress among motor-cars if she is beautiful, and among eye-flies if she isn't – was alien to his own emotions...
>
> (p.242)

*Straightforward* – how British! I'm reminded of Quiller Couch's injunction that you can tell a man by his use of the straight verb (quoted by Roger Day in Block 3 paragraph 1.25).

*5.9* These details are aspects of a larger issue, for they occur during the time when Fielding puts pressure on Aziz not to sue Adela for damages. Surely a desire for compensation, even for retribution, would be understandable and justifiable – though not a very pukka reaction. Fielding may be at odds with all the Club but in this instance he out-Englishes the lot of them: 'The insensitiveness about Adela displeased him. It would, *from every point of view*, be right to treat her generously' (p.259, my italics).

*5.10* *Every* point of view? And surely Fielding's moral high ground is unpleasantly compromised by the methods he uses to get his own way:

> ...Fielding was not ashamed to practise a little necromancy. Whenever the question of compensation came up, he introduced the dead woman's name. Just as other propagandists invented her a tomb, so did he raise a questionable image of her in the heart of Aziz, saying nothing that he believed to be untrue, but producing something that was probably far from the truth.
>
> (p.259)

*5.11* Together these details suggest not only that 'the Oriental' (as Aziz is repeatedly supposed to call himself) lacks moral refinement, but that he ('she' doesn't come into it) cannot be trusted to reach a right decision without a set of colonial administrators; but at the same time Forster is deftly insinuating that a more subtle breed of adviser is still necessary. He has shifted and internalized the colonial terrain. In place of the overt policing which he pillories, he substitutes a dominion of morality and manners. The Oriental's coarseness must be refined, his sense of propriety adjusted. No matter if the white man has to use a duplicity that could never be permitted in the subject people: it is for their own good.

*5.12* Above all, it is the Oriental's sexuality that must be checked. I suggested at the beginning that the comedy of the trial scene 'all but hides' Aziz's point of view. On every other occasion, Forster feels entitled to enter his mind; but at the crisis of his life he is silenced. The beautiful, mindless punkah-wallah presides over the scene like the voiceless ghost of exotic sensuality – and strangely genderless sexuality. At the trial, it is the oppressive farce of the law of the Turtons and Burtons that mutes him. But Adela's sudden release from aphasia releases Aziz to the more insidious tyranny of an unwritten law. 'You always get the scale wrong, my dear fellow' (pp.269–70) says Fielding with unbearable condescension. And Aziz always will, because this law is a tribal secret; and the only way he will ever know he has transgressed it is when he incurs his so-called friend's displeasure. The reader, it is assumed, is also privy to the secret.

*5.13* Aziz, we are pushed towards thinking, has much to learn from Fielding – but never the other way round. Fielding is quite immune to the satire applied to the other British characters: he and the authorial voice are at one. And this voice is seriously infected with racist condescension. To show the extent of this I've taken a single chapter (II) and listed some of the phrases which imply the superiority of the authorial voice. You'll remember similar tones from the first paragraphs of the novel. The italicized phrases attempt to decode the standard which Forster presumes he shares with his reader:

> Abandoning his bicycle, which fell before a servant could catch it (*careless and hasty*); 'thank you, Dr Aziz, I am dying' (*melodramatic self-indulgence*); 'We are having a very sad talk' (*naive emotionalism*); The hookah had been packed too tight, as was usual (*inefficient*); He lay in a trance (*self-indulgence*); the bitter fun (*childish word*); 'Hookah is so jolly now' (*funny foreign English*); Servants … meant that they wished [the dinner] was ready… (*inefficient, unreliable*); 'Queen Victoria was different' (*naive*); angelic ministration (*inability to distinguish between details and essentials, no sense of proportion*); He, too, generalized from his disappointments – it is difficult for members of a subject race to do otherwise (*lofty intimation that those of us who are not subjects do better*); It was difficult to get away, because until they had had their dinner she would not begin hers, and consequently prolonged her remarks in case they should suppose she was impatient (*pointless, hampering etiquette*); while the tale was in progress it convinced the two men (*so swayed by the moment, they cannot take a longer view*); a gentle, happy, and dishonest old man (*by whose standard?*); never stopping to analyse (*would they be better if they did?*); Between them they took [the bicycle] over a tintack (*careless*); he had neither light nor bell nor had he a brake (*dangerously reckless*); he dallied furthermore to clean his teeth (*dalliance is never good*); he was an athletic little man, daintily put together (*not really a man at all – that 'little' is a term of abuse is confirmed at the bottom of page 40*); the temple of another creed … would have bored him (*a better man would not have been bored, as Mrs Moore is not bored by a temple of another belief*); he … decked it with meanings the builder had never intended (*emotional and uninformed*); he always held pathos to be profound (*we know better*); tears in his eyes (*too easily moved by the trite*); 'I am just a subordinate' (*self pity, over dramatizing*); he was excited … by his wrongs … that led him to repeat, exaggerate, contradict (*making a childish fuss*); he did not expiate on his wrongs now, being happy (*childish, lives too much in the moment, too easily swayed*).

*5.14* Of course Forster was trying to create in his Indian characters men whose thoughts and attitudes had been created out of circumstances fundamentally different from even his own liberal perspective, let alone that of the governing class. (He doesn't even try to depict an Indian woman – and must have been grateful for purdah.) Technically, he had set himself an impossible task, because the only language available to him was that of the intellectual wing of the white middle class – and the attitudes embodied in that language ran contrary to so many of the aspects of Aziz, which he needed to endorse in order to make his critique of the white, male middle class.

*5.15* The cumulative effect of this constant undercutting (which continues throughout the novel) suggests that Aziz is unstable and incomplete. Indeed, compared with Fielding's inner certainties, Aziz is made to seem not fully a man as the prevailing standard would have him be – both in the sense of not being mature, and in the sense of sharing the inconsistencies and butterfly emotions conventionally associated with women. This latter is enhanced by the half-sexual *frisson* which runs through the relationship between Fielding and Aziz: a powerful attraction punctuated by tiffs and misunderstandings in which Aziz seems to play the part of the charming but not quite suitable woman who needs to be put right about a few things before she will do.

*5.16* Violation is not after all the only sexual metaphor appropriate to the imperial scene. Seduction is just as important, though not as prominent in Forster's view, which tends to suggest that the British loathed being in India. Perhaps some of them did, but even a collection of reminiscences as upright as Charles Allen's *Plain Tales from the Raj* suggests that many of the colonials loved India (even if they didn't understand it) with a most un-British ardour. In Block 4 Section 2 I tried to suggest something of the pleasures of the imperial adventure. And Kipling's India is much sexier that Forster's. It is steeped in the rich currents which only rouse Ronnie and Adela so briefly. Chandrapore is an arid and even a barren, childless community, and Forster can attribute only negative values to the landscape in which he sites it. The catastrophically explosive mixture of sexual and racial fears that erupts in the caves takes place in an almost sexless vacuum.

*5.17* The Marabar caves can be read as signs of an ambivalent sexuality (there will be more to say on this in Block 7), but among all the possibilities they signify something about the novel's own text: the hiatus in the narrative. Whatever happens or does not happen in the cave is inscribed only on the blank paper between chapters XV and XVI. Aziz's silence at the trial is a reflection of this central gap. British paranoia about oriental sexuality lies at the novel's heart, yet Adela Quested's aberration is never accounted for, just obscured in a cloud of perhaps rather spurious mysticism.

*5.18* You'll remember that earlier drafts of *A Passage to India* suggested a less ambiguous assault. Eventually Forster moved towards saying that it was all in Adela's mind; but not quite. When Fielding tries to press her for an account of what really happened she suggests that it might have been the guide or 'one of that gang of Pathans' (p.242). When he returns to the theme her last 'indifferent' words are 'Let us call it the guide … It will never be known' (p.261). Fielding treats her rather like Aziz, with the rights of one 'naturally' her superior to question and suggest. She never decided whether anyone followed her into the cave, but still she is given to say 'Let us call it the guide'. Forster allows a calumny to remain alive, like a half-killed snake. When there is no explanation, when no one can be accused, 'Let us call it the guide' – and blame an Indian.

*5.19* It is not just that Adela Quested does not know whether she was attacked: the narrative does not know either; the author has refused to know. This is shocking in a fiction where nothing else is withheld from us, and where the narrator assumes an unusually godlike stance – claiming, indeed, to see the world over the shoulders of several different gods. In Bloomsbury circles, wanting to know may be considered impossibly vulgar, but where the crisis of a novel is a court-room drama, a little detective curiosity is naturally triggered. It is not only the reader's desire for an explanation that is frustrated, but the desire for an exoneration that we ought to feel if we are not benighted in the very prejudices that the novel ostensibly – and in one way ostentatiously – attacks. There are two ways in which fictitious Indians are constructed in the novel. The first is the way of the British enclave that creates caricatures and monsters out of its own fears and narrow self-interest. The other way is the narrator's, and though that is far from untainted by prejudice it also stops far short of construing an Indian who might be guilty of rape. The denizens of the Club, on the other hand, are only too willing to see all Indians as potential rapists – as Forster makes clear in the scorching scene where they rally round the 'women and children' flag (p.190). It is out of *their* paranoia that such a hideous delusion might convincingly spring, and only to that can the possibility that Miss Quested was hallucinating satisfactorily be attributed. Then we could say that her delusion is the moment when the poison of Anglo India finally infected her.

*5.20* But Forster refuses this explanation, grimly satisfactory though it would be. Perhaps he was trying for something more profound but the result is that the novel remains trammelled with the very prejudices it sought to attack. None of the Indians that Forster has invented could possible be guilty; only those that the Club has invented. 'Let us say that the guide did it' and we are saying that the bogeymen the Club has dreamed up are real after all. 'Let us say that the guide did it' and all Forster's own well-intentioned efforts to see India without prejudice have been futile, because lurking in the hills is still the motiveless attacker, nameless and featureless save for two things: he is male – and he is Indian.



# 6 A study guide to 'Serjeant Musgrave's Dance'

*6.1* Because the version of the play recorded on Audio-cassettes 5 and 6 was originally broadcast, the text has been cut slightly to fit into the original time slot. You will probably find it useful to mark these cuts in your text. Listen to it once or more without the text if you wish, but also listen scene by scene with the following notes. You may find it difficult at first to make distinctions within the groups of miners and soldiers. Don't worry too much about this. Although the three soldiers represent different qualities or aspects of the argument, they also function collectively, as do the miners. Arden's notes on the characters will help you.

### Act I, scene i

*6.2* As you listen to this scene, mark the lines that stand out as specially significant in any way even if you do not know why.

*6.3* Though the basic elements are laid down clearly and confidently there is an air of mystery rather than exposition about this scene: we do not quite know what is going on, and a variety of symbolic elements (the ballads, the card-playing, the references to blood and roses) add a portentous quality.

*6.4* The soldiers are very jumpy. Attercliffe and Hurst both react nervously to Sparky's song: 'God-damned devil of a song to sing on this sort of a journey!' *What* sort of a journey? We don't know, though we might guess that the song offers some kind of clue either to the past or the future:

> When first I deserted I thought myself free
> Til my cruel sweetheart informed upon me...
> Court martial, court martial, they held upon me
> And the sentence they passed was the high gallows tree...

*6.5* The bargee, 'crooked old Joe', seems to belong to a long tradition of apparently innocuous tradesmen who turn out to be harbingers of death or the devil: the button-moulder in Ibsen's *Peer Gynt* is another example. His song ('Michael Finnegan') comes to represent the interminably cyclical nature of conflict which not even Musgrave can interrupt. Musgrave himself is introduced as if he were one of the most potent figures in the deck – Black Jack Musgrave. He is an archetypal soldier, who 'works his life to bugle and drum', and instantly takes command when he appears.

*6.6* There is another presence too in the scene. On stage, I doubt if anyone fails to guess what is in the box ('an old red rag stretched over four pairs o' bones'). There is a powerful melodramatic element in the play: the 'secret of the black magic box' is a theatrical motif as old as the hills. As with Brecht,

Arden's innovation lies not so much in discarding old forms, but in realizing the inherent power in simple devices. The suggestion of boxed-up death (there are guns on the other boxes) is made the more chilling by the constant references to the cold: 'there's ice coming on the water too'.

*6.7* When you have worked through the play once, you should return to this opening scene. Then you will see how much of it is *proleptic* (see Block 2 Section 3). What drives the drama on is a need for an explanation of these foreboding notes in the early scenes. What Musgrave has come about seems likely to be rather more sinister than 'beating up for recruities' as the bargee thinks.

### Act I, scene ii

*6.8* As Mrs Hitchcock puts it, there is more than one point of view about the strike: 'The owner calls it a strike, the men call it a lock-out, we call it starvation'. Arden does not go into detail. All he wants to convey is an archetypal industrial conflict between the bosses and the workers. But the situation also reveals the repressive instincts of other authorities: the parson wants to close the pubs.

*6.9* The scene introduces three representative authority figures who all see the arrival of what they think is a recruiting party as 'useful' – or in the mayor's words, 'bloody convenient'.

> 'There's two ways to solve this colliery – one is build a railway here ... The other is to clear out half the population, stir up a diversion, turn their minds to summat else.'

The justice of any war or 'rebellion' is of little importance. To the ruling classes the army is a kind of poultice that will draw off what they see as social infection.

*6.10* Annie has a very different perspective on 'for what a soldier's good' and her story and her thematic significance are developed in this scene. 'She talks a kind of truth' says Musgrave. Mrs Hitchcock sees joining the army as a drastic way of avoiding marriage: 'He gave her a baby and he went straight off to the war' is the message of her song.

### Act I, scene iii

*6.11* This is a good opportunity to look at Arden's dramatic language. After the briefest scene of barely articulated antagonism between a miner and a soldier, the soldiers muster from the four corners of the town, returning to the stage from different directions so that their movements, and not just their words, are part of the play's language. The episode is highly patterned. Phrases are repeated: 'Coldest town I ever was in ... Hardly a thing.' These lines are like the refrain in a poem in which the soldiers' vignettes are the successive verses.

*6.12* At first the scene seems to promise an explanation: 'Isn't it time you brought out clear just what you've got in mind?' Hurst demands, and he's probably speaking for the audience too. But the scene moves through a crescendo of rhetoric which conveys an impressive sense of the presence of power, but a frustrating absence of simple meaning.

*6.13* Still, we learn that the four are not an official recruiting party. Far from it, because they are all deserters. Hurst has murdered an officer, though it was 'put ... to the rebels'. And that has put him in Musgrave's power, and 'my power's the power of God'.

*6.14* Hurst wants to leave God out of it. It is the army's oppression of its own ('treat-you-like-dirt-but-you-do-the-dirty-work') that he has rebelled against. The standard he marches to is a crude democracy: 'Rights of man. Rights o' the Rebels.' And with this he has come to tell the people 'there'd be no more war'.

*6.15* But for Musgrave 'Our message without God is a bad belch and a hiccup'. Yet he has identified himself with God, and that his God is not some simplistic notion of righteousness becomes plainer in the course of the scene as he systematically browbeats all his men and reduces both their protests and their support to incoherence.

*6.16* Arden maintains the suspense by interrupting what looks like another explanation with the colliers, who remind us that a fighting spirit is not the sole prerogative of the army. The miners think the soldiers are the enemy – 'You see a strike: you see soldiers: there's only one reason' – though we now know they have some kind of pacific intention. What it might be is rendered mysterious by the belligerence of Musgrave's manner. He refers obliquely to the actual incident that Arden has said was one of the impetuses that made him write the play: 'One night's work in the streets of one city, and it damned all four of us and the war it was part of.' An off-duty soldier was killed in Cyprus and in rounding up suspects the reprisals got out of hand. The play is not, of course, *about* this incident, and Arden's generalizing and unspecific tactics will be discussed later.

*6.17* The bargee's song has already subliminally suggested that the play is about circularity. Sparky, who is inspired neither by Hurst's ragged principles nor by Attercliffe's simple 'All wars is sin' has come because of his 'dead mucker', Billy, the father of Annie's misshapen child, whose bones are in the box. As Musgrave says, 'We've come to this town to work that guilt back to where it began.'

*6.18* The scene ends very dramatically, with a long near-monologue by Musgrave which, although powerfully written, depends on the actor's power to give it the mesmeric qualities it needs. It is clearly a vision. Its language is quasi-mystical rather than mundanely meaningful. Vivid phrases stand out, but we cannot tell what they mean: 'the new, deserter's duty ... My regiment was my duty, and I called Death honest, killing by the book ... but it all got scrawled and mucked about and I could not think clear'. It's a terrific part for an actor – and what actors mean by that is a role where the power does not reside in the text alone, but requires their additional skills and presence to complete it. Here, perhaps, we could summarize that additional quality as conviction. The reader may be sceptical, worrying after a meaning. But the actor who plays Musgrave as a man supremely sure of the righteousness of his vision and his mission renders that kind of quibble irrelevant, and compels the audience not just to acknowledge but to experience his power.

### Act II, scene i

*6.19* If you have worked carefully through the first act you will need less guidance with the development of the themes in this one, so in these notes I shall concentrate more on the structure of the play. This scene elaborates on elements that have already been introduced and sets up the next crucial stage of the action. It is important in the rhythm of the play, and forms a kind of bustling interlude that is a relief from the high emotion that ended the previous act and will make an effective contrast with the starker patterning of the scenes to come.

*6.20* In the theatre, of course, it will probably follow an interval. Notice how lost Musgrave becomes amid the babble. He seems half submerged until the final episode with Annie, which you should listen to carefully: '...there's work is for women and there's work is for men: and let the two get mixed, you've anarchy.' We shall be discussing questions of gender in this play later.

### Act II, scene ii

*6.21* Walsh, the only miner capable of an argument rather than a reaction, cannot believe there can be any common interest between the soldiers and the colliers. But the bargee intimates that the soldiers' new Gatling gun could be useful to the miners.

### Act II, scene iii

*6.22* Again, notice the patterning in this scene. By an almost diagrammatic succession of variations Arden is able to give a semblance of universality to his theme. This is not just a whore with three soldiers but a kind of exploration of the relation and conflicts of the encounter between love and death in war. The inevitable consequence of the encounter between Annie and the instinctive, affectionate and life-loving Sparky is the urge to desert yet again – and equally inevitably it costs him his life. Significantly, it is not the fanatic Hurst who kills him, but the more muddled, life-wearied Attercliffe.

*6.23* In a highly dramatic piece of stage-craft, the love scene in which basic human instincts assert themselves is cut across by what is curiously like another kind of love-scene between Musgrave and Mrs Hitchcock. She brings her comforts to his lonely monomaniac vision of an apocalypse as steady as a parade ground.

*6.24* This is a play in which different blocks of feeling constantly cut across each other, interrupting their resolution. The death of Sparky is an obstacle to Musgrave's mysterious plan; the colliers' attempt to steal the gun is another. It brings the news that the dragoons are on their way – and precipitates Musgrave's great confrontation.

### Act III, scene i

*6.25* Again, remember the interval. By now a considerable part of the audience will have had two drinks.

*6.26* The scene begins with a charade. *We* know this is not going to be a recruiting drive, but that's what it looks like. At first it must seem to those on stage that Musgrave is speaking by the book, extolling all the conventional macho virtues of army life; but we know he has a more sinister purpose. It is after a speech of rousing phrases ('I'm the Queen of England's man'), when the Gatling gun is loaded and trained on the audience and his men have their rifles primed, and the drums are rolling – a moment of great dramatic tension – that Musgrave pulls off his great *coup de théâtre*. Notice the stage direction here: *his face contorted with demoniac fury*. Is he God or is he the devil?

*6.27* The audio-cassettes will help you appreciate the power of a stage performance here and how much is added to the text by production. When we read the text the dance seems a feeble even a ludicrous idea. But the drum has quickened our pulses; a skeleton, powerfully lit, hangs over the scene like a grisly banner; and the actor is able to command the audience's tense respect. Then the three soldiers (Musgrave, Hurst and Attercliffe) effectively re-enact the horror of the 'incident' that has driven Musgrave to this course. The savagery which is innate in the text is brought to life by the actors' presence, and all the while the audience on stage, like the audience in the theatre, is held mesmerized and at gunpoint.

*6.28* Then the tension is broken, when Musgrave turns to Walsh, who gradually backs away from any alliance with the soldiers during the next stages of the scene: 'You mend your own heartache and leave us to sort out ours – we've enough and to spare.' But Musgrave raises the pitch again, by revealing who the skeleton was: and just as Billy Hicks has been brought home, so what he calls the 'logic ... brings the wheel round'. It is then, though Attercliffe tries to restrain him, that he reveals his purpose.

*6.29* It is Annie, and all she stands for, who interrupts him, and from that moment his defeat begins. It is concluded by the arrival of the dragoons, which again looks insignificant in the text but is, of course, a moment of great drama. As the officer says, 'the winter's broken up. Let normal life begin again'. The scene ends with the impressive stage-spectacle of the drunken dance, presided over by the sinister bargee, in which the miners and the authority figures join together. The hollowness of this new alliance, forced upon them by the danger that is past, is something that a director would surely stress in the staging.

**Act III, scene ii**

*6.30* The final scene is perhaps summarized in Attercliffe's line, 'You can't cure the pox by further whoring', which is what Musgrave had tried to do. His song ends the play on a strange note of possible fruitfulness.

## The play's theatrical and political context

*6.31* Please note that TV9 *'Serjeant Musgrave' at the Court* is particularly relevant to this section.

*6.32* In an interview with Ronald Hayman published in *The Listener*, 4 September 1980, John Arden said:

> I wrote a play attacking the complacency with which the British public was prepared to regard actions undertaken by the British Army in foreign parts. The play becomes famous. It is presented as an examination piece for schoolchildren. And the British Army continues to do exactly the same things in Ireland, and has been doing so for ten years.

*ACTIVITY*

Does the first sentence of this quote summarize your reaction to the play?

*DISCUSSION*

I've tried to show in the study guide how the notion of 'bringing it home' is repeatedly emphasized. The masters think of the army as an instrument of social control; the miners think they could use the army's weapons to force their cause; the women see soldiers as a source of grief. But no one thinks that the wars and atrocities committed in their name have anything to do with them. However, the quotation is more important for the general emphasis Arden lays on his political purpose. He clearly believes that the theatre is a political instrument.

*6.33* When *Serjeant Musgrave's Dance* was first performed in 1959 (directed by Lindsay Anderson), only the *Manchester Guardian*'s critic admired this now thoroughly canonized play. Harold Hobson (far from the least enlightened critic of his day) wrote disparagingly:

> Another frightful ordeal. It is time someone reminded our advanced dramatists that the principal function of the theatre is to give pleasure ... It is the duty of the theatre, not to make men better, but to render them harmlessly happy.
>
> (*The Sunday Times*, 25 October 1959)

He clearly did *not* believe that theatre had a political role. Yet the play's reception on its revival at the Royal Court theatre in 1965 was much more sympathetic, and it eventually attained the ultimate *imprimatur* when it was 'set' as an A-level text.

*6.34* How often does the radically new gain immediate acceptance? And then prove durable? Arden was not the only playwright of this period to suffer initial hostility but gain respect a relatively short time later. Pinter, Osborne, Bond and Orton all met similar receptions at first. But other playwrights, apparently just as innovatory in their techniques or themes, were almost immediately and durably successful. Arnold Wesker's first play *Chicken Soup with Barley* appeared in 1958. By 1960 he was respectable enough for a commendatory survey of his work to be published in a learned journal. A.R. Jones writing in *Critical Quarterly* declared that Wesker had 'rewritten the myth of our time'. Academic acceptance is another of the ways in which 'literature' is established. In the theatre the intellectual climate around 1960 was becoming receptive and ready for change.

*6.35* What has frequently been described as a renaissance in British drama may be said to have begun on 8 May 1956 when John Osborne's play, *Look Back in Anger,* launched the Royal Court theatre. Many subsequent playwrights have acknowledged that it was this play that made would-be writers of the time want to write specifically for the theatre. Before that almost the only new drama on the British stage was the now notorious 'well-made play', technically as perfect as a reproduction antique, and just about as morally conservative. Priestley, Rattigan and Coward were competing with a succession of dazzling American musicals for the same audience. 'Serious' theatre mostly consisted of revivals of Shaw and the social-problem dramas of Galsworthy. In a symposium, 'Cause Without a Rebel', held at the Royal Court in 1956, the American dramatist Arthur Miller said: 'the British theatre is hermetically sealed against the way society moves' (printed in *Encore,* 9 November 1956). The theatre was middle class and middle brow, and audiences expected to be entertained and not offended. And the West End theatre owners exercised a commercial stranglehold at least as stifling as the still operative Lord Chamberlain's Office which subjected new plays to censorship.

*6.36* 1956 was the year of both Suez and Hungary. If the Left in Britain enjoyed the Conservative's acute discomfiture over Suez, they were appalled when Soviet tanks rolled into Budapest. *Look Back in Anger* attacked both traditional Conservative values and the post-war Labour government that had tried to replace them. To launch such an attack from the stage was like turning a machine-gun on the audience – as happens in the third act of *Serjeant Musgrave's Dance.* What was perhaps less obvious to audiences at the time, whether they were hurt or exhilarated by its onslaught, is that Jimmy Porter – the play's main protagonist and the original 'angry young man' – was hankering after something to fill the void created by his generation's disillusion. (Perhaps a comparable sense of nihilistic despair ends Arden's play, though he challenged that view in his introductory note. Musgrave wants to inflict the guilt of war on those who have allowed it to happen.)

*6.37* The language of *Look Back in Anger* was also shocking, not just because it included some of the milder expletives but because it seemed so 'realistic'. In fact, it is densely rhetorical. It is a curiously recurrent feature of literary history that significant innovations are felt to be marked by a rediscovery of 'real' language, which in its turn comes to seem so artificial that it is incapable of saying anything and has to be replaced. The drawing-room dramas that Osborne and his successors were to oust had themselves been thought of as a new realism, but in post-war Britain the political realities for the majority were very different. 'Kitchen-sink drama' is another phrase associated with the plays written in this period: before Osborne, the place where the cocktail glasses and the teacups were washed up was strictly off-stage. The following extract from one of Jimmy Porter's many lengthy diatribes is characteristic:

> Why, why do we let these women bleed us to death? Have you ever had a letter, and on it is franked 'Please Give Your Blood Generously'? Well, the Post-Master General does that on behalf of all the women in the world. I suppose people of our generation aren't able to die for good causes any longer. We had all that done for us, in the thirties and forties, when we were still kids. There aren't any good, brave causes left. If the big bang does come, and we all get killed off, it won't be in aid of the old-fashioned grand design. It'll be just for the Brave New Nothing-very-much-thank-you. About as pointless and inglorious as stepping in front of a bus. No, there's nothing left for it, me boy, but to let yourself be butchered by the women.

*6.38* It was in its attitudes to the sanctities of class and sex that the play was felt to be most sensational. It's hard to say now which was most shocking: that the heroine should be seen on the stage in her petticoat (*not* a Noel Coward style négligé), or that she was doing the ironing while wearing it. Censorship in the 'public' theatres had effectively banned the airing, not just of sexual issues, but of religious and political topics too. Yet as the extract above will have shown, what may then have looked very advanced was really very reactionary. The fifties were characterized by a deep misogny which was to necessitate the re-emergence of feminism in the sixties. What was happening was a kind of forcible repatriation of women once the war that had allowed them to take a wide range of unaccustomed roles was over, and the men returned to take up the places that were traditionally theirs. The chauvinism of *Look Back in Anger* went unremarked at the time, of course.

*6.39* The causes of change are seldom simple or single. It was not only the content, but also the forms of drama that were worn out and needing to be renewed. You can get some idea of how old-fashioned were the forms of British drama by thinking back to *Yerma* in the last block. The British theatre had to wait nearly thirty years before European innovation in form as well as content had any significant impetus. Osborne's three-act play is in fact still quite conservative in form. Arden's play on the other hand shows in its form and language the influences of Becket and Brecht.

*6.40* In 1955 Peter Hall (in his mid twenties) directed the first London production of Beckett's *Waiting for Godot*. Like *Endgame, Godot*'s language seems to hover on the edge of meaning. Its sparseness is a quality reflected in Arden. But Brecht was an even more powerful influence, and 1956 brought his Berliner Ensemble to London. You will be studying *Mother Courage* in Block 8, but we need to anticipate a little. Like Beckett, Brecht had rejected naturalism. His plays are performed on a bare stage, rather than against a realistic backdrop, and he makes no pretence of imitating 'real life' speech. The snatches of ballads that you find in *Serjeant Musgrave's Dance* are also characteristic of Brecht. Like Beckett, Brect was fiercely anti-bourgeois; unlike him, Brecht worked to an explicit political agenda – Marxism. And Arden sympathized not just with Brecht's politics, but with his theatrical ideology.

*6.41* One of the most notorious attributes of Brecht's theatrical technique is what he called the *Verfremdungseffekt* (literally, the 'making strange effect'). Nowadays this is usually referred to as 'alienation'. But when it first crossed the Channel it was known rather ludicrously as the 'A-effect'. (Curious, this penchant for certain initials. Older readers may remember A- and H-line dresses from the same period. And A- and H-bombs.) What Brecht was trying to achieve was neither very difficult to understand, nor entirely successful, though it has been the subject of much critical huffing and puffing. When the word 'alienation' was first used in a theatrical context it was perhaps too closely identified with that kind of spiritual alienation best exemplified in Camus' *The Outsider*. It's important to remember that although first published in French in 1942, that novella was extremely influential in Britain throughout the fifties. Jimmy Porter is in one respect very much a literary descendant of Meursault: he shares Meursault's sense of moral and spiritual disengagement, even though he expressed himself through anger and not indifference. But Brecht's alienation had nothing to do with feeling out of sympathy with the times. He wanted to establish a distance between the audience and the play, and break down the illusions of involvement. The notion that each member of the audience should somehow 'become part' of the play, and 'identify' with the feelings expressed by its actors, was, he believed, a debased subjectivity which indulged the emotions and prevented a detached objective engagement with the play's ideas. To achieve this end, his productions stressed their theatricality. When they weren't performing, his actors remained on stage, in full view of the audience.

*6.42* There will be more to say about this in Block 8. But one common misunderstanding needs to be dispelled. Alienation did not make for drab or unengrossing theatre. Because Brecht was a Marxist, he is sometimes half-expected to be a boring social realist. But his drama was 'epic'. Indeed, visitors to his theatre in East Berlin, which reopened very soon after the end of the Second World War, were amazed by its richness of spectacle in a ruined city. And interestingly, Arden says that one of the first promptings he felt to write his play was a reaction to the drabness of British society and its new theatre in the fifties: 'I visualized the stage full of scarlet uniforms' (quoted in *Encore*, August 1961). So it was not in fact only a desire to 'distance' his theme which lead him to set it in the vaguely Victorian past, even though the catalytic incident in the narrative had actually taken place in recent Cyprus, but a powerful theatrical preference for scarlet over khaki.

*6.43* If you now read the following passages from 'Telling a true tale', a piece Arden wrote in *Encore* in May 1960, you will see how permeated his thinking was with ideas similar to Brecht's:

> What I am deeply concerned with is the problem of translating the concrete life of today into terms of poetry that shall at the one time both illustrate that life and set it within the historical and legendary tradition of our culture ... costumes, movements, verbal patterns, music must all be strong and hard at the edges. If verse is used in the dialogue it must be nakedly verse as opposed to the surrounding prose, and must never be allowed to drop into casual flaccidities. That is the Brechtian technique, more or less...
>
> Social criticism ... tends in the theatre to be dangerously ephemeral and therefore disappointing after the fall of the curtain. But if it is expressed within the framework of the traditional poetic truths it can have a weight and an impact derived from something more than contemporary documentary facility.
>
> ...habits of playgoing have lead [audiences] to expect that they are going to have to begin by forming judgements, by selecting what they think is the author's 'social standpoint' and then following it to its conclusion. This does not happen in the ballads...

*6.44* The play's rhetoric not only generalized its issues but imparted the crucial distance which would enable the audience to see beyond merely anything that the author or even the actors might want to say and engage with a wider spectrum of ideas. I think you will have found it quite difficult to identify let alone paraphrase the argument Arden is making. John Russell Taylor summarized some of the confusion which greeted the play in 1959:

> At the time it was often found confusing because the liberal spectator saw in it a tract about pacificism which seemed to show that pacificism did not work. For the naive this was simply because Musgrave and his men are defeated at the end. For the more perceptive it was because the motives and methods of the soldiers are so at odds with each other and often so apparently wrong-headed that it might be interpreted as an attempt to

> discredit pacifism by discrediting pacifists. Either Arden is for the pacifists, the argument would run, or he is against them, but if he is for them why has he not made them largely creditable and heroic, while if he is against them why has he made their opponents so discreditable and unheroic?
>
> (Taylor, 1962, pp.93–4)

*6.45* This suggests that it is not just the forms of Arden's play that are Brechtian. He has also refused to prejudge moral issues. There is no character with whom the audience can identify, no emotional wave they can ride. 'Alienated', or distanced from subjective engagement, the audience have to make up their own minds. In 1959 this was, perhaps, an unnerving rather than an exhilarating position to be in. All kinds of authoritative structures were tottering, but the prospect of a future without these moral props could look as grim as Arden's mining town in the snow.

*6.46* It is not simply an anti-imperialist play, though political attack undoubtedly was (and is) one of Arden's intentions. He redoubled his efforts when *Serjeant Musgrave* was revived at the Royal Court in 1965, declaring in the programme that he was donating all his royalties from that production to the aid of political prisoners in South Africa, 'because South Africa is the worst reminder we have of those historical grandfathers of ours who sent the legendary Serjeant Musgrave and his men off to the wars'. The 1966 New York production coincided with the height of another imperialist debacle: the war in Vietnam. It forced Arden to contemplate the usefulness of his work and come to conclusions that were sometimes despairing but never less than passionate:

> Protest is a sort of futile activity in the Theatre ... it is ... unlikely that a couple of hundred people in the Theater de Lys [venue of the New York production] are going to suddenly get up and rush out of the theatre and start a revolution ... Yet I think it's very necessary that it should be ... One will at least be able to say, 'Well, I did get up and say so before it was too late.'
>
> (interview with Ira Peck, *New York Times*, 10 April 1966)

A month later he put an advertisement in the same paper:

> If *Serjeant Musgrave* fails in his attempt to bring the war to an end it is not because I believe such an attempt to be objectively impossible. Indeed I believe it is not only possible but mandatory for citizens in a democracy to use their voices in this cause.
>
> (*New York Times*, 15 May 1966)

## Themes

*6.47* This is obviously a play relevant to the study of drama and ideology in the previous block. You could use material and thinking from here to enhance any further work you do on this and related topics in Block 8 and in the examination. Do you agree that protest via the stage, while 'mandatory', is nevertheless futile? In the first extract quoted above, Arden seems dangerously close to the petulant tones of 'Don't blame me'. And, of course, as the interview with Ronald Hayman (quoted in paragraph 6.32) emphasizes, the play had no discernible effect on either British or American foreign policy. Look at Philip Larkin's poem 'Homage to a Government' (in the Poetry Anthology). Are the more pragmatic reasons for 'bringing the soldiers home' really 'all right'? Arden's play, and the theatrical renaissance of which it was part, testify to a deep need for change in the prevailing forms, but maybe his yearning for 'scarlet uniforms' is hankering for the glamour of the past.

*6.48* But it is a very unspecific past. The play's subtitle is 'An *un-historical* parable'. The stage directions suggest a date around 1880, but frankly the period is as vague as the geography. Arden's own introductory note refers vaguely to a Kipling era – thus indicating, by the way, what Kipling meant in 1960. Think back to Block 1 and what Martin Esslin had to say about the semiotics of drama. Both the 'pastness' and the setting operate as generalized *signs*. A northern mining town (which will probably be indicated on stage by the actors' accents, a few pick-axes, mining lamps, and a lot of coal dust about the face, and possibly – in an implausible, corny production – silhouettes of winding gear on the backdrop) does not in this case mean that the play has much to do with mining: it is a sign of that class's cultural values, and the women are signs of its moral values. What we are given is not a careful analysis, but a broad sketch. And by setting his play in the unspecific past, Arden is able to make his contrasts even broader, not just because the scarlet uniforms allow him to deploy an elemental colour scheme (the coal, the snow and the blood red), but because 'pastness' operates as a sign for *parable*.

*6.49* All kinds of signals hint that this is not going to be a naturalistic play even before the house lights go down or we get into our reading of it. The title could be misleading: you might think you were in for a comedy – strains of Glenn Miller at the Palais – rather than a dance of death. But the cast list would subdue you with its anonymous colliers and its representative authority figures – the parson, the constable and the mayor. Some of the characters have names, but the first few minutes of playing will suggest that categories are more important than characters. The songs and the symbolic references all quickly disillusion the audience of any expectations of naturalism which they were much more likely to have had in 1959 than today.

*6.50* In other sections of this block you will see how other writers evoke the past. A nostalgic hankering for past glories seems to have affected even those clear-sighted enough to have seen through the delusion. Obviously that is not what is happening here, but nor are we being shown a past which Evelyn Waugh recalls in *Officers and Gentlemen*. In Block 8 this question will be discussed in more depth. There, Ballard's *Empire of the Sun* is in some respects a case of 'telling what it was like', whereas Brecht's *Mother Courage* (more like *Serjeant Musgrave's Dance*) gives us little information about the Thirty Years' War but enables the play to make a time-free statement.

*6.51* Yet of course this is an impossibility. As we saw in Block 4, every literary work is inevitably shaped by the time and conditions in which it is produced. We have already noticed some of the ways in which *Musgrave* was of its time. But the play avoids directing its fire at any specific contemporary instance. An actual incident in Cyprus, in which a soldier's death was avenged with an out-of-control reprisal was the catalyst that inspired the play. But that is not what the play is about.

*6.52* I hope the recording on the audio-cassettes will have convinced you of the play's dramatic power. But it may have left you even more unsure of its meaning. Arden's own remarks suggest that he sees the play as pacific in intention: but its very excitement and momentum derive from the militaristic ethos. Is Arden having his moral cake and eating it too? If militarism is what you are attacking, then either it is morally dubious to make soldiering the source of nearly all the play's excitement, or the work is deeply ambiguous. Musgrave may be wrong, he may be crazy; but he's compelling, and perhaps only the women manage to embody any coherent challenge to what he stands for. In his introductory note Arden says that 'I know that if I am hit I very easily hit back'. What he means is that our intellectual position on a moral issue may be compromised by a gut-reaction. The play exploits this essential ambiguity. It is violence itself that reveals the endlessly self-perpetrating nature of violence.

*6.53* This is a very *macho* ethic. Later in the 1960s Arden's message may have seemed hopelessly compromised. Indeed, the play possibly achieved its ironic establishment status because it so emphatically does not endorse the more subversive 'peacenik' code of the anti-Vietnam, hippie generation a decade later. But Musgrave's crazy logic, by which each successive reprisal is a geometric multiplication,was appropriate in the frustrated, angry age of Jimmy Porter.

*6.54* But there is another war going on in this play, and this one Arden does not bring to any kind of dramatic resolution: the class war. What the miners call a strike, the bosses call a lock-out. They are only too eager to think that Musgrave has come on a recruiting drive, which they see as a way of getting rid of agitators. Naturally they assume that Musgrave is on their side. The miners have their own attitudes to the soldiers. They are tempted by the money and the glamour, and they also plot to steal the gun so that they can turn it on their masters. But when Walsh sees Musgrave threatening to shoot the establishment figures one by one, he can't countenance an action that would involve an alliance of pitmen with the military:

> That's coal-owners and it's pitmen – aye, and they battle, and the pitmen'll win. But not wi' no soldier-boys to order our fight for us. Remember their trade: you give 'em one smell of a broken town, you'll never get 'em out!
>
> (Drama Anthology, pp.225–6)

*6.55* Ironically, of course, the Mayor, the parson and the constable (and the audience, on whom the Gatling gun is trained) are saved by the dragoons. Not all of the army has been driven to Musgrave's logic. But the issue of the strike (or lock-out) isn't resolved. As Walsh says 'We're all friends and neighbours for the rest of today' (Drama Anthology, p.232). The miners and the authority figures all join arms in the dance. But in the original production they did so with a wall of dragoons behind them.

*6.56* So why did Arden not bring this theme of the play to a resolution? Walsh is the most intelligent and articulate of the miners – and the only one dignified by a name. And he was perhaps ultimately a very reassuring figure to the middle-class audience. He suggests that the working classes won't machine gun their masters when they get the chance, and that even among the starving, desperate men can be led to a moderate course by an articulate leader. What I am suggesting is that this apparently radical play still contains some very conservative elements. And nothing is really dislodged by its passion. The establishment figures are all preserved unscathed. The only casualties are Musgrave's band who came with Billy Hick's skeleton to bring war home, and to stop it by what came to be known as 'overkill'.

*6.57* Perhaps the conflict between radical pressures and lingering conservatism that I'm suggesting was characteristic of the late fifties and early sixties in Britain. This can be seen more clearly if we look at the female characters in the play. The scene in the stable (Act II scene iii) in which Annie comes to offer herself to Hurst, is pawed about by Attercliffe, and shares a love-scene with Sparky, would have been very startling when it was first produced. (You may have noticed that what happens between Annie and Sparky when the lights shift to Musgrave is left to the discretion of the producer.) Such relative frankness about sexuality was thought to be very progressive. Yet the shock-value of such scenes effectively disguised just how conventional were the roles played by the female protagonists. The shrewd but kindly landlady – provider of one kind of creature comfort – and the whore 'with a heart like a horsecollar' (and not quite right in the head) – who provides another – are cliché figures, and the moral responsibilities they carry in the play's argument can seem equally orthodox. If you refer back to what I said earlier about *Look Back in Anger* you may agree that while both these plays seem sexually progressive, a superficial shockingness hides an innate conservatism. Annie and Mrs Hitchcock are not the most simplistic figures in the play, of course. They are complex and rounded compared with those cardboard flat authority figures – the parson, the mayor and the constable.

*6.58* Perhaps what seems most old fashioned (but very much of its time) is the location of alternative values almost entirely among the women. That men fight and women weep now seems an over-simplification. But the dialectical structure of drama (see Block 1) tends to produce a simplification in the individual character that does not necessarily result in a simplification of the overall argument and certainly does not inevitably lessen the power of the case. It may be that Shakespeare has had a baleful influence in this respect. The psychologically complex and plausible characters which we find in his mature work are in fact rare in drama as a whole, but those raised in the British tradition still tend to think that character complexity and life-likeness are essential to profundity.

*6.59* Are Annie and Mrs Hitchcock archetypes or stereotypes? Annie's songs help to give her the dignity of a ballad figure but she is still a formulaic character – a source of comfort, but also a source of death. Look at the brief scene between her and Musgrave at the end of Act II scene i.

> MUSGRAVE ...Our work isn't easy, no and it's not soft: it's got a strong name – duty. And it's drawn out straight and black for us, a clear plan. But if you come to us with what you call your life or love – *I'd* call it your indulgence – and you scribble all over that plan, you make it crooked, dirty, idle, untidy, *bad* – there's anarchy.
>
> (Drama Anthology, p.184)

*6.60* Musgrave's chilly 'duty' brings him to the gallows in the end, but Annie's 'life and love' (and also Annie's words to Hurst in Act II scene iii) seem to be incapable of effecting any good. It is she who inspires Sparky's desire to escape – and hence his death. And it was she who was the lover of the skeleton that dominates the crucial scene, and the mother of his deformed child. On the 'life' side, however, it is she who reveals that 'They buried the other one in Ma Hitchcock's midden' thus completing Walsh's revulsion from Musgrave's cause:

> WALSH ...If you want to stand by 'em when they've done for their own mucker and not one of the bastards can tell ye the same tale, well, you're at your damned liberty and take it and go!
>
> (Drama Anthology, p.229)

But this decision leads the miners back to the 'Michael Finnegan – begin agen' stalemate symbolized in the dance with the masters.

*6.61* Of course, we should not expect that a playwright who practises a Brechtian detachment from his central character would attribute any special emotional weighting to the women. All I am suggesting you should register are the limits of Arden's progressiveness. There is no attempt to rethink women's traditional roles in the debate of peace and war. Mrs Hitchcock is even a kind of nurse, adminstering soothing potions in Act II scene iii as well as in the final scene. And Annie's influence on the action is quite outside the rational dimension.

*6.62* I wonder if you felt that the religious dimension in Musgrave's character was also rather old fashioned? Arden says in his notes that he might have served under Cromwell. He sees his retributive mission as the work of God. Did you feel that the inclusion of this element in his make-up was an indictment of religious values?

*6.63* Certainly the time of writing was a period of aggressive secularization among the British intelligentsia. The church was yet another traditional authority that had to go. Religion was an arm of the state, a colonial power. The pacifist clergyman was a relatively new phenomenon, and the presence of many clerical figures on the early Aldermaston marches was felt by many to be startling and subversive. Now, I think, we would expect Christian and

Jewish leaders to be associated with international peace movements. Arden's drum-beating parson seems a very anachronistic figure. Musgrave, on the other hand, surely remains more familiar. The religious zealot is perhaps an even more chilling figure today.

*6.64* Arden does not bring the peculiar, specific evils of colonial warfare into sharp focus. Instead he concentrates on the generalized power of the military ethos, embodied in Musgrave, which seems to mesmerize society. I have suggested that this was ambiguous, but maybe that is inevitable at a point of transition. What it is difficult to remember now is that savage attacks on military values were new in the British theatre. Until then when audiences saw a red coat, they expected a romantic hero. Arden's play coincided with the beginnings of a new cynicism about the army that reached its popular apogee a few years later with Joan Littlewood's bitter music-hall collage *Oh, What a Lovely War!*.

# 7 A study guide to British poetry, 1950–c.1980

*7.1* The principal aim of this study guide is to consider a selection of the work of four English poets, Philip Larkin, Ted Hughes, Geoffrey Hill and Tony Harrison, and one Scottish Gaelic poet, Sorley MacLean, in relation to the theme of this block, the end of the British Empire.

*7.2* A secondary aim is to encourage you to think further about the way that poetry engages with historical and cultural change. To this end, this study guide builds on your familiarity with the theme of Block 3, 'Englishness', and the poetry discussed in that block. Your knowledge of the theme of Block 4, 'Literature and Ideology', is essential in understanding how the legacy of empire could be argued to be implicit in the poems you will be studying here.

## Poetry and the end of empire

*7.3* Of the three literary genres which you are studying in this course, poetry is the one that appears to register historical events and ideological conflicts most obliquely. Equally, it could be argued that poetry demonstrates more starkly than either drama or fiction that literature does not simply mediate or reflect history; it transforms it. But a poem may best exemplify a latent paradox in the relationship between literature and history. That is, its form and content may express an emotional or psychological state quite distinct from the historical experience out of which it arose. It may transmute the actuality of an experience into something symbolic or allusive. It may aspire to communicate a metaphysical feeling which transcends the material condition that occasioned its creation. Eliot's *The Waste Land*, for example, communicates a cultural crisis in the aftermath of the First World War, but does so without direct reference to the historical context in which it was written.

*7.4* Critics who venture to read a poem with reference to the historical pressures which it disguises or conceals are often accused of mere speculation. Why should they impose their own preoccupations on writers of the past, or even of the present? What about the intentions of the authors themselves, and the reception which the first readers give to a literary text? Don't these factors provide a surer indication of how to interpret a poem's meaning? These issues are central to A319 and you will have begun to equip yourselves with the relevant arguments in both the course material and the Reader. You will also be aware of how the language of a text can often subvert a single reading. A certain kind of historical contextualist might offer a rather deterministic reading of a text without due attention to the way that its language displays ambiguities or, in Macherey's terms, reveals gaps and silences, which provide an insight into other, possibly contradictory, readings (see Reader, pp.215–22). It is essential that you bear these wider issues in mind as you work through this study guide. Because poems tend to be particularly economical and often elliptical in their use of language, your full engagement in the exercise of close reading is imperative.

*7.5* My own declared aim, as stated above, is to read the poems in this study guide with the particular historical and cultural fact of the end of Britain's empire in mind. But I want to register at the outset that this does not mean that all the poems are being read simply to establish how far they state this bald fact, because that would produce disappointing results and be a futile exercise anyway. Because literature does not reflect history in a reductive, deterministic sense, there is no simple, causal relationship between the demise of the British Empire and the work of the five poets discussed in this section. The argument here is that all these poets are preoccupied with authority, be it the endurance of national or regional myths of pastoral splendour or individual heroism, or the ideological and linguistic dominance of one kind of culture over another, or of the power of native roots and origins to transcend time and place, or of the dominant hold of physical and animal nature over human history. Furthermore, many of the poems you will study in the following pages reveal that their authors' imaginations are concerned with the past, and with either the loss of power or its reassertion in the face of an actual political authority which no longer exists. A forceful and persuasive exposition of this argument is given in Seamus Heaney's essay, 'Englands of the mind', an abridged version of which is reprinted in the Reader. I shall ask you to consider it in the conclusion of this study guide, but it would be useful if you read it now.

*7.6* Below are some examples of the kinds of questions which we will be asking you to consider as you read the poems:

What is notable about the language and form of the poems, compared with the poetry you studied in Blocks 2 and 3?

What views of the past are expressed? Are they nostalgic, elegiac, ironic or propagandist?

How is nature presented, and does it shape the historical sensibility in the poems you are reading?

Is a sense of national or regional identity expressed through a pastoral literary idiom, examples of which you studied in the Georgian poets examined in Block 3?

What is the importance of myth in the poems you are examining?

Could the poems be described as imperialistic and, if so, how?

## *ACTIVITY*

To give you an idea of how these questions can be applied to your reading of the poems themselves, I would like you now to read the following poems, one by each of the authors to be studied in this block: 'At Grass' by Philip Larkin; 'Hawk Roosting' by Ted Hughes; I 'The Naming of Offa' from *Mercian Hymns* by Geoffrey Hill; 'On Not Being Milton' by Tony Harrison; 'Heroes' by Sorley MacLean.

You will find the first four poems in the Poetry Anthology; 'Heroes' is reprinted in the Broadcast and Cassette Notes. When you have read these poems, please answer the following specific questions in the form of brief notes. Please note that there will be further, more detailed discussion of each of these poems later in the study guide, so don't worry too much at this stage if you feel you would like to pursue some of the points raised in more detail.

(a) What in your own words is the poem about? (Remember to be brief.)

(b) What is notable about the language and form of the poem, compared with the other poetry you have examined so far in this course?

(c) Which, if any, of the themes or issues in the list of questions above (the past, nature, national or regional identity, or myth) best applies to your interpretation of the poem? In the light of your view, can you suggest ways in which the poem has a bearing on the block theme of end of empire?

(Note: If you have listened to Radio 9, you will have heard Donald Davie and Tom Paulin discussing their responses to the first two of these poems – which are read aloud by their authors – so you can use this exercise as a way of finding out how far you agree or disagree with their interpretations.)

## *DISCUSSION*

### 'At Grass'

(a) As the title suggests, the poem is about retirement. But given the contrast between the racehorses' present anonymity and their past fame, it could be said to be as much about release and escape as about coming to terms with loss.

(b) Its language is a subtle combination of prosaic and lyrical diction and it has a dignified, classical form. The mood of elegiac pastoral may have reminded you of the Georgian poetry you studied in Block 3.

(c) The glorious past evoked in stanzas 2 and 3 is conveyed through horse-racing, crowds, and hot summers. This imagery is presented in terms of a snapshot of English culture. This means that the theme of retirement is linked, in albeit ambivalent ways, with images of what it is, or was, to be English. The poem can thus be seen, on one level, to allude to a vanished glory of which the empire was part.

### 'Hawk Roosting'

(a) The poem is about perfecting authoritarian power, though its effect seems almost as ironical as it is menacing. Whether the portrayal of the hawk serves as a serious critique of dictatorship, or whether it parodies the self-inflated delusions of a petty despot, is difficult to determine.

(b) The language of the poem, like its subject, is excessive and frequently brutal, but it also has a dynamic exhilaration as you will have found in listening to Hughes reading the poem in Radio 9.

(c) If power and authority are the basis of imperial rule, then the conviction that there is no alternative is necessary to sustain that political imperative. Yet the poem could be seen to expose the comically exaggerated claims of its speaker. The very excess of this fantasy of unproblematical authority carries with it an implicit qualification of its boasts, and therefore the poem cannot be seen simply to endorse the imperial dream.

### I 'The Naming of Offa' from *Mercian Hymns*

(a) This differs from the others in that it is the first of a sequence of thirty closely connected poems, so it doesn't stand alone in the way that the others do. But the title of the sequence and the proper name in the final line suggest that this is a hymn of praise to Offa, the Anglo-Saxon King of Mercia, by an apparently twentieth-century speaker who is registering Offa's mythical influence on the West Midlands from the Anglo-Saxon period until the present day.

(b) The hymn is without regular stanzaic divisions and rhyme, and although there is a perceivable momentum to the catalogue of titles, there is no formal rhythm either. Its language is knotty and allusive. The irony derives from the blatant anachronisms, the fact that, for example, Offa is 'overlord of the M5'. The apparent incongruity of the language of modern-day England and its past is accentuated in order to emphasize Offa's transcendence of his own historical period.

(c) Through Offa, Hill seems to make the historical past bear upon the present in a peculiarly mythical way, as if the roots of this region of contemporary England can be understood through this eighth-century figure of feudal authority. The historical sensibility of this hymn seems imbued with imperial resonances.

### 'On Not Being Milton'

(a) As its title suggests, this poem describes the struggle of the inarticulate and dispossessed to challenge the political and linguistic privileges of those in power. This struggle to give voice to social protest is perceived in the context of the struggle against economic oppression in the industrial age.

(b) The poem is in an unusual sonnet form of sixteen lines, which is both eleborately formal in rhythm and rhyme, but also colloquial in idiom.

(c) In this poem, Harrison expresses a parallel theme to that of the decline of empire, that is the way in which the voices of those from working-class and regional cultures within England have found independence from the language and values of the metropolis. As London weakens its hold as the hub of the empire, so the composite identity of what is called 'England' becomes more apparent.

### 'Heroes'

(a) This poem is a critique of the kind of spurious heroism often associated with battle. Compared to the Gaelic heroes this English soldier, who dies unremembered in the North African desert in the Second World War, has few redeeming qualities, but nevertheless the poet finds himself moved at his unnoticed heroism – 'he took a little weeping to my eyes'.

(b) The language of the poem sets off, in the first and final verses especially, the nobility of Gaelic warriors against the anonymity and prosaic death of the Englishman.

(c) MacLean's poem takes issue with military heroism, and in so doing exposes the mythology implicit in his own Gaelic culture. The Englishman is seen as a victim of, as well as an accessory to, the ideology of imperialism.

*7.7* As you can see from this exercise, each of the poets in this study guide employs a distinctive language and is preoccupied with different issues. No attempt will be made to make the poets into a homogenous group, nor could they be described properly as 'representative'. There are many other distinguished poets who are not discussed. You will have noticed expecially that these are all white, male poets. There have, of course, been many distinguished black male and/or female poets writing in English during the period spanned by these five poets, and you will be studying some of them in Blocks 6 and 7. It is important to emphasize that the end of empire is registered in the poetry of those who have experienced life under colonial rule, and by women who have criticized the male ideology complicit in the concept of empire.

## The Movement

*7.8* The aim of this sub-section is to provide a brief introduction to a group of poets of the 1950s known as the Movement. Of the poets you will look at in this study guide, however, only Philip Larkin can be said to have been influenced by the Movement, and only in a relatively small number of his poems of the fifties. Therefore, this sub-section will be of use primarily in indicating the literary and historical context of poets who began writing in the fifties, and in questioning whether their sensibility was influenced by the end of empire.

*7.9* Like other labels you have encountered in A319, such as Georgianism (to characterize some poetry of the period roughly 1912–22), Modernism (to describe some of the major literary works of 1922 and after), or the social and political themes of poetry of the thirties, the Movement needs some qualification as a way of identifying the poetry of the fifties. Unlike the other terms, it is also possibly more contentious both in its journalistic origins and in the self-conscious irony of its title. It was coined in 1954 by the literary editor of the *Spectator*, J.D. Scott, to describe the work of Kingsley Amis (1922–), Donald Davie (1922–), Philip Larkin (1922–85), John Wain (1925–), D.J. Enright (1920–), Elizabeth Jennings (1926–), and others, 'but after 1956 it was no longer possible to think of the Movement writers as being united in a common cause' (Morrison, 1980, pp.238–9). The Movement was a self-assured denial of the value of grand themes and goals for poetry; it was a negative *movement* against implicitly self-proclaiming 'literary movements'. Robert Conquest, another poet associated with the Movement, described it as 'little more than a negative determination to avoid bad principles' (Conquest, 1956, p.xv). But it can best be characterized by a plain language and uncomplicated syntax, a desire to recover what was perceived to be the rightful tradition of English poetry from the Modernists and from the neo-Romantics (metaphysical poets of the 1940s) and among some writers, by an insular, 'Little England' mentality.

### *ACTIVITY*

The most celebrated document of the Movement's poetic principles is Robert Conquest's introduction to his anthology of nine fifties poets, *New Lines*, published in 1956. The anthology included poems by Amis, Davie, Enright, Jennings, Larkin, Wain, Thom Gunn (1929–), John Holloway (1920–) and

Conquest himself (1917–). Please read the following extract from Conquest's introduction and note down the key characteristics of Movement poetry:

> In one sense, indeed, the standpoint is not new, but merely the restoration of a sound and fruitful attitude to poetry, of the principle that poetry is written by and for the whole man, intellect, emotions, senses and all. But restorations are not repetitions. The atmosphere, the attack, of these poets is as concentratedly contemporary as could be imagined. To be of one's own time is not an important virtue, but it is a necessary one.
>
> If one had briefly to distinguish this poetry of the fifties from its predecessors, I believe the most important general point would be that it submits to no great systems of theoretical constructs nor agglomerations of unconscious commands. It is free from both mystical and logical compulsions and – like modern philosophy – is empirical in its attitude to all that comes. This reverence for the real person or event is, indeed, a part of the general intellectual ambience (in so far as that is not blind or retrogressive) of our time...
>
> On the more technical side, though of course related to all this, we see refusal to abandon a rational structure and comprehensible language, even when the verse is most highly charged with sensuous or emotional intent.
>
> (Conquest, 1956, pp.xiv–xv)

## *DISCUSSION*

The key characteristics of Movement poetry according to Conquest are the following: 'the restoration of a sound and fruitful attitude to poetry'; the fact that it 'is empirical in its attitude to all that comes' and a 'refusal to abandon a rational structure and comprehensible language'. The first of these three statements concerns the unequivocal rejection of the Modernists and their successors of the thirties; the second two concern the proper themes and language of poetry.

*7.10* Many of the poets of the Movement saw their writing in the context of the history of English poetry in the twentieth century. They were deeply conscious of the major voices of twentieth-century poetry including Eliot, Yeats, Auden and, most recently, Dylan Thomas. All were preoccupied however, with the tradition which the Modernists and thirties' poets had interrupted. Conquest commented:

> All of us were brought up in the tradition of the supposed poetic revolution of the 1920s and 1930s. All our predilections and original partisanships were for this 'modernism'. It is only now, with the advantage perhaps of perspective, that the innovations of that time are seen to be peripheral additions to the main tradition of English poetry, in so far as they are valuable at all, and for the most part as wholly useless.
>
> (Conquest, 1963, p.xxiv)

*7.11* Modernism was also to be criticized by the Movement because it represented the corruption of a native literary tradition by American and European literature. Kingsley Amis's comment typifies the aggression of the 'Little England' viewpoint:

> ...nobody wants any more poems on the grander themes for a few years, but at the same time nobody wants any more poems about philosophers or paintings or novelists or art galleries or mythology or foreign cities or other poems. At least I hope nobody wants them.
>
> (in Enright, 1958, pp.17–18)

*7.12* Larkin, Amis and Davie were less interested in innovation and experiment in poetic form and language than in restoration and recovery. This concern with an identifiable and essential Englishness in their concept of tradition is manifest in the predisposition in Kingsley Amis's recent *Amis Anthology* (1988) for pre- or anti-Modernist English poets, such as Newbolt, Kipling, Masefield and Betjeman. Larkin's selection for *The Oxford Book of Twentieth-century English Verse* (1973) reflects a similar taste, however much his own poetry belies that stance in its Romantic and even Modernist tendencies. Davie too, despite his receptive view of Pound and Eliot and his keen interest in translation, published an important critical work entitled *Purity of Diction in English Verse* (1952), which was perceived as an indirect manifesto for the Movement, advocating a return to the clarity of the language of late eighteenth-century (that is, pre-Romantic) poetry. In terms of the theme of the block, the cultural insularity of some members of the Movement and their common desire to recover a lost tradition of English poetry reveals an anxiety about England as the empire began to disintegrate.

## *ACTIVITY*

By way of reviewing the above summary of the characteristics of the Movement, please read Amis's 'Against Romanticism' (first published in 1956) in the Poetry Anthology. What views of the content and technique of poetry is the poem criticizing?

## *DISCUSSION*

As the title suggests, the poem criticizes an idealized way of looking at the function of poetry, and its language is unembellished. The 'Romanticism' of the title does not describe simply the literary-historical period of Romantic poetry but, implicitly, any kind of idealism. In short, the poem attacks the idea that poetry has to participate in an unreal world, be it imagined or prophesied. Look at how the first stanza attacks this view of poetry with a particularly sharp irony in its final lines. In the second stanza, the poet makes plain his own preferences for poetic form and subject matter, and formulates this preference in terms of an uncomplicated, transparently clear landscape, 'Woods devoid of beasts, roads that please the foot'. This desire for 'a temperate zone', a lack of extremity and an attention to empirical reality ('Better, of course, if images were plain, /Warnings clearly said') is directed against more recent poetry than that of the Romantic poets. Amis implicitly identifies and criticizes those, to him, tiresome elements in Modernist and neo-Romantic poetry which continue a Romantic preoccupation with symbol and prophecy.

*7.13* 'Against Romanticism' also expresses an impatience with and hostility to the socialist ideals of much of the poetry of the thirties. Many Movement poets did not simply reject Modernism but, like Amis, were sceptical of the political and social dimension of the poetry of the thirties. In this respect some instructive comparisons have been made between the Movement and the Georgian poets, through the figures of Larkin and Edward Thomas, by the critic Edna Longley:

> From a cultural point of view, before one war and after another, the Georgians and the Movement signalled, if nothing else, an important sensibility-shift. As the Georgians rejected Victorian rhetoric, 'Hectoring large-scale verses' on public themes, the propaganda of Kipling: so the Movement poets reacted in part against the propaganda of Auden and the

> socio-political orientation of much thirties poetry. At the other end of the spectrum they repudiated the oddly equivalent psychic wallowings of the *fin de siècle* and the Apocalypse.
>
> (Longley, 1986, p.116)

Longley thinks of the two literary groupings as parallel in their rejection of an elevated social or political role for poetry, and their advocation of a return to empirical reality and experience, though with different emphases: 'Whereas the "empirical" base to which the Georgians returned was observation of Nature; the Movement was more grounded in observations on human nature...' (p.117).

## *ACTIVITY*

Please now read 'Remembering the Thirties' by Donald Davie, reprinted in the Poetry Anthology. How far does it reflect Longley's account? Does it recommend the neutral tone it describes?

(Note to line 13: *Anschluss* was a term applied to the union of Austria and Germany, achieved through the forced annexation of Austria by the Nazis in 1938; Guernica was the Spanish town bombed by the Nazis in the Spanish Civil War in 1937, and is now most famous as the title of a painting by Picasso based on that event which depicts the inhumanity of war.)

## *DISCUSSION*

In the first part, the poem examines the historical events of the thirties through the perspective of the poet's own, younger generation. Davie's self-critical tone rebukes the distortions of memory, 'And in the process some-one is betrayed. /Ourselves perhaps'. The first few verses of the second section of the poem challenge the accusation that in their commitment to political causes the poets of the thirties were half-hearted:

> They played the fool, not to appear as fools
> In time's long glass. A deprecating air
> Disarmed, they thought, the jeers of later schools;
> Yet irony itself is doctrinaire,
>
> And curiously, nothing now betrays
> Their type to time's derision like this coy
> Insistence on the quizzical, their craze
> For showing Hector was a mother's boy.

The idea here that the very ironies which they attempted to anticipate in their writing about contemporary history deflected back onto themselves is offset by the recognition that in Davie's own era, that of the Movement of the fifties, the self-conscious position of the intellectual in relation to politics is equally questionable:

> A neutral tone is nowadays preferred.
> And yet it may be better, if we must,
> To praise a stance impressive and absurd
> Than not to see the hero for the dust.

The critic, John Press, has pointed out that:

> As originally printed, the poem bore as its epigraph a quotation from Paul Tillich: 'Courage is an ethical reality, but it is rooted in the whole breadth of existence and ultimately in the structure of being itself.' Read in conjunction with the final verse, this epigraph should have alerted Davie's readers to the poem's many reservations, qualifications and courtesies.
>
> (Press, 1971, p.252)

*7.14* There were contemporary critics of the Movement poets, such as Charles Tomlinson, who said that 'They seldom for a moment escape beyond the suburban mental ratio which they impose on experience' (1957, p.215). Tomlinson's criticism is from the viewpoint of an advocate of high Modernism, but the Movement was exclusive in other senses, too. With one exception, they were all male, white poets, and most were Oxbridge-educated. The contrast between the more or less solitary voice of Elizabeth Jennings (who you will meet in TV14 *Changing Voices*) in the mid-fifties and the much greater number of women who published poetry in the sixties is evidence, surely, of a pervasive cultural climate in which women poets found it difficult to gain recognition. If we survey the qualities of Movement verse, empirical in content, forthright and straightforward in language and style, preoccupied with the traditions of the predominantly male canon of English poetry, and acknowledge the promotion of aggression and pathos in male characters in texts of the fifties such as Osborne's *Look Back in Anger* (1956) and Amis's *Lucky Jim* (1954), some of the reasons why women writers were excluded and marginalized become apparent. The ideology of the Movement was conservative and its preoccupation with an imagined literary past purified of alien linguistic forms from Europe displayed a fundamental reaction against the literature of the twenties and thirties which you studied in Blocks 2 and 3.

## Philip Larkin

*7.15* Philip Larkin was born in Coventry in 1922. During the war he studied for a degree in English at Oxford, where he started writing poetry. He published four slim volumes of poetry in his lifetime: *The North Ship* (1945), *The Less Deceived* (1955), *The Whitsun Weddings* (1964) and *High Windows* (1974). The poems in the course's Poetry Anthology come from the latter three collections. His early poems, and other uncollected or unfinished poems written between 1946 and the end of his life are published in *Philip Larkin: Collected Poems* (1988), edited and introduced by Anthony Thwaite. Larkin also wrote two novels: *Jill* (1946) and *A Girl in Winter* (1947), and published two volumes of essays, one on jazz, *All What Jazz* (1985), and the other a collection of critical essays and reviews, *Required Writing* (1983). He also edited *The Oxford Book of Twentieth-century English Verse* (1973). Larkin spent much of his working life as the librarian of the Brynmor Jones Library at Hull University. He died in 1985.

### *ACTIVITY*

Now please read the poems by Larkin reprinted in the Poetry Anthology, referring back to the general questions in paragraph 7.6 as you do so.

### *ACTIVITY*

'At Grass' was completed on 3 January 1950, according to Anthony Thwaite's recent edition, and was published in *The Less Deceived* (1955). Please read it again. This time I'd like you to concentrate in more detail on the form and language of the poem. You should be familiar with the kind of features to look for. Work out the rhyme-scheme and consider how it contributes to the poem's rhythm and effect. Are there any features of the final stanza that disrupt the otherwise regular rhyme-scheme? Decide which words in the poem you think are particularly unusual, and think about how they contribute to the poem's sense. Are there any images which stand out and, if so, why?

## DISCUSSION

The rhyme-scheme is intricate (*abcabc*) but creates a less obtrusive rhythm than rhyming couplets. This contributes to the undemonstrative way that the narrative is presented in the poem. Indeed, the narrative technique is foregrounded in the second and third stanzas which take the form of a flash-back to the glorious fame of the racehorses. There is a slight deviation in the rhyme-scheme, which Donald Davie comments upon at the opening of Radio 9: the final words of the third stanza and sixth line of the last stanza, 'home' and 'come' make an 'eye-rhyme', that is, a rhyme to the eye but not to the ear. Instead of the poem 'clanging home with a close', Donald Davie sees it as ending on 'a fading echo which, after all, is what the whole poem is about'. Larkin also inverts the syntax of the last line, 'With bridles in the evening come', making it stand out as lyrical where some other lines of the poem are emphatically prosaic and conversational in idiom. His plain diction is effortlessly enriched by such touches as the pun in the third line, 'distresses', and his masterful use of negatives, 'the long cry /Hanging *unhushed*' in the third stanza and 'the *unmolesting* meadows' in the fourth. The image which is particularly effective in summoning up the wider themes of the poem is that of a royal crown at the end of the second stanza to suggest the past fame of the racehorses' names, 'artificed /To inlay faded, classic Junes'. Through metonymy, a figure of speech in which the name of an attribute is substituted for the thing it refers to, this image in particular associates the memory of the horses with the authority of the Crown. The atmosphere of 'faint afternoons / Of Cups and Stakes and Handicaps' is achieved through a snapshot evocation of the excitement of a public sporting event, and a careful use of alliteration and assonance, 'fable', 'faint', 'faded', which contribute to the process of constructing an image which has the authentic grain of an old photograph.

*7.16* In the first exercise on 'At Grass' we established that one of the themes of the poem was retirement. But how are we to interpret the perspective that the poem provides on this subject? In Radio 9 Donald Davie argues that 'the theme of the poem is universal, outside of history, if you like, and that this is part of what people respond to in it', whereas Tom Paulin expresses the view that 'a poem of retirement is always addressing a society by turning its back on it'. It is important for you to decide on the merits of each view. Because the poem is popular with most readers, it would not be surprising if you agreed with Donald Davie. Notice that he does not dismiss the possibility of reading the poem in different ways but he does believe that its true meaning resides in an appeal to a common human experience. But Tom Paulin reads the poem with its date of composition in mind, and attends to the significance of the social order it describes in the second and third stanzas. He calls it 'an elegiac poem' which is summoning up an image of a 'past glory, presumably empire'. There are two different ways of reading the poem: one sees its allegorical significance in social and political terms, the other in terms of a supposedly common human experience.

## ACTIVITY

Would you describe the mood of the poem as nostalgic? If so, what do you think the nostalgia is for? Are there any elements that counter its nostalgia? Don't be worried if you find contradictions in your response.

## DISCUSSION

Nostalgia, in common usage, means a wistful memory of, or sentimental yearning for, some period of the past. Although the poem does not succumb to sentimentality, I think it does display nostalgia in stanzas 2 and 3 for the idea that moral values and the social order were stable in the past.

Horse-racing was, and is, a popular national pastime. What is significant about the old-photograph imagery of stanzas 2 and 3, already discussed above, is that it suggests a common spectacle, a collective form of public entertainment with which most of us can identify, not necessarily because we have first-hand experience of it but because the imagery is so familiar. If we take the date of composition into account, then this memory is of the years before the Second World War and the paradoxical loss of empire and national identity which occurred in the aftermath of the allied victory (to which both speakers refer in Radio 9). In other words it invokes the kind of Englishness that you studied in Block 3. Larkin does not describe individual faces in the crowd but rather the institutionalized aspects of group behaviour on such occasions. The imagery carries a pathos because what we see are the poignant, empty signs of life, 'Squadrons of empty cars, and heat, /And littered grass', what we hear is a collective cheer quickly transformed into newspaper print, 'then the long cry /Hanging unhushed till it subside /To stop-press columns on the street'. In contrast to the individual loneliness of the horses in the opening stanza, there is a sense of collective warmth in the following two stanzas. But, as Tom Paulin points out in Radio 9, Larkin's depiction of the race-meeting preserves the status quo in social terms. In stanza 3 we move down the aesthetic and social hierarchy from 'Silks at the start' in the first line, to 'stop-press columns on the street' in the last. This epitomizes, for Tom Paulin, 'the old organic hierarchy that is so much a part of conservative discourse'. But it should be emphasized, I think, that the crowd transcends the boundaries of social class and that the poem manages to be populist at the same time as confirming the status quo.

You may have noted several elements in 'At Grass' which make it difficult for us to see it as an entirely nostalgic poem. The two victorious horses are shown to be oblivious to the past: 'Do memories plague their ears like flies? / They shake their heads'. In fact the last two stanzas of the poem describe the way the horses have come to enjoy their retirement: 'Summer by summer all stole away, /The starting-gates, the crowds and cries – /All but the unmolesting meadows'. The enjambment , or running on of the last line of the penultimate stanza into the first line of the final stanza, mimes this process of freedom and lack of restraint, 'Almanacked, their names live; they /Have slipped their names, and stand at ease, /Or gallop for what must be joy'. Larkin refuses the sentimental option of anthropomorphizing (that is, attributing human feelings to) the horses, so that the lonely and vulnerable figures in the first stanza come to appear somewhat deceptive, necessary to the development of the poem's narrative suspense. Yet I wonder if you felt that the final two lines of the poem revealed a further twist to the tale?

While we are aware that the horses are being properly cared for with dignity and respect, there is a rather melancholy sense of resignation as if the prosaic fact of the end of another day is something that all forms of life have to acknowledge, and this registers symptomatically the way that mortality awaits us all. The fact that the groom and his boy are carrying bridles suggests that complete release and unfettered freedom of the kind suggested in the last two stanzas are impossible. Referring to 'At Grass', the critic George Fraser remarked that Larkin's poetry suggested 'a chastened Yeats – a Yeats "done over again" in water-colour' (1956, p.24), as if Larkin can never indulge that transcendent move characteristic of Yeats but wishes he could.

---

*7.17* How does 'At Grass' fit with the block theme? It has been read very literally as an allegory of the end of empire: the horses in retirement are seen as colonial administrators displaced from the glorious days of empire before the war; there are military images, 'Squadrons of empty cars' in the third stanza, and in the last stanza the horses 'stand at ease ... And not a field-glass sees them home'. Such a view, however, seems altogether over-deterministic, and to distort the allegorical subtlety of the poem.

*7.18* Blake Morrison, the poet and critic, has commented that 'At Grass' was 'one of the most popular post-war poems':

> The reason for its popularity is surely that, by allowing the horses to symbolise loss of power, Larkin manages to tap nostalgia for a past 'glory that was England': it is a poem of post-imperial *tristesse*.
>
> (Morrison, 1980, pp.82–3)

Morrison goes on to comment that:

> ...to see in the poem any intentional allegoric design would be misleading. What can be claimed is that 'At Grass' taps and expresses feelings of loss and regret that might, for a certain section of the British populace at least, have been unusually pronounced around 1950 (when the poem was written), and that it finds for those feelings an acceptable public outlet.
>
> (pp.83–4)

*7.19* How far the poem articulates a sense of the loss of power depends partly on whether you think that its mood is elegiac. It does not fit the formal definition of an elegy, a poem of mourning for an individual or a lament for a tragic event. But there is a sense of loss, and its opening emphasis on anonymity and twilight ending suggest one of the most famous of English poems, Gray's 'Elegy Written in a Country Churchyard' (1751). For Seamus Heaney, the poem is representative of 'a late Augustan Larkin, the poet of decorous melancholy moods, of twilit propriety and shadowy melody ... it could well be subtitled "An Elegy in a Country Paddock"' (Reader, p.256). Larkin's skill is to know that poems about animals are always popular, while incorporating the immensely popular English poetic tradition of elegy. Heaney's point about the echoes of Gray suggests how the anonymous becomes elevated to the exemplary in 'At Grass'. In relation to the theme of end of empire, the poem yields a recognition of temporality, but also a nostalgia for the images of England which offered security, and for a historical identity which is at once factitious and seductive.

## *ACTIVITY*

Please now read 'MCMXIV'.

---

*7.20* 'MCMXIV' was composed in 1960 and published in *The Whitsun Weddings* in 1964. The title was explained by Larkin when he made a recording of the poem:

> I should really announce the next poem 'Nineteen Fourteen' as 'MCMXIV' because that is the way the title is printed, in roman numerals. I printed it that way because I wanted to remind the reader of the date on a monument and because I felt the emotional impact of 1914 in arabic numerals was too great for anything I could possibly write myself. The other thing is that when I finished the poem I found it had no main verb in it but this was a complete accident and not an attempt at experimental literature, so I left it.
>
> (Larkin, 1965)

Its untranslatable force stands as testimony to the inability of any poem to testify to the horror of the First World War.

## *ACTIVITY*

What do the images of the poem say about the kind of society which is being projected? Why does the lack of a main verb in the poem lend it power?

## *DISCUSSION*

The consequence of omitting a main verb reinforces the effect in the poem of contemplating a series of stills of a film which are run together to form a fictional narrative, a hypothetical world in which the gaps and absences are filled in by the poet's 'as ifs' in the first stanza: 'Standing as patiently /As if they were stretched outside /The Oval or Villa Park' and 'moustached archaic faces /Grinning as if it were all /An August Bank Holiday lark'. 'Those long uneven lines' with which the poem opens are most probably queues of volunteers at the outbreak of the First World War, and the faces have all the more pathos because they are grinning with an innocence, remarked upon in the final stanza, that is tragic in the light of our knowledge of subsequent events. Larkin's diction is so sensitively attuned to the spirit of the scene that we may be inclined to overlook the attention to detail and his self-conscious acknowledgement of period, for example, 'the moustached archaic faces'. What the first stanza emphasizes is that the collective spirit of national loyalty expressed here is akin to the sense of group identity apparent in other public, institutionalized events such as bank holidays, football and cricket matches. The public forms of group behaviour, identifiably English, are interchangeable with the more serious forms of group loyalty which characterize nationhood necessary for the purposes of war.

As in 'At Grass', the poem achieves its force by association of images, hence the impact of not having a main verb. This world consists of business and commerce: 'And the shut shops, the bleached /Established names on the sunblinds, /The farthings and sovereigns'; and fuses innocent childhood with the authority and stability of the monarchy: 'And dark-clothed children at play /Called after kings and queens'. Above all, this is a depiction of leisure: 'The tin advertisements /For cocoa and twist, and the pubs /Wide open all day'. Even though the images have an authenticity, they remain isolated from any historical context. The third stanza adds to this by presenting a straight pastoral, an England the spirit of which resides with indolent largesse in the landscape: 'And the countryside not caring: /The place-names all hazed over'. It is also the vision of an eternal England, which dates from the Norman Conquest: 'fields /Shadowing Domesday lines /Under wheat's restless silence', an England that has remained untouched by any alien culture, and essentially unchanged through all those centuries. The hint of aristocratic privilege and superfluous luxury also becomes part of this elegiac vision and commits the poem to an ideal order based upon social hierarchy: 'The differently-dressed servants /With tiny rooms in huge houses, /The dust behind limousines'.

## *ACTIVITY*

How do you interpret that curious phrase, 'Never such innocence, /Never before or since'?

## *DISCUSSION*

That the final stanza should begin with this phrase seems highly contentious. Like 'At Grass', the poem projects a public image of the past the resonances of which most readers can identify either from literature or the 'period' dramatizations of film and television. Yet the innocence is not projected without a taint of irony: 'Never before or since' confesses that this age of innocence is fabricated and mythical. Even though the lines suggest a betrayal of this innocence, 'As changed itself to past /Without a word', the poem shows the needs and motivations for investing in this hypothetical, transient, innocent moment to be related to a sense of disillusion with the present. Larkin reveals that the greatest loss is that of a collective understanding of what it is to be English, and what it is to share that identity. In this visionary world, such an identity serves as an implicit criticism of present values: 'the men /Leaving the gardens tidy, /The thousands of marriages /Lasting a little while longer: /Never such innocence again'. This association of tidiness and marital fidelity with innocence seems as curiously naive as the rest of the poem in its insistent refusal to confront the reasons why the social order of England has changed during this century, or to acknowledge that in some respects it might have changed for the better.

---

*7.21* 'MCMXIV', however, offers itself up knowingly as myth and uses 1914 as a focus for several kinds of displacement. Angus Calder has commented in Block 3 on the significance of 1914 in the work of Edward Thomas (see, for example, his reading of 'As the team's head brass'), and the date can also be seen as the watershed between Georgianism and Modernism described by Graham Martin in Block 2. As several critics, including Morrison, point out, 1914 serves for Larkin as a date that symbolizes the decisive break-up of the England to which he alludes so frequently. Yet the symbolic force of this date is in fact part of a displacement of the causes of discontinuity registered in his own lifetime in terms of the decline of empire; it could be seen as a poem about 1945 and the post-war world he inhabits in the guise of a yearning for the pre-Modernist, English poetic tradition from which he feels separated.

*7.22* Like 'At Grass' the poem seems to be fundamentally elegiac. In 'MCMXIV', Larkin uses his powers of literary evocation to create a notional past purified of conflict which, though a travesty of historical accuracy, makes a bid to appeal to a collective consciousness of nationhood. Although we can see the poem as participating in a common and understandable kind of delusion about the golden age before the modern world, the displacement out of which it issues can be seen as the post-1945 anxiety, in Heaney's words, of 'being forced to explore not just the matter of England, but what is the matter with England' (Reader, p.257). Larkin is elegiac about the loss of status and order because nothing will ever quite be the same, the same, that is, as the myth he has successfully perpetuated.

### Larkin and the Movement

*7.23* Larkin's volume *The Less Deceived*, in which 'At Grass' appeared, was accused by Charles Tomlinson of an 'intense parochialism' (1957, p.214), and his famously mischievous reply to the critic who asked him if he read much foreign poetry, '*Foreign* poetry? *No!*' (Hamilton, 1964, p.77), is often taken to confirm his principled insularity in literary tastes. His defence of an English literary tradition, exemplified by his controversial selection for *The Oxford Book of Twentieth-century English Verse*, was motivated by his attack on Modernism and three of its principal culprits ('the three P's'), Pound, Picasso and Parker:

> No, I dislike such things not because they are new, but because they are irresponsible exploitations of technique in contradiction of human life as we know it. This is my essential criticism of modernism, whether perpetrated by Parker, Pound or Picasso: it helps us neither to enjoy nor endure. It will divert us as long as we are prepared to be mystified or outraged, but maintains its hold only by being more mystifying and more outrageous: it has no lasting power.
>
> (Larkin, 1983, p.297)

(Note: Charlie Parker, 1920–55, was a jazz saxophonist and improviser.)

*7.24* He justified his preferences in poetry in the following way:

> The poetry I've enjoyed has been the kind of poetry you'd associate with me, Hardy pre-eminently, Wilfred Owen, Auden, Christina Rossetti, William Barnes; on the whole, people to whom technique seems to matter less than content, people who accept the forms they have inherited but use them to express their own content.
>
> (in Hamilton, 1964, p.71)

*7.25* His own manifesto in the fifties was one that accorded very much with fellow Movement poets:

> I believe that every poem must be its own sole freshly-created universe, and therefore have no belief in 'tradition' or a common myth-kitty or casual allusions in poems to other poems or poets, which last I find unpleasantly like the talk of literary understrappers letting you see they know the right people.
>
> (in Enright, 1958, pp.77–8)

*7.26* All these statements suggest Larkin's association with the characteristic scepticism of the Movement towards high culture. But despite what he says, Larkin's debts to Romantic, Symbolist (that is, foreign) and Modernist poets and their idioms are discernible. Yeats was an acknowledged influence on his first volume *The North Ship*, and despite his subsequent conversion to Hardy, is a presence in much of his subsequent work. In talking about his own poetry Larkin sees himself as writing out of areas of common human experience with which the reader can identify: 'I didn't invent old age and death and failure and disillusion: they're there, and I don't see why I shouldn't write about them if they seem writeable-about' (in Haffenden, 1981, p.122). Whether this is an adequate account of the mood of his poetry deserves further examination.

## *ACTIVITY*

Please now read 'Here', written in 1961, and reprinted in the Poetry Anthology.

How long is the first sentence of the poem and what effect does this have? What is the subject of the poem 'swerving' from and towards? Is the poet dismissive of the 'cut-price crowd, urban yet simple' in line 17? Which 'here' does the poem finally approve – that of the second stanza, or the final one?

## *DISCUSSION*

'Here' is one of Larkin's 'railway-carriage poems', so-called because they describe England from the window-seat of a train. (The others include 'I Remember, I Remember', 'The Whitsun Weddings' and 'Dockery and Son'.) Its structure reflects the journey it describes. The first sentence ends in the first line of the last stanza and is without a subject or a main verb. Added to the present participle of motion with which the poem begins, an impression of seamless movement is conveyed, a constantly changing perspective which adjusts the shape and syntax of the verse. This makes the poem, in Larkin's words, 'frightful to read aloud' (in Haffenden, 1981, p.127). The train is 'swerving' from the world of industry and commerce, 'rich industrial shadows', towards the isolation and tranquillity of 'unfenced existence' in the final stanza. Between the first line and the last is what Douglas Dunn has described as a 'wonderful, panoptic, sentient, subjective realism' (1987, p.9), a combination of the details of consumer life, 'Electric mixers, toasters, washers, driers', and subjective insight. Certainly part of the vitality of the poem's impetus is its movement towards nature, anticipated slightly in the last four lines of the first stanza by a pastoral interlude between the 'rich industrial shadows' and the urban detail of stanzas 2 and 3. Larkin is unafraid of compounding the vocabulary of everyday existence and of poetic self-consciousness: for example, the 'cut-price crowd' are 'dwelling ... Within a terminate and fishy-smelling /Pastoral of ships up streets' in stanza 3. We shall come back to this expression in the following section.

The poem brakes with beautiful composure, as the inverted syntax is slowed to a halt by the enjambment between stanzas 3 and 4 'where removed lives / Loneliness clarifies'. These last two words with which the final stanza opens suggest a moment of clarity as the speaker leaves the town behind and moves towards the freedom of the countryside. As the poem moves towards resolution, and the narrative trajectory towards clarification, so the syntax moves into a new phase. The concentration of 'heres' in this final stanza emphasizes that we have moved beyond the 'here' of line 10 into an unspecified region of transcendence, a place of silence and solitary communion, the poem's apparently desired conclusion. Yet the poem also seems to acknowledge the ambiguity of the speaker's predicament. Instead of 'swerving' he is in the final line 'facing', but the 'unfenced existence' of 'Here' is 'untalkative, out of reach'. Thus the 'Here' of the commonplace crowd remains something from which he is ineluctably isolated as well as liberated. But what does 'Here' reveal about Larkin's attitude to contemporary England?

---

**Larkin's 'condition of England' poems**

*7.27* Larkin has been described by Donald Davie as 'the effective unofficial laureate of post-1945 England':

> ...we recognize in Larkin's poems the seasons of present-day England, but we recognize also the seasons of an English soul – the moods he expresses are our moods too, though we may deal with them differently. On the literal level at any rate, no one denies that what Larkin says is true; that the England in his poems is the England we have inhabited.
>
> (Davie, 1973, p.64)

*7.28* Yet Davie also takes Larkin to task for submitting too easily to an acceptance of the spiritual and physical impoverishment of contemporary England in his phrase, 'Larkin's poetry of lowered sights and patiently diminished expectations' (Davie, 1973, p.71). Davie's criticism is essentially of what Heaney describes as Larkin's 'urban and pastoral visions' (Reader, p.252) encapsulated in the 'terminate and fishy-smelling /Pastoral of ships up streets' in 'Here'. 'Pastoral' refers to an ancient literary tradition of poetry which invokes the values and strengths of the country and its folk. Heaney accounts for the way that Larkin makes his vision of industrial landscape and urban society, often from the window of a railway carriage, into an invocation of the commonality of being and its happiness. But the position in the window-seat of a train from which Larkin comments on England is ambiguous. It is a vantage point which is both aloof and cut off, so that he can speak dismissively of the popular crowd, the 'jewellery-substitutes' in 'The Whitsun Weddings', while casting a loving benediction over contemporary society in the image of 'London spread out in the sun, /Its postal districts packed like squares of wheat'. The vistas of a mythically typical middle of England (both geographically and as a figure of the essence of England) in 'Here' and 'The Whitsun Weddings' use the detail of modern industrialization and consumerism as a backdrop not only for musings about the self, but more provocatively to assert a central continuity with the literary representation of the pastoral in English literature.

## *ACTIVITY*

Please now read 'Cut Grass', reprinted in the Poetry Anthology.

How would you describe the language and formal features of this poem? What is peculiarly English about the vision evoked in the poem?

## *DISCUSSION*

The poem is a lyrical evocation of a summer scene of beauty and order. This is achieved through the poem's diction and imagery, but also through alliteration and assonance. Notice how the rhyme-scheme is heightened by the brevity of the lines, and how the force of alliteration ('Brief ... breath' and 'Lost lanes of Queen Anne's lace') amplifies the sense of these words capturing a brief, intense, magical moment. The vision summoned up is of an English summer; Queen Anne's lace, a roadside plant which produces white flowers during the summer months, suggests the celebrated monarch of the early eighteenth century, and the stable hierarchies noted in 'At Grass' and 'MCMXIV'. Although nothing much happens in this poem, it does address the wider themes of mortality; the grass dies yet the clouds continue to move.

Each of the first four lines of the poem dwells on mortality and transience (the first line echoes 'All flesh is grass', Isaiah 40:6), and each reminds us of the cutting of grass as equivalent to a dying human body ('frail ... breath ... exhale ... death'). But the second stanza plays off the dying grass against the fecund and abundant beauty of the rest of nature. The hours are 'white' because of the intensity of heat and light, 'Of young-leafed June'. The rest of the poem builds with confidence in a long sentence stretching from the first stanza to the poem's end, suggesting deference, 'White lilac bowed', socially dignified beauty, 'Lost lanes of Queen Anne's lace', and finally the overarching confirmation of this secular beauty in the sky, 'And that high-builded cloud /Moving at summer's pace'. As you may have noticed, that penultimate line recalls, appropriately enough, 'the high cloudlets in the sky' in Edward Thomas's 'Adlestrop'.

'Cut Grass' can be seen as a version of pastoral elegy subsumed within a more confident assertion of an image of the undying essence of organic England.

### Conclusion

*7.29* The effect of the decline in Britain's status as an imperial power is registered bitterly in 'Homage to a Government', where the consequences of the Labour government's withdrawal of British troops from Aden in 1969 will be that, 'The statues will be standing in the same /Tree-muffled squares, and look nearly the same'. Both this poem and 'Going, Going' (both in the Poetry Anthology) are unconvincing not so much because they evince sentiments that are controversial but because they remain statements willingly confined by prejudice. They also exemplify Larkin's sense of duty to his country, evident in 'Naturally the Foundation will Bear Your Expenses', a poem whose ironic anger was not at first grasped. In this poem the speaker who scorns the tradition of Armistice day ('their solemn-sinister /Wreath-rubbish in Whitehall. /It used to make me throw up, These mawkish nursery games: /O when will England grow up?') is the target of Larkin's quite genuine anger at what he perceived as a fashionable, cosmopolitan and intellectual contempt towards patriotism.

*7.30* Larkin can be considered as a poet preoccupied with various forms of alienation, principally from a notional past in which the identity of England was established and understood. His poetry about England has a private quality contained in its frequently elegiac mood, but this is in fact partly a matter of his self-consciousness about literary convention. Both in terms of its language and form, and in terms of the assimilation of a traditional aesthetic in which nationhood is invoked through nature, the poetry seeks covertly to recover a literary tradition which can be most readily described in terms of pastoral, and to apply it to modern, urban life. The public, popular and usually joyful occasions (the weddings, seaside holidays, shows and races) through which he often establishes the identity of England, paradoxically issue from the deeply private and isolated position of a late twentieth-century individual, for whom the orderings of the monarchy, the Empire, and the Church in an earlier period would have been clearer and more believable than the complexities of contemporary England. The act of memory, and the investment in the convenient illusions of order which it brings, are the mainsprings of this desire to identify an innocence in being English. Consider the final lines from 'Show Saturday', published in *High Windows* (1974), in which Larkin describes the ritual of an annual agricultural show:

> Let it stay hidden there like strength, below
> Sale-bills and swindling; something people do,
> Not noticing how time's rolling smithy-smoke
> Shadows much greater gestures; something they share
> That breaks ancestrally each year into
> Regenerate union. Let it always be there.

*7.31* The ritual here is seen as a necessary part of society and culture but Larkin achieves this in a heavy-handed and moralizing way. Contrast 'The Whitsun Weddings' in which the 'urban pastoral' is realized in the image of London in the penultimate verse through what the critic John Lucas terms an 'intensely democratic' vision (Lucas, 1986, p.203). Davie remarked that Larkin, in contrast to Betjeman, was the least nostalgic of poets (Davie, 1973, p.65). But nostalgia is one of the primary features of 'Cut Grass', 'At Grass' and 'MCMXIV', and of 'The Whitsun Weddings', as Tom Paulin's analysis of the patriotic overtones of the 'arrow-shower /Sent out of sight, somewhere becoming rain' shows (in Radio 10 *Englands of the Mind?*). However, Larkin's oeuvre, with a few impoverished exceptions such as 'Going, Going', cannot be regarded simply as a blinkered nostalgia for a bygone England. His poetry plays upon the irrational and uncomfortable longings which many people feel about their native roots, be they English or not, but the way he invokes an emotional security in his readership, through articulating the feelings of isolation and loss which have resulted from the end of empire, seems peculiarly English.

## Ted Hughes

*7.32* Ted Hughes was born in West Yorkshire in 1930. He met Sylvia Plath, a poet whose work you will be studying in Block 7, at Cambridge University and they married in 1956. He has published many volumes of poetry, as well as plays, stories for children and some translations. The poems by Hughes in the Poetry Anthology are taken from four volumes: *The Hawk in the Rain* (1957), *Lupercal* (1960), *Wodwo* (1967), and *Crow* (1970). His more recent volumes of poetry include *Moortown* (1979), about his experience as a farmer in Devon, and *Wolfwatching* (1989). He was appointed Poet Laureate in 1984.

*7.33* In this sub-section we shall be looking at four principal issues in Hughes's poetry: his distinctive poetic language, the themes of war and nature, and the issue of gender. In conclusion, we shall examine the block theme in relation to his poetry.

## *ACTIVITY*

Please now read the poems by Hughes reprinted in the Poetry Anthology, referring back to the general questions in paragraph 7.6 as you do so.

## *ACTIVITY*

Please re-read 'The Hawk in the Rain' (the first, and title-poem of Hughes's first published volume). First we shall concentrate on the language and form of Hughes's poetry.

How would you describe the language of this poem? Is there an identifiable rhyme-scheme or rhythm? What formal features does the poet rely upon to achieve his effects? What are we to think of the hawk, are we to view it with fear or admiration, or a combination of both?

## *DISCUSSION*

The language of this poem is forceful, even abrasive: 'While banging wind kills these stubborn hedges, /Thumbs my eyes, throws my breath, tackles my heart, /And rain hacks my head to the bone'. There is no rhyme-scheme and the rhythm seems closest to the 'sprung rhythm' of Hopkins's verse. It is irregular and strongly reliant upon alliteration and the stress-patterns of its forceful diction: 'I *dr*own in the *dr*umming ploughland, I *dr*ag up /*Heel* after *heel*'. The hawk has explicit associations with violence; the sky it inhabits is described as, 'the master – /Fulcrum of violence where the hawk hangs still'. Like Hopkins's 'The Windhover', which those of you who studied A102 will remember, this poem expresses wonder at the bird it describes. Violence and physicality may seem appropriate because the poem describes a bird of prey, but looking at it closely, is it the bird alone that is the source of this violence? The answer seems to be that it is nature. Don't we sympathize, or even identify with the bird in the final stanza when we realize that it too may become a victim of the elements?

When it is introduced, the hawk is tranquil, in fact, rather than violent: 'the hawk /Effortlessly at height hangs his still eye. /Steady as a hallucination in the streaming air'. That effortless, weightless quality of its flight is contrasted to the heaviness which drags the human speaker downwards, literally, to the earth ('With the habit of the dogged grave'). The violence that develops from the third stanza to the end of the poem emanates from the elements, the wind and the rain, and it is this violence that the hawk seems initially to be able to resist, and from which it offers the speaker refuge: 'the hawk hangs /The diamond point of will that polestars /The sea drowner's endurance'. 'The master – /Fulcrum of violence where the hawk hangs still' is like the pole-star, a guide, a governing principle towards which the speaker strains in order to resist the chaotic, up-ending qualities of nature. Yet 'maybe in his own time' the hawk too will succumb to these chaotic forces experienced by the speaker, losing his statuesque pre-eminence as he 'suffers the air ... Fall from his eye'. The vision at the end of the poem suggests that the airy supremacy of the bird of prey will itself fall victim to the predatory powers of the earth, 'the ponderous shires crash on him, /The horizon traps him; the round angelic eye /Smashed, mix his heart's blood with the mire of the land'.

If the violent end of the hawk is envisaged then the forces which could destroy him appear to manifest themselves out of the very mire that constrains the speaker. So that despite describing power in terms of an ostensible contrast between human and animal in the first two stanzas, by the end of the poem both human and animal are aligned against a third, overarching force, that of an indiscriminate violence from the earth and the elements.

## Hughes and poetic language

*7.34* A comparison of their dates of birth will indicate that Hughes is of a different generation from the poets published in Conquest's *New Lines* anthology of 1956. Indeed, his work marked a break with the poetry of the mid-fifties. For Al Alvarez, the editor of an anthology entitled *The New Poetry* (first published in 1962), Hughes represented a new, vigorous and un-English awareness of the need for poetry to tackle themes beyond the conventional civilities of the Movement. In a rather clumsy effort to demonstrate Hughes's talents, Alvarez compared Larkin's 'At Grass' adversely with Hughes's poem 'A Dream of Horses' (not reprinted in the Poetry Anthology but published in *Lupercal*) which although 'not all that good',

> is unquestionably *about* something; it is a serious attempt to re-create and so clarify, unfalsified and in the strongest imaginative terms possible, a powerful complex of emotions and sensations. Unlike Larkin's, Hughes's horses have a violent, impending presence. But through the sharp details which bring them so threateningly to life, they reach back, as in a dream, into a nexus of fear and sensation. Their brute world is part physical, part state of mind.
>
> (Alvarez, 1966, p.31)

*7.35* This 'nexus of fear and sensation' is part of that 'new depth poetry' (Alvarez, 1966, p.32) which Alvarez associated with the poetry of American poets such as Robert Lowell and John Berryman. Even if you disagree with Alvarez's value-judgement, you could profitably compare Hughes's 'The Horses', reprinted in the Poetry Anthology, with Larkin's 'At Grass' to test the validity of his point.

*7.36* For Alvarez, Hughes's work broke new ground in terms of the kinds of poetry to which he was receptive. This included the work of Hopkins, D.H. Lawrence and Dylan Thomas as well as Donne, Blake and Yeats. It was an antithetical tradition to the one invoked by Larkin and the Movement partly because it was not exclusively English and partly because it was typified by writers concerned to foreground their innovative formal techniques. But Hughes's literary bearings contrast with Larkin in another explicit sense in his indebtedness to American poets, particularly during the mid-fifties:

> Up to the age of twenty-five I read no contemporary poetry whatsoever except Eliot, [Dylan] Thomas and some Auden. Then I read a Penguin [book] of American Poets that came out in about 1955 and that started me writing. After writing nothing for about six years. The poems that set me off were odd pieces by Shapiro, Lowell, Merwin, Wilbur and Crowe Ransom.
>
> (in Faas, 1980, p.203)

*7.37* It is significant that Hughes's first collection, *The Hawk in the Rain*, was published first both in America and Britain in 1957 as a result of having won a New York poetry competition in 1956, judged by Auden, Spender and Marianne Moore – Sylvia Plath had entered Hughes's work for the competition (Sagar, 1975, p.12). Metaphorically, in terms of literary influence, Hughes had married the modern American poetic tradition and further defined himself against the Movement in a way that made him stand out as the exemplary hope of his generation for Alvarez.

*7.38* But Hughes's own sense of the determining influences on his poetic language and style has less to do with literary sources than with the language he felt he had absorbed from his native roots:

> I grew up in West Yorkshire. They have a very distinctive dialect there. Whatever other speech you grow into, presumably your dialect stays alive in a sort of inner freedom ... it's your childhood self there inside the dialect and that is possibly your real self or the core of it ... Without it, I doubt if I

> would ever have written verse. And in the case of the West Yorkshire dialect, of course, it connects you directly and in your most intimate self to middle English poetry.
>
> (in Faas, 1980, p.202)

*7.39* In 'Englands of the mind', Heaney uses this passage as evidence for his own argument that Hughes conjures up a stratum of language rooted in Anglo-Saxon or early medieval England and its geographical hinterland. The simple ruggedness of the language he employs is related by Heaney to a historical period in which nature's elements exercised a compelling hold on life:

> Its sensuous fetch, its redolence of blood and gland and grass and water, recalled English poetry in the fifties from a too suburban aversion of the attention from the elemental; and the poems beat the bounds of a hidden England in streams and trees, on moors and in byres.
>
> (Reader, p.253)

*7.40* Hughes's poetic language can thus be seen, on the one hand, as revolutionary in that, as you can see, it is radically different from the poetry of the Movement. But, on the other hand, the language of his poetry seems preoccupied with an attempt to reach back into the past, to recover and preserve an authenticity unfettered by literary convention. As we have seen from his own words, this is part of a quest to articulate his native roots, but also to link his own dialect with a notional historical period before the Renaissance, after which the language of English poetry became more standardized. So his poetic identity is to be linked with a pre-civilized period in which his sense of nature rather than culture determined the shape of human life. In a sense, then, the content of his poetry, as well as the language he employs, are shaped by his desire to express a primary, elemental condition, which he thinks of as closest to nature.

*7.41* Hughes describes his poetic language as aspiring to 'the dream of an ideal vernacular' (in Faas, 1980, p.202), that is, a simple elemental language based upon Shakespeare, folk poetry, dialect and rhyme. These sources are themselves interesting for they suggest that Hughes's linguistic resources are founded on an ideal of the English common tongue. But Hughes also wants to communicate the idea that his poetic language is *natural*. It is worth considering for a moment how far Hughes's work accords with Jakobson's definition of the poetic function, which you studied in Block 2. Since the poetic function involves the foregrounding of linguistic elements related through phonology or grammar, we might conclude from the two poems you have read so far that although Hughes does not use regular rhythm or rhyme, the force of alliteration and stress draws attention to the literary qualities of his language. But Hughes's own 'dream of an ideal vernacular' seems to refuse the idea that poetic language has to be referential in any sense, be it through metaphor or symbol, and he seems to reject the idea that it should be self-referential. In short, his sense of 'elemental', 'direct' or 'simple' language is opposed to theoretical or academic notions of literariness. Yet his desire that his poetry should simulate nature is close to the Modernist idea of language as gesture.

### War in Hughes's poetry

*7.42* Hughes had direct and personal experience of the effects of war. His father was one of seventeen men from his regiment who, in the First World War, returned from the disastrous Gallipoli campaign of 1915–16 on the Eastern Front.

## *ACTIVITY*

Please now read 'Six Young Men' in the Poetry Anthology.

In Block 1 you studied a famous poem of the First World War, 'Dulce Et Decorum Est', by Wilfred Owen. Are there any points of comparison between the two poems by Hughes and Owen?

Is Hughes simply horrified by the deaths of the six young men in war, or is there more to his response than that? Look carefully at the final stanza.

## *DISCUSSION*

Both 'Dulce Et Decorum Est' and 'Six Young Men' are poems about the death of young soldiers in war. One shows itself to be based upon direct experience and the other speculates on the fate of the six figures in an old photograph. Hughes's poem works through a set of dramatic contrasts between his own knowledge of how the men might have lived, and the imagined horror of what they suffered; the pathos of Owen's poem is achieved through a detailed memory whose gravity speaks for itself. One of the most salient images in Hughes's poem is of nature's permanence in contrast to the cruel deracination of these men from their native land: 'I know /That bilberried bank, that thick tree, that black wall, /Which are there yet and not changed'. The simple image of the photograph preserving an image of a Sunday jaunt contrasts brutally with their subsequent deaths: 'And on this one place which keeps him alive /(In his Sunday best) see fall war's worst /Thinkable flash and rending, onto his smile /Forty years rotting into soil'.

It seems to me that 'Six Young Men' stops short of being an anti-war poem, which I think 'Dulce Et Decorum Est' is. Whereas the final lines of Owen's poem expose the falsity of justifying war in terms of patriotic honour, the final stanza of 'Six Young Men' confronts the 'contradictory permanent horrors' released by war. That is, war can offer us insights into the 'permanent horrors' of humankind, as well as shocking us. Hughes makes the men in the photograph assume a reality comparable with a living old man and a dead 'prehistoric or fabulous beast'. In fact there is 'No thought so vivid as their smoking-blood'. The clinching ambiguity of the word 'exposure' in the penultimate line suggests that the photograph is being contrasted with the viewer's fascination with their deaths which amounts to an almost physical epiphany ('and shoulder out /One's own body from its instant and heat'). It is almost as if the photograph invites the poet to go beyond the conventional threshold between life and death, and contemplate how death in war might feel. Although it is admitted that the happy photograph has the power to 'dement', the contrast between the smile of the men and the actual pain of their suffering is one that exercises a kind of demonic attraction.

The view of war expressed in the final stanza of 'Six Young Men' contrasts sharply with that of the Movement poets, as Hughes himself was aware:

> One of the things those poets had in common I think was the post-war mood of having had enough ... enough rhetoric, enough overweening push of any kind, enough of the dark gods, enough of the id, enough of the Angelic powers and the heroic efforts to make new worlds. They'd seen it all turn into death camps and atomic bombs. All they wanted was to get back into civvies and get home to the wife and kids and for the rest of their lives not a thing was going to interfere with a nice cigarette and a nice view of the park. The second war after all was a colossal negative revelation. In a sense it meant they recoiled to some essential English strengths. But it set them dead against negotiation with anything outside the cosiest arrangement of society. They wanted it cosy. It was an heroic position. They were like eskimos in their igloo, with a difference. They'd had enough sleeping out. Now I came a bit later. I hadn't had enough. I was all for opening up negotiations with whatever happened to be out there.
>
> (in Faas, 1980, p.201)

It is important to emphasize, as Donald Davie does in Radio 10, that whereas some of the Movement poets, such as Davie, had served in the war, and others, such as Larkin, had experienced its effects (which contribute in important ways to both his novels, *Jill* and *A Girl in Winter*), Hughes came from a different generation. While he describes the Second World War as 'a colossal negative revelation', there is also a sense in which the passage above is compatible with the curiosity in the final stanza of 'Six Young Men'. Hughes did not *need* to take refuge from the horrors of the war by retreating into domestic comfort and gentility as Tomlinson had accused the Movement of doing: '"moderation" ... has found yet another cosy corner for itself in our watered-down, democratic culture' (Tomlinson, 1957, p.216). Donald Davie has commented that the preoccupation with violence in Hughes's work is in part a consequence of having missed out on the direct experience of war: 'Hughes ... in some poems seems to regret having been excluded, by being born too late, from the carnival of violence which World War legitimized' (Davie, 1989, p.220).

### Hughes and nature

*7.43* Having discussed the forceful language of Hughes's poetry and his fascination with war, I now want to consider the presentation of nature in his work. From the poems you have read, you will have noticed that there is a deliberate lack of idealization or value-judgement of nature. Unlike Larkin's poetry in which nature is often represented within an identifiable literary convention, broadly that of elegiac pastoral, Hughes gives us nature, 'red in tooth and claw', as a Darwinian struggle for survival.

## *ACTIVITY*

Please now read 'Relic' in the Poetry Anthology.

What evidence is there to suggest that the view of nature expressed in this poem is of constantly warring elements? How does the language contribute to this view?

## *DISCUSSION*

Several words in the poem reveal Hughes's perception of nature to be influenced by the language of war, most obviously the word 'cenotaph' in the final line. A cenotaph (from the Greek – literally an 'empty tomb') commemorates those dead whose bodies lie elsewhere. The Remembrance Day service to those who died in the two world wars takes place on the site of the Cenotaph in London (remember how the service is mocked by the speaker in Larkin's 'Naturally the Foundation will Bear Your Expenses'). A cenotaph both signifies the dignity accorded to those who die in battle and symbolizes the need to preserve the memory of what they fought for. The 'jawbone' that is found at the sea's edge is itself then both a surviving trace of life, a relic, and a cenotaph, a material sign of a war or struggle which has occurred beneath the surface of the sea. 'Relic' also has a specifically religious meaning, referring to 'part of [a] holy person's body or belongings kept after his [or her] death as [an] object of reverence' (*OED*), and the poem's title elevates the commemorative force of the jawbone into a language of honour. Yet what the jawbone honours is the ceaseless war which takes place beneath the surface of existence in which destruction prevails: 'The deeps are cold: /In that darkness camaraderie does not hold; /Nothing touches but, clutching, devours'.

The language does not follow any recognizable or consistent syntactical pattern. There is a variation between extremely short sentences, 'None grow rich /In the sea': lists, for example, the catalogue of 'the sea's achievement'; 'shells, /Vertebrae, claws, carapaces, skulls', and a menacing obscurity, 'Before … their stretched purpose /Slacken, go down jaws; go gnawn bare'. While the line-breaks ostensibly break up the syntax, in its internal rhymes, and the use of alliteration and assonance, the poem is leant a coherence which accords with the self-consuming cycles it describes.

---

*7.44* The obsessive parallel between the sea as a consuming monster and human mastication and consumption is present in 'Mayday on Holderness' (reprinted in the Poetry Anthology), where the unremitting destruction of war and animal life is made explicit in the final two stanzas:

> The North Sea lies soundless. Beneath it
> Smoulder the wars: to heart-beats, bomb, bayonet.
> "Mother, Mother!" cries the pierced helmet.
> Cordite oozings of Gallipoli,
>
> Curded to beastings, broached my palate,
> The expressionless gaze of the leopard,
> The coils of the sleeping anaconda,
> The nightlong frenzy of shrews.

The sea becomes the repository of a historical memory which includes the machinations of war, 'Curded to beastings', which are tasted along with the potential and alien destruction of wild animals. It is interesting to note that whereas the sea at Holderness in Larkin's 'Here' is the site of a transcendent meditation on the self, for Hughes it is the starting-point for a recovery of primal violence which joins the human and animal worlds.

## *ACTIVITY*

If there is a violence contained by the sea then 'Hawk Roosting', which you read at the beginning of this section, affirms that the animal world also possesses a violent, mythical power in Hughes's work. Please read this poem again, and answer the following questions:

(a) Do you think that the poem is metaphorical? If so, what is the hawk a metaphor *for*?

(b) What are we to make of the hawk? Could the tone of the poem be interpreted as being ironical, and if so, why?

## *DISCUSSION*

(a) The poem has created something of a controversy because the hawk has appeared to some critics to be a metaphor for the totalitarian political power of a dictator ('I kill where I please because it is all mine', 'I am going to keep things like this'). Hughes has answered his critics in the following way:

> The poem of mine usually cited for violence is the one about the Hawk Roosting, this drowsy hawk sitting in a wood and talking to itself. That bird is accused of being a fascist … the symbol of some horrible totalitarian genocidal dictator. Actually what I had in mind was that in this hawk Nature is thinking. Simply Nature. It's not so simple maybe because Nature is no longer so simple. I intended some Creator like the Jehovah in Job but

> more feminine. When Christianity kicked the devil out of Job what they actually kicked out was Nature ... and Nature became the devil. He doesn't sound like Isis, mother of the gods, which he is. He sounds like Hitler's familiar spirit. There is a line in the poem almost verbatim from Job.
>
> (in Faas, 1980, p.199)

Even though he denies that the hawk is a political symbol, the logic of Hughes's response equivocates somewhat with the accusation that the poem celebrates the instinctive violence it portrays. Can the hawk be 'Simply Nature' as he puts it? He acknowledges the need to qualify his assertion almost immediately, but nevertheless demonstrates that he is tempted to view that notoriously complex word, 'Nature', as signifying something straightforward. His comments seem to suggest that he is aware of the ironies inherent in using the word 'Nature': if the hawk is like Jehovah berating Job, then he is involved in *'kicking Nature out'* (to use Hughes's language) of a human being and this is what makes him sound like 'Hitler's familiar spirit'.

(b) The hawk seems a little crazy, a demonic representation of human paranoia. So I think recognizing the possibility of irony in the tone is essential to any interpretation. The poem's narrative consists of the inner dialogue of the imagined animal; we are presented with no other persona or voice to contradict or question it. Its very excess seems monstrous: 'It took the whole of Creation /To produce my foot, my each feather: /Now I hold Creation in my foot /Or fly up, and revolve it all slowly'.

But is the irony sufficient to allay the misgivings which many readers feel? John Lucas comments that: 'The absurdity of this entirely solipsistic view is not challenged from within the poem because the consciousness of violence comes to us unmediated. It is all seen from the hawk's point of view' (Lucas, 1986, p.195). Lucas's comment implies that the poem endorses the hawk's position, and his criticism is one to which we shall return in the conclusion. But for the moment it is worth noting what a forcefully ambiguous poem this is.

---

## Hughes and gender

*7.45* The use of myth in Hughes's poetry has been increasingly prominent. Please now read 'A Childish Prank' from *Crow* (1970), reprinted in the Poetry Anthology.

*7.46* 'A Childish Prank' is part of the sequence of poems published in *Crow* which tells the story of the adventures of a mythical creature of that name. Some of the malevolent characteristics of Crow are evident in 'Hawk Roosting', and in terms of gender it's important to note that in the hawk he 'intended some Creator like the Jehovah in Job but more feminine' (in Faas, 1980, p.199). This poem exemplifies the language and idiom of the sequence in its elliptical, almost casual, treatment of sadistic cruelty. The prank of the poem's title is a highly revisionary reading of Genesis in which sexuality, instead of being punished, is ignored by God, and ridiculed by Crow. Sexuality is predicated here on a male principle; Crow bites 'the Worm, God's only son, /Into two writhing halves' and the wish of the halves to rejoin symbolizes sexual desire. The fact that the bodies of Man and Woman are passive and unconscious in this process makes them the helpless victims of this practical joke, and Hughes subverts the conventional gravity of the Christian story. Note that the Woman is not the agent of evil, as Eve is in Genesis, but the poem as a whole hardly serves as a feminist critique of the male principle in the Old Testament.

## Hughes, history and empire

*7.47* Several critics have noted the way that Hughes's poetry embraces the theme of empire. The hawk, cognate with the fascist insignia of the eagle, symbolizes, to the Indian critic M.G. Ramanan, a specifically imperialist as well as totalitarian consciousness for whom Hughes's 'masculinity' is one aspect of the imperial character (the other half being a Larkinian gentility):

> What Hughes seems to be saying is that this is no time for self-pity or nostalgia. This is the time to assert ourselves as we did in the good old days of empire. Hughes's violent imagery is closely aligned with authoritarian politics...
>
> (Ramanan, 1985, p.67)

By way of reviewing this criticism, and considering the relationship between gender and empire which Ramanan suggests in Hughes's work, I would like you now to read 'Pike' in the Poetry Anthology.

*7.48* One of the central features of this poem is its movement from a meditation on the disturbing physical power of the fish to a wider existential reflection. Towards the end, the pike seems to drop out of the poem altogether so that the narrator is no longer fishing for real fish but they, as it were, are fishing for him. Read the last three stanzas closely. The dream freed by the night's darkness comes from that mythical depth in which there is menace and violence. Even the depths of this vision, however, do not seem to be political or historical, but rather mythical and elemental as in the description of the pond: 'Stilled legendary depth: /It was as deep as England'. Consider John Lucas's argument that the poem represents a questionable political vision:

> The dream which is as 'deep as England' is expressed through the rapacious pike. It is a dream of violence. This is not without justification. The English have always been a great deal more warlike and belligerent than they like to believe, and the imperialism which both proves and is a self-condemnation of such belligerence is perhaps as near to the heart of England as the sweet dream of Adlestrop. But the point I want to make is that here, as elsewhere, Hughes's fascination with what Ramanan calls his 'masculinity' amounts to an endorsement of it. In their ruthless predatoriness the Thrushes, the Hawk and the Pike all say 'there is no alternative'.
>
> (Lucas, 1986, p.195)

*7.49* Like Ramanan, Lucas sees 'something very suspect about this use of birds and fish to explore issues as complex as the history and use of power and violence'. Often nature simply *is* violence and empire in Hughes's work, it represents accretion and domination, an endless process of absorption and consumption (see, for example, the poem 'Thistles', reprinted in the Poetry Anthology).

*7.50* Hughes's poetry manifests a desire to recover something from beneath the surface of human life, in the world of immediacy and animal sensations, even if that involves cruelty. Stan Smith thinks that this signals a nostalgia for a primal myth of England and Englishness:

> Hughes's poems are haunted by a nostalgia for a lost world of being in which the feudal, the archaic, and the prehistoric are associated with the instinctual and automatic, with a brutal realm of primary responses which, as here, is equated with the most ancient and abiding recesses of England itself. The mythos of all these poems, in fact, is a *recherche* for a lost unity of being back before the modern era, before two world wars which overthrew, as if for good, the real England.
>
> (Smith, 1982, p.163)

In Hughes's desire to establish an autonomous sphere for his poetry in which he can invoke nature and mythology, and in his preoccupation with the struggle to recover and extend the dominion of the physical world, Smith sees lurking an anxiety about the loss of power. Even as his poetry represses history, history seems to reassert itself, in displaced forms.



## Geoffrey Hill

*7.51* Geoffrey Hill was born at Bromsgrove, Worcestershire in 1932. His first collection, *For the Unfallen*, was published in 1959. He has published four more volumes of poems to date: *King Log* (1968), *Mercian Hymns* (1971), *Tenebrae* (1978) and *The Mystery of the Charity of Charles Péguy* (1983) as well as a book of critical essays, *The Lords of Limit* (1984). He has taught English at the universities of Leeds and Cambridge and now teaches in America. In this sub-section, we shall concentrate principally on *Mercian Hymns*.

### *ACTIVITY*

First, though, please read three short poems by Hill reprinted in the Poetry Anthology, 'Requiem for the Plantagenet Kings', 'Ovid in the Third Reich' and 'September Song'. You will remember reading part of this last poem in Block 2, page 75 (we shall return to it again in Block 8), and you probably found that the densely allusive quality of the verse made special demands on you as readers. But the three poems have in common a rigorous interrogation of the past (the latter two poems allude to the atrocities committed by the Nazis).

### Hill and history

### *ACTIVITY*

Now please re-read 'Requiem for the Plantagenet Kings'.

(a) What does the poem commemorate? Does it glorify the Plantagenet kings, or is it critical of them? Do you think it comments on the way we think about the past?

(b) What would you describe as the main characteristic of the language of the poem? How does the language contribute to the meaning of the poem?

### *DISCUSSION*

(a) The title tells us that this poem is a formal and religious tribute (a requiem is a special Mass for the repose of the souls of the dead) to the bloody achievements of the Plantagenet kings, the royal house of England from 1154–1485, the latter part of whose reign saw the civil strife known as the 'Wars of the Roses'. But it is manifestly critical of the means by which they won their renown. In the opening lines of the second stanza their death is described in ambivalent terms: 'Relieved of soul' suggests a welcome abdication of spiritual responsibility rather than a justifiable repose which would more properly befit the dignity of the requiem service. Theirs is, in fact, a material death – 'the dropping-back of dust' – and it is only their vanity and corruption that is honoured –

'Their usage, pride, admitted within doors'. The title of the poem is then ironical, tongue-in-cheek. What this poem tells us about is the deception that is part of any investment in the heroic moments of a nation's past.

(b) The main characteristic of the language of the poem is its ambiguity. Take 'They lie; they lie' in line 9 as a straightforward example. The repetition stops us short by drawing attention to the fact that the words 'They lie' do not simply describe the carved figures lying in the church but the possibility that they are also deceiving us. The lower case of the second 'they' also brings these royals down to earth. There is a further ambiguity in the lines, 'secure in the decay /Of blood, blood-marks, crowns hacked and coverted'. This suggests that the kings are secure *because of* the wars they have caused, that they do not have to worry about the end of earthly life, but it also exposes the authority of kingship to be founded on human greed and a lust for power. The final four lines carry a reference to the vision of the day of judgement in the Bible: 'and the sea /Across the daubed rock evacuated its dead' can be compared with the sea giving up the dead in it in Revelation, 20:13. The fact that these kings 'lie' suggests that their sense of immunity to God's final judgement is misplaced. The kings may seem to have attained a statuesque repose and sanctity while the dead bodies of the soldiers have been consigned anonymously underground, but when the day of judgement comes their greed will be punished.

The ambiguity in the poem is not simply that of a word having two different, possibly opposed, meanings but that the poem employs one kind of language, ostensibly suitable for its formal subject matter and ceremonial occasion, which is undermined by another kind, often colloquial and anachronistic. The word 'Budge' in line 13 has a modern ring, as does the neat play 'within doors; /At home' in lines 6–7 which suggests that the protected place of rest for the kings is rather prosaic. The use of modern-day language exposes the hollowness of the kings' stature, but it also makes the poem about more than simply medieval history. The lines 'To sound the constitution of just wars, /Men, in their eloquent fashion, understood' suggest the cutting wit and cadence of Auden in the way that they draw attention to the crudeness with which all history is begotten and justified. There is also a sense in which the poem is about the way that art deceives our historical sensibility; the sculptured figures of the kings appear noble and tranquil, and thus conceal the brutality of their reigns.

---

### *Mercian Hymns*: some close readings

#### *ACTIVITY*

You will notice from the Poetry Anthology that we have only been able to reprint twenty out of the thirty poems that make up *Mercian Hymns*. However, these twenty hymns divide into four self-contained sequences. If you have access to the whole text, then do consult it but this discussion will limit itself to the hymns in the Anthology. Please read them through now.

This first exercise will involve you in a close-reading exercise looking at one hymn from each of the four sequences (I, XIII, XXV, XXVII). (In the next section, I will discuss *Mercian Hymns* as a whole.)

Please now re-read I, the first of two poems entitled 'The Naming of Offa'.

(a) What is unusual about the language and form of the hymn?

(b) What kind of picture do we get of Offa and his authority in this hymn?

## *DISCUSSION*

(a) The most obvious point about the form of the hymn is that it resembles prose; the main paragraph is indented after the first line and the hyphenation of words within justified margins gives the poem a physical shape on the page. So can the hymn be properly considered as poetry? I think so for several reasons. The title of the sequence is *Mercian Hymns*, the last word specifying that these are songs of praise. There is also a tradition of prose-poetry to which Hill is indebted. Furthermore, the first verse of the hymn has a rhythm and structure provided through the catalogue of Offa's achievements, and the resonances of proper names.

(b) My sense, from the final line of this hymn, is that the first verse is contrived as a eulogy for a vain and despotic king by a court bard. Offa, however, is not simply a historical figure nor is the hymn simply dramatizing his need for approval. His authority extends beyond the confines of Anglo-Saxon England to the present day. One of the humorous, if slightly chilling, facets of this hymn is the exaggerated legacy of his achievements which give rise to its apparent anachronisms.

Many of the allusions cover a wide period of history from the eighth-century Offa's Dyke he constructed, 'architect of the his- /toric rampart and ditch', to the Welsh Bridge at Shrewsbury (1791), and the Iron Bridge (1778) nearby, down to the M5, the motorway that runs from Birmingham through Worcestershire towards the South West, which dates from the 1970s. There are also ambiguities about many of Offa's titles: 'contractor to the desirable new estates' suggests one who is legally obliged to a landed class (presumably the feudal nobility), as well as a builder providing accommodation for the less well-off in post-war Britain, and 'martyrologist' suggests not simply a historian of martyrs but a brutal king who has created martyrs. Even if you did not pick up these allusions (although you may have noticed several which I haven't mentioned), you will have understood that Offa is not simply a historical figure but a mythical presence.

## *ACTIVITY*

Please now read XIII, the last in a sequence of three hymns entitled 'Offa's Coins'.

What does the description of the coins reveal about Offa's authority?

## *DISCUSSION*

This poem begins with a specialist of recent times examining the rare coins of Offa's reign. Close scrutiny of the King's 'masterful head' which emerges 'out of England's well' becomes an interrogation of the myth of his authority. Implicitly his mortality and earthly reign, 'his underkingdom of crin- /oid and crayfish', is contrasted with his self-inflated title, which translates as 'King of the Whole Country of the English'. Yet the endurance of the myth he has created is depicted, albeit ironically, as triumphant: 'coiffured and ageless, / portrays the self-possession of his possession, /cushioned on a legend'. So, while there is plenty to alert us to the hollow basis of Offa's authority as represented on this coin, its lasting power triumphs. Moreover, because he appears 'ageless' and self-possessed, his legendary force illustrates how a deep subliminal myth of authority in England's distant past can persist. The poem does not necessarily endorse the myth but rather anatomizes the way it is perpetuated.

## ACTIVITY

Now please re-read XXV, the final poem in the sequence of three poems entitled 'Opus Anglicanum'.

Hill's note to this poem informs the reader that 'Opus Anglicanum' ('English Work') is the term 'properly applicable to English embroidery of the period AD 1250–1350', adding that he has 'with considerable impropriety, extended the term to apply to English Romanesque sculpture and to utilitarian metal-work of the nineteenth century'. This is another example of that tendency we noted in the first poem, for Offa's reign to extend to our own day. Hill speaks here in his own voice, apparently, remembering his grandmother's work making nails (*darg*: 'a day's work, the task of a day...', *OED*). Heaney's interpretation of this poem, and of the significance of Ruskin's letter in which the exploitation of factory labour is criticized can be found in the Reader, pages 254–5. But the injustice that Hill feels about the way his grandmother and many other nineteenth-century factory workers were treated means that her inclusion in the 'Opus Anglicanum' is bitterly ironic rather than celebratory. 'English work' includes not only embroidery but exploitation. Once again Hill seems clear-sighted about what is involved in the construction of tradition.

## ACTIVITY

Finally please read XXVII, the first in a sequence of four poems entitled 'The Death of Offa'.

(Note: *gleemen*: 'travelling minstrels'; *Merovingian*: 'member of the Frankish dynasty founded by Clovis and reigning in Gaul and Germany *c*.500–750; *shire tree*: 'a tree marking a meeting place for a shire-court' (*OED*); *Thor* is the Norse God of Thunder.)

Like the rest of the hymns, this one contains word-play, 'defunct ... perfunctory', and modern allusions, 'Merovingian car-dealers'. The death of Offa is marked by a shady, slightly comical, commemoration. Perhaps most significant in this hymn, and characteristic of *Mercian Hymns* as a whole, is the elaborate description of nature. The dramatic account of the storm in which 'Earth lay for a while, the ghost-bride of livid /Thor' makes Offa's death an almost apocalyptic occasion.

### *Mercian Hymns*: a brief study guide

*7.52* In the acknowledgements to *Mercian Hymns*, Hill cites two sources for his sequence. An Anglo-Saxon poem gave him the title, and he found a precedent for the form in the Latin prose-hymns or canticles of the early Christian Church. Asked why he chose to write the sequence on the form of prose-poems, Hill replied:

> They're versets of rhythmical prose. The rhythm and cadence are far more of a pitched and tuned chant than I think one normally associates with the prose poem. I designed the appearance on the page in the form of versets. The reason they take the form they do is because at a very early stage the words and phrases began to group themselves in this way.
>
> (Haffenden, 1981, pp.93–4)

'Verset' suggests both music and religious liturgy, and the hymns have a fastidious, ceremonial quality.

*7.53* You may feel that the density of allusion, even in the first hymn, suggests that the reader needs to have a thorough knowledge of Anglo-Saxon history before being able to understand the sequence. In fact, I do not think this would help very much. In the acknowledgements, Hill provides us with an account of Offa, and some explanation of the key significance of anachronism in *Mercian Hymns*.

> The historical King Offa reigned over Mercia (and the greater part of England south of the Humber) in the years AD 757–796. During early medieval times he was already becoming a creature of legend. The Offa who figures in this sequence might perhaps most usefully be regarded as the presiding genius of the West Midlands, his dominion enduring from the middle of the eighth century until the middle of the twentieth (and possibly beyond). The indication of such a timespan will, I trust, explain and to some extent justify a number of anachronisms.

*7.54* Hill suggests here that Offa became as much a creature of legend as a figure of history. The particular Offa that interested Hill is regarded as 'the presiding genius of the West Midlands', and his 'dominion' is of interest not simply for the geographical area it circumscribes but for its historical legacy. Hill explains, and 'to some extent' justifies, anachronism in the poem in quite formal terms by describing Offa's dominion provocatively as 'enduring from the middle of the eighth century until the middle of the twentieth (and possibly beyond)'. He remarks further with apparent self-deprecation that 'I have a duty to acknowledge that the authorities cited in these notes might properly object to their names being used in so unscholarly and fantastic a context'. In *Mercian Hymns*, then, the historical Offa is less important than the legendary figure which Hill constructs, to borrow and adapt his own word, as a fantasy.

*7.55* So what kind of fantasy is wrought around the figure of Offa in *Mercian Hymns*? Reading the first group of hymns reprinted in the Poetry Anthology, it seems that Hill is interweaving his own autobiography with a projection of Offa's character. Take, for example, III, the first poem of the three entitled 'The Crowning of Offa'. This is a quite straightforward memory of a modern-day coronation ('hankies /and gift-mugs'), that of George VI in 1937 during Hill's childhood ('we chorused our re- /mission from school'). The child's perspective is enforced through the apparent regality of the chef because of his hat and the food he dispenses, and the effect of this appears comically incongruous in relation to the hymn's title. In this superficial pageantry, the child implicitly finds a confirmation of himself as a poet, and of the power of Offa as a true King.

*7.56* The relationship of the twentieth-century childhood of the poet to King Offa is continued in hymns IV–VII. The ambivalence towards royal authority and towards the child's *amour-propre* are the subjects of irony and self-ridicule in V: 'I wormed my way heavenward for /ages amid barbaric ivy, scrollwork of fern', and 'Dreamy, smug-faced, /sick on outings – I who was taken to be king of /some kind, a prodigy, a maimed one'. Even as the parallel is developed, it is also undermined by the careful construction of two discourses at odds with one another, the formal liturgical seriousness of the hymns, and the modern idiom of the children's playground. Hill's description of the flaying of 'Ceolred' in VII exemplifies this where *Albion*, the trademark of the old lorry he plays in, is synonymous with the name of much of the *patria* over which Offa rules. The child's play and the kingdom of Offa are paralleled; the child is capable of the humiliation of others, the very essence of the brutal, pre-civilized regime of Offa.

*7.57* By way of concluding this brief summary I want to refer you to other parts of the sequence for closer study. The description of digging for coins in Hymns XI and XII demonstrates Hill's affinity with Hughes's attention to the earth and soil in descriptions of physical nature. For Hill 'Coiled entrenched England', as he terms it in Hymn XX, can be discovered best beneath the ground. The association of 'charabancs' and 'evergreen albums' in Hymn XXI suggests a late Victorian or early twentieth-century pastiche of fascination with the 'real Camelot', the mythology of ancient England, and this is followed in Hymn XXII by his own memories of childhood excitement in an air-raid shelter during the Second World War. Even as the legacy of Offa, 'Tracks of ancient occupation', is described in Hymn XXVIII, Hill shows himself capable, like Larkin and Hughes, of a powerful nostalgia. The 'solitary axe-blow that is the echo /of a lost sound' is a fitting symbol of Offa's bequest, which by the final hymn is a haunting, quasi-religious vision of blood and soil, imaged in terms of 'traces of red mud'.

### *Mercian Hymns*: criticism

*7.58* The element of autobiography in *Mercian Hymns* has led the American critic, Harold Bloom, to perceive the poem as 'a kind of *Prelude*-in-little' (in Hill, 1975, p.xxii), implying that writing about Offa is for Hill an oblique way of describing his own election to the status of poet, as Wordsworth did in his famous poem. When confronted with this view, Hill deflects it by saying that 'I was genuinely interested in the phenomenon of King Offa and of the rise and fall of the Kingdom of Mercia', but concedes that 'My feeling for Offa and Mercia can scarcely be disentangled from my mixed feelings for my own home country of Worcestershire' (Haffenden, 1981, p.94).

*7.59* Hill seems to see Offa as both a creator of order and beauty and a brutal murderer. Offa is therefore not simply the means for writing about his own poetic vocation but for meditating on political authority and imperial or national identity, in short, patriotism:

> Since Offa seems to have been on the whole a rather hateful man who nonetheless created forms of government and coinage which compel one's admiration, this image of a tyrannical creator of order and beauty is, if you like, an objective correlative for the inevitable feelings of love and hate which any man or woman must feel for the *patria*. The murderous brutality of Offa as a political animal seems again an objective correlative for the ambiguities of English history in general, as a means of trying to encompass and accommodate the early humiliations and fears of one's own childhood and also one's discovery of the tyrannical streak in oneself as a child. Here again one is speaking of those characteristics which one holds in common with one's fellow beings.
>
> (Haffenden, 1981, p.94)

Of the many revealing features of this passage, I want to draw your attention to the way that Hill identifies Offa with a fundamental aspect of our relationship to what he terms the *patria* (literally the fatherland, not simply country or nation).

*7.60* Your response to much of Hill's poetry will depend to a great degree, I think, on how you perceive the relationship of the individual to his or her national identity. It is possible to argue that in Britain in the 1990s national identity is challenged, though not necessarily excluded, by other kinds of cultural identity based on religion, ethnic group, region and gender. We might then take issue with Hill's view of the *patria*. Is patriotism 'natural', and do we find both the use and possible abuse of political authority in the name of a nation, however ugly, a basic and inevitable fact of existence? Hill seems to think so since he says, 'the inevitable feelings of love and hate which any man or woman must feel'. The image of Offa as an 'objective correlative' (the phrase, you will remember, is Eliot's) for the complexity of our relationship to political authority, and of Offa's brutality as another 'objective correlative' to describe 'the ambiguities of English history in general', make the use of the Anglo-Saxon king explicitly ideological. In other words Offa, for Hill, is a symbol of the nature of our feelings towards our native culture and history.

While Hill has clearly not chosen Offa to celebrate feudal violence, he identifies our relationship to the past in terms of what he perceives as a permanent longing to celebrate the *patria*. The question seems to be whether Hill offers a critique of the need for tradition, or whether he is enforcing an ideal, organic sense of culture as normative or natural.



**Hill and history**

*7.61* If there is a recurrent theme in Hill's work, reflected both in the choice of historical period for his subject-matter and the kind of language he uses, it is that of loss. In an interview, Hill makes it clear that there is a parallel between the recurrent preoccupations with a lost innocence in the subject-matter of his work and the kind of language he uses. The language of Hill's poems is often dense and tortuous because he seeks to articulate the gap between an innocent and a corrupted usage:

> I think there's a real sense in which every fine and moving poem bears witness to this lost kingdom of innocence and original justice. In handling the English language the poet makes an act of recognition that etymology is history. The history of the creation and debasement of words is a paradigm for the loss of the kingdom of innocence and original justice.
>
> (in Haffenden, 1981, p.88)

*7.62* This heavily-weighted view of poetic language is intrinsic to that attachment to historical period in his work. While Hill's poems can be seen to interrogate nostalgia, exposing the temptation to imagine a past grandeur where merely squalor exists, it has been argued that there is an 'obstinately archaic' quality about his work:

> The fraught anachronism of Hill's poetry represents the imaginative pull of the past for a poet obsessed above all by the persistence of what has been lost, and the impossibility of reappropriating it; the idea of continuity – and the stark fact of distance.
>
> (Haughton, 1985, p.131)

*7.63* Clearly this sense of loss and rupture is a means of self-examination in a way that it isn't in Larkin's 'MCMXIV'. Hill could not have written Larkin's lines 'Never such innocence /Never before or since' because he does not hold to Larkin's dehistoricized images of loss. Though Hill meditates on loss, and his poetic language alludes to that 'lost kingdom', he refuses Larkin's flagrant recourse to historical mirages. Where Larkin's poetry is characteristically dehistoricizing, Hill identifies a historical sensibility through recourse to myth.

*7.64* So is Hill's obsession with the past a nostalgia for the violence which feudalism and empire legitimized? Hill has defended himself in the following way from this charge:

> If one writes lyrics of which nostalgia is an essential element, naive or malicious critics will say that the nostalgia must be one's own. There are, however, good political and sociological reasons for the floating of nostalgia: there's been an elegiac tinge to the air of this country ever since the end of the Great War. To be accused of exhibiting a symptom when, to the best of my ability, I'm offering a diagnosis appears to be one of the numerous injustices which one must suffer with as much equanimity as possible.
>
> (in Haffenden, 1981, p.93)

*7.65* For the critic David Norbrook, Hill's work remains ' a symptom of the problem it so intensely seeks to diagnose' (Norbrook, 1987, p.23). Hill's sentiments in the passage above situate his nostalgia and concomitant patriotism, like Larkin's, in a crisis of English identity recognized in the post-World War II world as having begun with the end of World War I and with the beginning of Modernism.

## Tony Harrison

*7.66* Tony Harrison (1937–) was born in Leeds and educated at Leeds Grammar School and Leeds University. His collections of poetry include *The Loiners* (1970), *From The School of Eloquence and Other Poems* (1978), *Continuous* (1981), and *v.* (1985) which was broadcast on Channel 4. He has also translated classical plays and written verse texts for the National Theatre including *The Misanthrope* (1973), *Phaedra Britannica* (1975), *The Oresteia* (1981) and *The Mysteries* (1985).

### *ACTIVITY*

Please re-read 'On Not Being Milton', which you studied at the beginning of this section.

What is the poem about and how does the language and form of the poem relate to its subject?

### *DISCUSSION*

The first things to notice are its form, an unusual sixteen-line sonnet (though not without precedent) and rhyme-scheme *ababcddceffeghhg,* with the poem divided into uneven units. The ironic title of the poem emphasizes that it paradoxically articulates the subject of what it is to be inarticulate, 'On *Not* Being Milton', and we shall discuss the title later. The dedication to 'Frelimo' (the Mozambique Liberation Front), which fought for the independence of the African colony from Portugal in the 1960s when Harrison was in Africa, makes the poem explicitly about political freedom. The poem is also an analysis of a literary self and its historical roots in terms of the long poem, 'Return to my native land' (1939), by the Martiniquan, Aimé Cesaire, about alienation and colonialism: 'these sixteen lines that go back to my roots /my *Cahier d'un retour au pays natal*'. This return to native roots and origins is a theme, as we have seen, of Hill's *Mercian Hymns,* and of Hughes's poetry. The subject of the poem is developed through the metaphor of the 'branks'. The *Oxford English Dictionary* defines 'branks' as follows: 'a scold's bridle: an instrument of punishment used in the case of scolds, etc. consisting of a kind of iron framework to enclose the head, having a sharp metal gag or bit which entered the mouth and restrained the tongue'. This crude instrument of silencing (women were often punished in this way) becomes for Harrison a symbol of the silencing of one class by another, 'of condescension, class and counter-class', while the stutter of the scold articulates the pent-up frustration of her class into ammunition with which to challenge both the instrument which traps her and, by implication, the industrialized machine age and the social and economic oppression it brings. Although the stutter in the branks represents the stifling of language, it nevertheless 'thickens with glottals to a lumpen mass /of Ludding morphemes closing up their ranks' suggesting a social struggle for liberation as well as a linguistic bid for articulation. These most basic sounds ('glottals') are the articulation of the smallest meaningful units of language ('morphemes') into a unified force, 'a lumpen mass /Of Ludding morphemes closing up their ranks'. The (derogatory) Marxist term, 'lumpen', for the 'ignorantly contented lower orders of society uninterested in revolutionary advancement' (*OED*) functions here to show the language as itself effecting a political challenge of a spontaneous kind just as the Luddites, the English artisans who rioted for the destruction of machinery in the early nineteenth century, in popular lore struggled against the imposition of an alien kind of labour. What the poem draws out is the violence of one kind of articulation, one kind of political language and form against another; the fine paradox contained in the word 'Enoch' in line 9, glossed by Harrison in his own note, symbolizes the irony of the confrontation. The sledge-hammer is made by the same man who makes the frames which it smashes; the language of destruction (the hammer) and the language of oppression (the frame) emanate from the same source:

> Each swung cast-iron Enoch of Leeds stress
> clangs a forged music on the frames of Art,
> the looms of owned language smashed apart!

Clearly Harrison's metaphor has wrought the economic struggle of ownership in terms of language and culture. This indeed becomes a source of celebration to him: 'Three cheers for mute ingloriousness! /Articulation is the tongue-tied's fighting'. Here the reference to Gray's famous line, 'Some mute inglorious Milton here may rest', in the 'Elegy Written in a Country Churchyard', explains Harrison's title; he is writing on behalf of the anonymous dead upon whom Gray speculates, those who might have been but aren't proficient employers of language, poets.

The ironic theme of Harrison's open-ended sequence, 'Sonnets from The School of Eloquence', is that it is not about eloquence, although the further irony is that the sonnets are poetically highly eloquent. Thus in this poem he uses highly wrought language to praise mute ingloriousness. The source for Harrison's quotation from Tidd in the final line is E.P. Thompson's book, *The Making of the English Working Class* (1982, p.787); the illiterate scrawl is both painful and humorous and yet powerful too.

---

*7.67* Tony Harrison comes from a different social and geographical background from the other poets we have been looking at in this block. He has also become well-known more recently than they have. By the late fifties Larkin, Hughes and Hill were all recognized as major contemporary poets; for Harrison, although he had published verse since the sixties, major recognition came in the late seventies. A major theme dominating his recent work, especially the 'Sonnets from the School of Eloquence' to which he is constantly adding material, is that of the relationship between language, class and power. In language, he finds class division, social disunity and a clashing of opposites. As a poet addressing contemporary cultural issues, and as a popular and novel phenomenon, a television poet, he has made his poetry accessible and contemporary through his facility with rhythm and rhyme.

*7.68* Defining a suitable language for poetry was, in a different way, a preoccupation of the well-educated grammar school generation of Larkin, Amis and the Movement, who argued for a plain-speaking use of English without either social or literary affectation. Unlike the other poets examined in Block 5 who are wedded to a literary tradition, Harrison seems rather to be rooted in his regional and class identity, to the life from which his grammar-school education in fact alienated him. He broods on the barely articulate, the Luddites, the Tidds and their heirs in the urban industrial working class, including his father.

*7.69* The empowering force of language lies at the heart of much of his verse. This echoes Harrison's own brief epigraph to 'The School of Eloquence' entitled 'Heredity', '*How you became a poet's a mystery! /Wherever did you get your talent from? /*I say: *I had two uncles, Joe and Harry – /one was a stammerer, the other dumb*'. As Harrison puts it in another poem, 'Fire-eater', 'Theirs are the acts I nerve myself to follow'. His own eloquence and articulation, his successful translations of dramatic works from several languages, dramatize a central conflict between a profound sentimental attachment to his working-class childhood and a relief that through his education and use of language he has escaped it. Yet Harrison is also a poet who describes various kinds of loss, both personal grief in the obsessive sequence of poems about the death of his parents and, in a wider sense, a nostalgia for a working-class culture and language which has disappeared. In a distinctive way his themes are comparable with the ones we have been exploring in Hill, Hughes and Larkin. Yet Harrison's position is more explicitly ideological than the others. His poetry sees itself as challenging the dominance of one kind of class and language over another.

### *ACTIVITY*

Please now read 'Them & [uz]', I and II, in the Poetry Anthology.

How is the conflict of the poem's title reflected in the poem itself?

### *DISCUSSION*

The class conflict signalled in the title of this poem is epitomized for Harrison in the division between Standard English and Received Pronunciation where 'us' is pronounced [^s] and the non-Standard English dialect and accent he speaks at home where it is pronounced [uz]. Thus the location of the conflict over language is of key importance too, for the battleground is English literature. Harrison, unlike Hill, Larkin and Hughes, does not write as heir to an English literary tradition of his own making. His models in collections like *Palladas: poems* (1975) and *U.S. Martial* (1981) are classical Greek poets. 'Them & [uz]' hints at the reason for this. His English teacher's denigration of his accent and dialect were to make him feel disqualified from participating in the high culture bequeathed by Shakespeare (except the 'prose bits') and Keats. This related very literally then to the Englishness of English literature discussed in Block 1, pages 52–5. But it also signals Harrison's criticism of an imperial attitude towards the dominion of English literature itself.

We have already discussed the significance of the inarticulate in Harrison's work. This poem begins with that very paradox of eloquence and inarticulateness around which many of these poems are wrought. It was said, according to popular tradition, that Demosthenes (384–322 BC), generally considered to be one of the greatest Athenian orators, 'overcame a speech impediment by declaiming on the seashore against the noise of the waves with a mouth full of pebbles' (Radice, 1973, p.102). Harrison puts himself in an analogous position as he begins to read the first line of Keats's 'Ode to a Nightingale' ('My heart aches, and a drowsy numbness pains /My sense...') before being interrupted by his teacher. Harrison's rendition of Keats is seen as an assault not simply on Standard English but on the English literary heritage – 'Poetry's the speech of kings'. Harrison's 'barbarian' tongue makes him only fit for the low parts in Shakespeare's plays which are usually not formally poetry at all, 'one of those /Shakespeare gives the comic bits to: prose!' With hindsight Harrison can undermine the claim that literature is the heritage and cultural property of those with one kind of accent known mysteriously as 'Received Pronunciation' by remarking that Keats himself was a victim of just such snobbery for being a 'Cockney'. The word that signifies a common identity [^s] becomes the source of this conflict. Harrison becomes by the end of the poem a dumb stammerer, like Demosthenes before his cure, deferring to this linguistic imposition, 'I doffed my flat a's (as in 'flat cap') / my mouth all stuffed with glottals, great /lumps to hawk up and spit out ... *E-nun-ci-ate!*'. The second part of the poem declares war on the 'Receivers' and rejects the linguistic imposition: 'I chewed up Littererchewer and spat the bones /into the lap of dozing Daniel Jones'. In his assertion of the validity of his own tongue, Harrison also points to those canonical poets, like Keats and Wordsworth, whose accent was also not 'RP'.



## *ACTIVITY*

Please now read 'Old Soldiers'. The poem was first published in *The Observer* in October 1986 and then reprinted in a collection of seven sonnets about Hiroshima and Harrison's childhood memories of the war entitled *Anno Forty Two*, printed on 6 August 1987.

What is the 'essence' that is destroyed in the poem?

## *DISCUSSION*

The poem refers to a childhood memory of staring at the picture on a bottle of coffee essence ('CAMP coffee extract') on the kitchen table, in which an Indian servant holds the drink on a tray before a British army officer, 'the breakfasting Scots hero'. The label represents the essence of empire but also, as the opening line suggests, an image of its imminent demise. The child stares and sees the picture on the label reproduced through its staring until it becomes minute, 'down to amoeba, atom, neutron size'. Yet still the image remains: 'but the turbaned bearer never lost his bearing /and nothing shook the bottle off his tray'. The immortal image represents an essence that can't be destroyed: 'Through all infinity and down to almost zero /he holds out and can't die or fade away /loyal to the breakfasting Scots hero'.

In the final lines, the poem describes the dropping of the two atomic bombs on Japan in 1945. Notice how Harrison plays lightly with the preposition 'on', so that 'the two high summer days' are not simply dates in the calendar but symbols of fruitful life itself destroyed by the bomb. Just as the child looked into the label, so the adult looks back to the child. What for the child was the wonder of an infinite reproduction or cloning 'through all infinity and down to almost zero' becomes now an interrupted and darkened vision. The immortal, self-perpetuating dream of the child is returned as a fragmentation. The essence has now been shaken off the tray by the blast of the bomb, the essence of the empire destroyed and finally an essence of the world itself has also vanished: 'from that child's forever what returns my gaze /is a last chuprassy with all essence gone'. The essence that is destroyed is of a set of dependable, though paradoxically related, realities of imperial authority and a pre-nuclear age. The sense of a loss of order which the empire brings is dwarfed by the more metaphysical yet real potential for the world to self-destruct. The loss of security and innocence in this poem is framed in terms of a childhood, imperial and pre-nuclear dream. Loss and nostalgia are themes with which Harrison's poetry, for all his indictments of social and linguistic injustice, is deeply infused.

## Sorley MacLean

*7.70* To begin with, look at Section 8, References. You will see that the list includes books by Sorley Maclean and by two other important Scottish poets, Tom Leonard and Edwin Morgan. Not one title was published in London. None of these writers has ever published a collection of poems in London. Yet the prizewinning work of Edwin Morgan is widely used in Scottish schools, and Sorley MacLean's work has been translated into several foreign languages. By the 1980s, a shift of the centre of gravity of poetry publishing had occurred, with Carcanet and Bloodaxe, based in northern English cities, accounting for a very high proportion of acclaimed new books. The day when one major Scottish writer, Hugh MacDiarmid, languished out of print for years on end, and another, Edwin Muir, relied on the recognition of his quality by T.S. Eliot at Faber, were clearly over. The power of the 'metropolis' in British poetry had significantly weakened. This corresponded to the political weakening of the London centre with the end of empire.

*7.71* In the twentieth century there has, in fact, been a conflict of two forces within British culture – one centripetal, making for a greater standardization of language and attitudes, the other centrifugal, involving the assertion of national and regional differences within the United Kingdom.

*7.72* Arguably, imperialism was at its apogee in Britain not before 1914, but from the 1920s through to the 1950s (see Mackenzie, 1984). Geographically the empire was larger than ever. The colonial civil service expanded markedly. And new means of communication – the aeroplane and, above all, radio – drew metropolis and possessions closer. While BBC broadcasts to the empire radiated the metropolitan viewpoint abroad, the BBC at home disseminated the 'BBC accent'. Such eminent Victorians as Gladstone and Tennyson, as early gramophone records show, had strong regional accents (Lancashire and Lincolnshire respectively). Now the bland BBC voice became the badge of respectability.

*7.73* Furthermore, as you saw in Block 3, there was a strong drive in education to elevate *English* literature from the 1920s – to impose a canon of Oxbridge approved 'classics' on the captive audiences in schools and universities. It is no accident that 'Hugh MacDiarmid' (the pen-name of C.M. Grieve) began a crusade on behalf of Scottish culture at just that time, nor that one of his chosen platforms was the *Scottish Educational Journal.*

*7.74* Of MacDiarmid's most important contemporaries in the so-called 'Scottish Renaissance' (a label attached to a very divergent body of work by men who often disagreed strongly with each other), the novelist Neil Gunn wrote in Standard English, as did the poet Muir. But 'Lewis Grassic Gibbon' (J.L. Mitchell) wrote fiction in modified Scots, and – perhaps, in the long run, most momentously – Sorley MacLean proved that Gaelic could be the vehicle for powerful poetry fully engaged with contemporary politics and society.

*7.75* An important outcome of MacDiarmid's renaissance was the growing widespread adoption of a pluralistic view of language and culture in Scotland. MacLean's first pamphlet was produced jointly with Robert Garioch (1909–81), who wrote in Lowland Scots (*Seventeen Poems for Sixpence*, 1940). But neither was necessarily more 'radical' or more 'Scottish' in attitude towards language than their friend Norman MacCaig (*b.*1910), Edinburgh-born but of Gaelic extraction, whose work is in elegant Standard English. The existence of fully accepted alternatives makes Standard English itself experimental! Other poets who have followed through the breach made by MacDiarmid include Edwin Morgan (*b.*1920), who writes as he pleases, in English, Scots and languages of his own invention.

*7.76* Morgan's 'First Men in Mercury' can be read as a witty parable about language and imperialism. There are two voices. The leader of the Earth men seeks to communicate with the Mercurians. At the outset, his Standard English is calm and assured:

> – We come in peace from the third planet.
> Would you take us to your leader?
>
> – Bawr stretter! Bawr. Bawr. Stretterhawl?
>
> – This is a little plastic model
> of the solar system, with working parts.

You are here and we are there and we
are now here with you, is this clear?

– Gawl horrop. Bawr. Abawrhannahanna!

Faced with Mercurian truculence, the Earth man moves into pidgin:

– I am the yuleeda. You see my hands,
we carry no benner, we come in peace.
The spaceways are all stretterhawn.

– Glawn peacemen all horrahanna tantko!
Tan come at 'mstrossop. Glawp yuleeda!

– Atoms are peacegawl in our harraban.
Menbat worrabost from tan hannahanna.

Eventually it is the Mercurian who speaks assuredly, the Earth man who mouths gutturally:

– Banghapper now! Yes, third planet back.
Yuleeda will go back blue, white, brown
nowhanna! There is no more talk.

– Gawl han fasthapper?

– No. You must go back to your planet.
Go back in peace, take what you have gained
but quickly.

– Stretterworra gawl, gawl...

– Of course, but nothing is ever the same,
now is it? You'll remember Mercury.

(Morgan, 1982, pp.259-60)

*7.77* This represents in miniature, one might say, the process (to be seen at work in Block 6 of this course) by which the colonized learn to handle the English language better than their increasingly muddled and demoralized former masters. But the poem also suggests the situation in Morgan's home city, Glasgow, where a proletarian version of Scots is spoken which the English (and even many Scots) profess to find uncouth and incomprehensible.

*7.78* Attempts to impose 'BBC Standard' through the educational system, on Glaswegians (or Geordies, or Liverpudlians, or Aberdonians) replicate the efforts of British colonialists educating élites to serve them in Africa. Nothing brings out the ruler-ruled factors of distance and domination better than the following poem in Glaswegian by Tom Leonard (*b.*1944):

**Unrelated Incidents**
(3)
this is thi
six a clock
news thi
man said n
thi reason
a talk wia
BBC accent
iz coz yi
widny wahnt
mi ti talk
aboot thi
trooth wia
voice lik
wanna yoo

scruff. if
a toktaboot
thi trooth
lik wanna yoo
scruff yi
widny thingk
it wuz troo.
jist wanna yoo
scruff tokn.
thirza right
way ti spell
ana right way
ti tok it. this
is me tokn yir
right way a
spellin. this
is ma trooth.
yooz doant no
thi trooth
yirsellz cawz
yi canny talk
right. this is
the six a clock
nyooz. belt up.

So resistance to the south-eastern metropolis within the United Kingdom is not by any means conducted solely in the surviving Celtic languages.

*7.79* Nevertheless, Sorley MacLean's work in Gaelic bears with special emphasis on our theme of 'end of empire'. From the sixteenth century, the drive of rulers in London (and Edinburgh) against Celtic cultures in the British Isles wore an aspect of cultural genocide. You may remember from the Open University course A205 *Culture and Belief in Europe 1450–1600* the animus displayed by that pioneer of Standard English, Edmund Spenser, against the Gaels whose land he was stealing in Ireland. At about the same time, James VI of Scotland attempted to colonize Lewis, in the Gaelic-speaking Hebrides, with Lowlanders. As Scottish Gaelic-speakers see their own history, they were deprived of their land, through the nineteenth century 'clearances' of people in favour of sheep and deer, by English and Anglicized capitalists, following which attempts to extirpate Gaelic culture intensified. Through acculturation and emigration Gaelic, a language once spoken over most of Scotland, is now reduced to some 80,000 speakers, chiefly resident in the Isles. Gaels find it easy to compare the fate of their people with those of West Indian Caribs, North American Indians and Australian Aborigines. Sorley MacLean, as the most famous of living writers in Gaelic, therefore represents not only a poetic tradition, but also direct resistance to capitalist imperialism. To use the language is to reject the empire and the muscle-bound metropolitan state which has survived it.

*7.80* But that cannot be the only reason for using it. Protest can be expressed in English. Through that medium it will reach more readers. Why should a small language have any right to survive? What would be lost if it disappeared? After all, tongues spoken across the whole landmass from Ireland to Bangladesh have evolved from one used in the Volga basin less than 5,000 years ago. During that relatively brief time uncountable languages have died out as the groups which have used them have succumbed to new or more successful cultures. Even endurance into the age of print technology did not preserve Cornish – or Pruzzian, which was spoken in part of Eastern Europe until the eighteenth century.

*7.81* Pruzzian was commemorated by the German writer Joannes Bobrowski (1917–65) in a poem which seems (to me) largely to answer my question. The italicized words are among the surviving fragments of that tongue:

**Dead Language**

He with the beating wings
outside who brushes the door,
that is your brother, you hear him.
*Laurio* he says, water,
a bow, colourless, deep.

He came down with the river,
drifting around mussel
and snail, spread like a fan
on the sand and was green.

*Warne* he says and *wittan*,
the crow has no tree,
I have the power to kiss you,
I dwell in your ear.

Tell him you do not
want to listen -
he comes, an otter, he comes
swarming like hornets, he cries,
a cricket, he grows with the marsh
under your house, he whispers
in the well, *smordis* you hear,
your black alder will wither,
and die at the fence tomorrow.

*7.82* What Bobrowski's poem suggests powerfully is that in our modern environments we are haunted by extinct languages. Only an extreme sentimentalist could argue that one language alone is appropriate to any one environment. But the fact is that cultures abiding for some time do create a language especially for the settled place. This has important implications for literature, especially for poetry. As a poet from Orkney, George Mackay Brown, has put it:

> If words become functional ciphers merely, as they are in white papers and business letters, they lose their 'ghosts' – the rich aura that has grown about them from the start, and grows infinitesimally richer every time they are spoken. They lose more; they lose their 'kernel', the sheer sensuous relish of utterance ... We are in danger of contenting ourselves with husks. For example, nowadays we say 'it rains'. The old Orkneymen had a range of words for every kind and intensity of rain – a driv, a rug, a murr, a hagger, a dagg, a rav, a hellyiefer. This is a measure of how language has coarsened in a generation or two.
>
> (Brown, 1973, pp.21–2)

*7.83* *A fortiori*, Mackay Brown's point applies to Gaelic. To lose the language would be to lose not only the Gaels' sense of their own history and culture which is conveyed in its oral and sung traditions, but also the meaning of places, the 'character' of landscapes. MacLean's distinction had been not only to conserve but to extend the significance of Gaelic; to give tradition and locality new 'aura', and language fresh purchase on experience.

**Grasping Gaelic**

*ACTIVITY*

Now please read the following poems by Sorley MacLean: 'The Turmoil', 'Kinloch Ainort', 'Heroes', 'Death Valley', 'A Spring', 'She to Whom I Gave ...'. 'The Turmoil' is reprinted in the Poetry Anthology; you will find the other poems in the Broadcast and Cassette Notes, where both Gaelic and English versions are printed (the English versions are by MacLean himself).

As you read, please consider the following questions:

(a) Looking at the Gaelic, do you see patterns in the verse which are not reproduced in English – likely assonance, for instance?

(b) What strikes you about MacLean's handling of landscape?

## *DISCUSSION*

Audio-cassette 3 Side 1, in which Sorley MacLean is recorded in conversation about these poems with Iain Crichton Smith, should enable you to check your own answers to these question against two cardinal authorities. (Crichton Smith is a most distinguished poet and novelist in both Gaelic and English. His translation of MacLean's book *Dain do Eimhir*, published in 1970, was a landmark in MacLean's belated public recognition.) But before you listen to the cassette, you probably need to know more about MacLean and the Gaelic which he uses.

---

*7.84* MacLean was born in 1911 in Osgaig, a small township on the Isle of Raasay, adjacent to Skye, the larger island where he went to school. His childhood was dominated by a majestic landscape. The woods of Raasay and the peaks of the Cuillin Hills on Skye are as central to his poetic universe as the hills of Cumbria to Wordsworth's. His father and mother combined work on a small croft with a tailoring business. The latter was severely hit by the great depression of the 1930s, and the family's relative poverty had a powerful effect on MacLean's early life. He studied English literature, not Celtic, at Edinburgh University because it offered better job prospects, and after he took a first class degree, he trained as a teacher so that he could help to support his family, rather than going to Oxford and Cambridge as a research student. He returned to Skye as a teacher, then moved on to the Isle of Mull, and then back to Edinburgh in 1939. In late 1940 he entered the Army. He was wounded three times in the North African campaign – the third experience at the Battle of El Alamein ended his war, since many of the bones in his feet were broken. After convalescence he returned to teaching English in Edinburgh, but in 1956 he went as headmaster to Plockton Secondary School in Wester Ross, a post from which he retired in 1972. For the greater part of his life, he was a hard-pressed and devoted teacher. Most of his poetry was produced in his twenties and thirties, during a long-term crisis when love affairs and politics tortured him equally.

*7.85* MacLean was powerfully affected in the 1930s by his admiration for the poetry in Scots of Hugh MacDiarmid, whose close friend he became. Just as MacDiarmid brought into the faltering tradition of Scots verse the consciousness – philosophical and political – of avant-garde Europe, so MacLean revolutionized Gaelic poetry.

*7.86* Gaelic, of which there are Scots and Irish variants, has the longest continuous literary tradition of any European tongue. It was in no sense a primitive or undeveloped medium.

*7.87* Elaborate verse forms and complex patterns of rhyming (both internal rhyme and end-rhyme) were nourished by a very rich vocabulary. Its lexicon was adequate, in the 1930s, to express a modern consciousness: 'I've invented a neologism once or twice, but very few', MacLean has said (in Ross and Hendry, 1986, p.216). It would seem, though, that MacLean's handling of the tongue owes less to his deep reading in the published Gaelic tradition of 'high' poetry than to oral influences.

*7.88* Though MacLean cannot sing, his family were musically gifted. From his earliest years he was devoted to the songs of his people. 'I am convinced', he wrote, 'that Scottish Gaelic song is the chief artistic glory of the Scots, and of all people of Celtic speech, and one of the greatest artistic glories of Europe'. He referred, in particular, to the songs 'of the two and a half centuries between 1550 and 1800 – the songs in which ineffable melodies rise like exhalations from the rhythms and resonances of the words'. He detected in them 'the simultaneous creation of words and music' *(Ris a' Bhruthaich,* 1985, p.106). You will notice, listening to the audio-cassette, that his manner of reading his verse is highly declamatory. Many who have heard him have found the sound of his verse immensely moving, though they are without Gaelic. It has been inferred that he wrote poetry of such oral power precisely because, frustratingly, he could not sing. Yeats, whose verse certainly influenced MacLean, also declaimed his verse in an incantatory fashion, and was 'tone deaf'.

*7.89* Another important influence on MacLean was the Free Presbyterian Church, dominant in the Gaelic-speaking areas after it split from the Free Church of Scotland in 1893. Though at a very early age MacLean rejected its doctrines in favour of socialism, he defends it against Lowlanders and others who sneer at its strict practices, which include a complete prohibition of social and private pleasures on Sunday. Unaccompanied Gaelic psalm singing, fiercely passionate, is a feature of Free Presbyterian worship and MacLean has paid tribute to the powerful tradition of Gaelic preaching. Scholars have shown that much of his own poetry is saturated in the vocabulary of this strenuous, sincere and deeply emotional tradition.

*ACTIVITY*

Now please listen to Audio-cassette 3 Side 1. I hope you will find that it brings to life the poetry which you have looked at on the page, and that it helps you to grasp some of the differences between Gaelic and English which affect MacLean's translation of his own work, as well as elucidating particular references which may have puzzled you. Perhaps the best plan, if you have time, will be to listen to the whole cassette once, and then go through it again, stopping and restarting as you take notes on particular points.

The discussion of the poems in the Broadcast and Cassette Notes will deal with them only as they appear in English.

## Conclusion to Section 7

*ACTIVITY*

Please now read Heaney's essay, 'Englands of the mind', in the Reader, pages 250–7. Let's consider the details of Heaney's account of how the acknowledgement of Britain's loss of imperial power is registered by these poets, outlined in the second paragraph of his essay (Reader, pp.250–1). Please read this paragraph carefully.

In what ways does Heaney see England as a literary and linguistic, as well as historical and political, entity for Larkin, Hughes and Hill? You should consider Harrison and MacLean in your answer, even though Heaney does not discuss either of them in this essay.

How does Heaney see Larkin, Hughes and Hill as manifesting a post-colonial mentality?

(Note: Donald Davie and Tom Paulin discuss Heaney's essay in Radio 10

*Englands of the Mind?*. It would be useful for you to listen to this programme before you do this activity.)

## *DISCUSSION*

It is the weight of a native literary tradition with its particular linguistic and stylistic forms which is manifested in the poetry of Larkin, Hill and Hughes. This literary canon acts as a culturally determining presence, often subject to irony and detachment, but nevertheless carrying the weight of deep attachments, loyalties and even duty:

> All of them return to an origin and bring something back, all three live off the hump of the English poetic achievement, all three, here and now, in England, imply a continuity with another England, there and then. All three are hoarders and shorers of what they take to be the real England.
>
> (Reader, p.250)

In that last phrase, 'the real England', you will remember the discussion of the appeal to the past made by the Georgian poets as described by Angus Calder in Block 3. The sense of a clearer identity existing in the past is itself a symptom of unease as well as a cause of nostalgia for the historical role of Britain as a colonizing power. This can be found in the quest for power and earthiness in Hughes, the blood and violence of Hill, or the mixture of frank vernacular and Augustan gentility in Larkin. Harrison seems to resist the imposition of a sense of order from within language itself. He asserts his ability as a poet, a craftsman of words, to defy linguistic imposition by challenging the mastery of Received Pronunciation and, by implication, challenging all forms of national dominant culture. Similarly MacLean's poetry challenges the linguistic and cultural control of one people over another.

Heaney also argues that the anxious desire to assert a regional difference, an identity detached from any centre, identifies these poets most closely with the mentality of the colonized rather than the colonizer. As an Irish poet, Heaney is in a good position to understand this:

> All three treat England as a region – or rather treat their region as England – in different and complementary ways. I believe they are afflicted with a sense of history that was once the peculiar affliction of the poets of other nations who were not themselves natives of England but who spoke the English language. The poets of the mother culture, I feel, are now possessed of that defensive love of their territory which was once shared only by those poets whom we might call colonial – Yeats, MacDiarmid, Carlos Williams.
>
> (Reader, pp.250–1)

It is paradoxical that this post-colonial, or rather colonized, consciousness is now registered in those writers of the once imperial, colonizing nation. The self-questioning that results is a frequent preoccupation of their work. In an entirely different way, it is also the preoccupation of those poets under discussion in Block 6.

---

*7.90* The Indian critic, M.G. Ramanan, also sees the work of Larkin and Hughes in imperial terms, but with a different emphasis:

> Indeed, it has been argued that Larkin and Hughes together make up what one might call a composite British poet, if such a creature were possible. One is soft, Norman French, concerned, nostalgic: the other is tough, Anglo-Saxon, assertive, imposing. One represents British gentility, the other British

> 'masculinity', virtues appropriate to the Imperial character. What Larkin in his neutral and modest way seems to be saying is that it is a pity the soldiers could not be maintained and had to be brought back from their duties abroad. What Hughes seems to be saying is that this is no time for self-pity or nostalgia. This is the time to assert ourselves as we did in the good old days of empire. Hughes's violent imagery is closely aligned with authoritarian politics, while Larkin's poetry is aligned with that other side of British society – the side which says 'keep England British'. Together these two poets are saying in their different ways the same thing. One does it with a smile, the other with anger. Together they are broadly representative of post-colonial British society, and together they represent the Anglo-Saxon, Norman French bases of English against which a Seamus Heaney, a R.S. Thomas or a Rushdie has to contend.
>
> (Ramanan, 1985, p.67)

*7.91* Ramanan's is a less subtle thesis than Heaney's, but is interesting to consider, given the critic's vantage-point. Like the criticism of John Lucas and Stan Smith, Heaney and Ramanan offer ways of understanding recent poetry through a historical context that takes into account the end of empire.

*7.92* I shall end this study guide by referring to a different perspective on the end of empire by a black British poet who came to England from the Caribbean in 1948.

## *ACTIVITY*

Please read James Berry's 'On an Afternoon Train from Purley to Victoria, 1955', reprinted in the Poetry Anthology.

*7.93* You will be examining the work of Caribbean poets in Block 6 but Berry's poem registers the end of empire in terms of Black British experience. End of empire in the writing we have examined by Larkin, Hill, Hughes and Harrison is mediated in terms of insecurity and loss. Yet the alienation which empire imposed upon the post-colonial consciousness was, and is still, a legacy of our culture, a facet of existence for many in our society, as you will find when you read the short story by Sam Selvon and the excerpt from one of his novels in the Prose Anthology. If the decline of empire created an insecurity about national identity in Hill, Hughes and Larkin, how much more profoundly did it and does it affect other British poets such as Berry, who have known life in post-imperial Britain from a different viewpoint. Thinking back to Larkin's 'At Grass', consider how that innocent faith in an eternal British hegemony, implied by the Quaker woman in Berry's poem, can seem painfully, if innocently, inhuman.

# 8 References

AHMAD, A. (1989) '"Third World Literature" and the Nationalist Ideology', *Journal of Arts and Ideas*, nos.17–18.

ALDINGTON, R. (ed.) (1950) *Selected Letters: D.H. Lawrence*, Penguin.

ALLEN, G.O. (1955) 'Structure, symbol and theme in E.M. Forster's *A Passage to India*' in SHAHANE, V.A. (ed.) (1968) *Perspectives on E.M. Forster's 'A Passage to India'*, Barnes and Noble.

ALVAREZ, A. (1966) *The New Poetry*, Penguin (first published 1962).

AMIS, K. (1956) *A Case of Samples: poems, 1946–1956*, Victor Gollancz.

AMIS, K. (ed.) (1988) *The Amis Anthology*, Hutchinson.

ARCHER, W. (1917) *India and the Future*, Hutchinson.

BELL, R. (ed.) (1989) *The Best of Scottish Poetry*, Chambers.

BOBROWSKI, J. and BIENEK, H. (1971) *Selected Poems*, Penguin.

BRADBURY, M. (ed.) (1970) *E.M. Forster 'A Passage to India': a casebook*, Macmillan.

BRADBURY, M. and McFARLANE, J. (eds) (1976) *Modernism*, Penguin.

BROWN, G.M. (1973) *An Orkney Tapestry*, Quartet.

BURKE, P. (1977) 'Tradition and experience: the idea of decline from Bruni to Gibbon' in BOWERSTOCK, G.W., CLIVE, J. and GRAMBAND, S.R. (eds) *Edward Gibbon and the Decline and Fall of the Roman Empire*, Harvard University Press.

CHANDRA, B., MUKHERJEE, M., MUKHERJEE, A., PANIKKAR, K.N. and MAHAJAN, S.(1989) *India's Struggle for Independence 1857–1947*, Penguin.

CONQUEST, R. (ed.) (1956) *New Lines: an anthology*, Macmillan.

CONQUEST, R. (ed.) (1963) *New Lines II: an anthology*, Macmillan.

CONRAD, J. (1973) *Heart of Darkness*, Penguin (first published 1899).

DAS, G.K. (1977) *E.M. Forster's India*, Macmillan.

DAVIE, D. (1952) *Purity of Diction in English Verse*, Chatto.

DAVIE, D. (1973) *Thomas Hardy and British Poetry*, Routledge and Kegan Paul.

DAVIE, D. (1989) *Under Briggflatts: a history of poetry in Great Britain 1960–88*, Carcanet.

DRAPER, A. (1981) *Amritsar: the massacre that ended the Raj*, Cassell.

DUNN, D. (1987) *Under the Influence: Douglas Dunn on Philip Larkin*, Edinburgh University Library.

EAGLETON, T. (1983) *Literary Theory: an introduction*, Blackwell.

ENRIGHT, D.J. (ed.) (1958) *Poets of the 1950s: an anthology of new English verse*, Kenkyusha (first published 1955).

FAAS, E. (1980) *Ted Hughes: the unaccommodated universe*, Black Sparrow Press.

FORSTER E.M. (1962) *Aspects of the Novel*, Penguin (first published 1927).

FORSTER, E.M. (1967) *Abinger Harvest*, Penguin (first published 1936).

FRASER, G.S. (ed.) (1956) *Poetry Now: an anthology*, Faber.

FREUD, S. (trans. Strachey, J.) (1976) *The Interpretation of Dreams*, Penguin.

FURBANK, P.N. (1977) *E.M. Forster: a life, vol.1*, Secker and Warburg.

FURBANK, P.N. (1978) *E.M. Forster: a life, vol.2*, Secker and Warburg.

GARDNER, P. (ed.) (1973) *E.M. Forster: the critical heritage*, Routledge and Kegan Paul.

HAFFENDEN, J. (1981) *Viewpoints: poets in conversation with John Haffenden*, Faber.

HAMILTON, I. (1964) 'Four conversations: Philip Larkin', *London Magazine*, November, pp.71–7.

HARRISON, T. (1970) *The Loiners*, London Magazine Editions.

HARRISON, T. (1978) *From The School of Eloquence and other poems*, Rex Collings.

HARRISON, T. (1981) *Continuous: 50 sonnets from The School of Eloquence*, Rex Collings.

HARRISON, T. (1981) *U.S. Martial*, Bloodaxe.

HARRISON, T. (1984) *Palladas: poems*, Anvil Press Poetry (first published 1975).

HARRISON, T. (1985) *v.*, Bloodaxe.

HARRISON, T. (1986) *Theatre Works 1973–85*, Penguin.

HARRISON, T. (1987) *Anno Forty Two*, The Scargill Press.

HARRISON, T. (1987) *Selected Poems*, Penguin (first published 1984).

HAUGHTON, H. (1985) '"How fit a title ...": title and authority in the work of Geoffrey Hill' in ROBINSON, P. (ed.) *Geoffrey Hill: essays on his work*, Open University Press, pp.129–48.

HILL, G. (1959) *For the Unfallen: poems 1952–1958*, Deutsch.

HILL, G. (1968) *King Log*, Deutsch.

HILL, G. (1971) *Mercian Hymns*, Deutsch.

HILL, G. (1975) *Somewhere is such a Kingdom: poems 1952–1971*, with an introduction by Harold Bloom, Houghton Mifflin.

HILL, G. (1978) *Tenebrae*, Deutsch.

HILL, G. (1983) *The Mystery of the Charity of Charles Péguy*, Deutsch.

HILL, G. (1984) *The Lords of Limit: essays on literature and ideas*, Deutsch.

HILL, G. (1985) *Collected Poems*, Penguin.

HUGHES, T. (1957) *The Hawk in the Rain*, Faber.

HUGHES, T. (1960) *Lupercal*, Faber.

HUGHES, T. (1967) *Wodwo*, Faber.

HUGHES, T. (1970) *Crow*, Faber.

HUGHES, T. (1979) *Moortown*, Faber.

HUGHES, T. (1982) *Selected Poems: 1957–1981*, Faber.

HUGHES, T. (1989) *Wolfwatching*, Faber.

HUTCHINS, F.G. (1967) *The Illusion of Permanence: British Imperialism in India*, Princeton University Press.

JAMESON, F. (1988) 'Modernism and imperialism' (Field Day Pamphlet No.14) in EAGLETON, T. *et al.*, *Nationalism, Colonialism and Literature*, Field Day Theatre Company Ltd.

KIPLING, R. (1963) *A Choice of Kipling's Verse made by T.S. Eliot*, Faber.

LAGO, M. and FURBANK, P.N. (eds) (1983) *E.M. Forster: letters, vol.1 1879–1920*, Collins.

LARKIN, P. (1946) *Jill*, Faber.

LARKIN, P. (1947) *A Girl in Winter*, Faber.

LARKIN, P. (1955) *The Less Deceived*, The Marvell Press.

LARKIN, P. (1964) *The Whitsun Weddings*, Faber.

LARKIN, P. (1965) *Philip Larkin Reads 'The Whitsun Weddings'*, The Marvell Press (cassette).

LARKIN, P. (1966) *The North Ship*, Faber (first published 1945).

LARKIN, P. (ed.) (1973) *The Oxford Book of Twentieth-century English Verse*, Oxford University Press.

LARKIN, P. (1974) *High Windows*, Faber.

LARKIN, P. (1983) *Required Writing: miscellaneous pieces 1955–1982*, Faber.

LARKIN, P. (1985) *All What Jazz: a record diary 1961–1971*, Faber (first published 1970).

LARKIN, P. (1988) *Collected Poems*, Faber and The Marvell Press.

LEONARD, T. (1984) *Intimate Voices 1965–1983*, Galloping Dog Press.

LONGLEY, E. (1986) *Poetry in the Wars*, Bloodaxe.

LUCAS, J. (1986) *Modern English Poetry from Hardy to Hughes: a critical survey*, Batsford.

MACKENZIE, J. (1984) *Propaganda and Empire ... 1880–1960*, Manchester University Press.

MACLEAN, S. (trans. Crichton Smith, I.) (1970) *Poems to Eimhir*, Northern House.

MACLEAN, S. (1981) *Spring tide and Neap tide: selected poems 1932–72*, Canongate.

MACLEAN, S. (1985) *Ris a'Bhruthaich: the criticism and prose writings*, Acair.

MACLEAN, S. (1987) *Poems 1932–1982*, Iona Foundation.

MACLEAN, S. (1989) *From Wood to Ridge: collected poems*, Carcanet.

MORGAN, E. (1982) *Poems of Thirty Years*, Carcanet.

MORRISON, B. (1980) *The Movement: English poetry and fiction of the 1950s*, Methuen.

MUKHERJEE, R. (1974) *The Rise and Fall of the East India Company*, Monthly Review Press.

NORBROOK, D. (1987)'Shaggy Fellows', *London Review of Books*, vol.9, no.13, 9 July, pp.22–3.

PLUMB, J.H. (1963) *England in the Eighteenth Century*, Penguin.

PRESS, J. (1971) *A Map of Modern English Verse*, Oxford University Press.

RADICE, B. (1973) *Who's Who in the Ancient World*, Penguin.

RAMANAN, M.G. (1985) 'Macaulay's Children', *London Magazine*, February, pp.59–67.

ROSS, R.J. and HENDRY, J. (eds) (1986) *Sorley MacLean: critical essays*, Scottish Academic Press.

RUMBOLD, A. (1979) *Watershed in India 1914–1922*, Athlone Press.

RUSHDIE, S. (1984) 'Outside the Whale' in *Granta 11*.

SAGAR, K. (1975) *The Art of Ted Hughes*, Cambridge University Press.

SAID, E.W. (1978) *Orientalism*, Routledge and Kegan Paul.

SAID, E.W. (1985) 'Orientalism reconsidered' in BARKER, F. *et al.* (eds) *Europe and Its Others: proceedings of the Essex Conference on the Sociology of Literature*, July 1984, 2 vols, vol.1, pp.14–27.

SALUSINSZKY, I. (1987) *Criticism in Society*, Methuen.

SEELEY, J.R. (1883) *The Expansion of England*, Macmillan.

SMITH, S. (1982) *Inviolable Voice: history and twentieth-century poetry*, Gill and Macmillan.

STALLYBRASS, O. (ed.) (1978) *The Manuscripts of 'A Passage to India'*, Edward Arnold.

STOKES, E. (1959) *The English Utilitarians and India*, Clarendon Press.

STONE, W. (1966) *The Cave and the Mountain: a study of E.M. Forster*, Stanford University Press.

TAYLOR, J.R. (1962) *Angel and After*, Methuen.

THOMSON, D. (1950) *England in the Nineteenth Century: 1815–1914*, Penguin.

THOMPSON, E.P. (1982) *The Making of the English Working Class*, Penguin (first published 1963).

TOMLINSON, C. (1957) 'The middlebrow muse' (review of *New Lines*, ed. R. Conquest), *Essays in criticism 7*, pp.208–17.

TRILLING, L. (1970) *'A Passage to India'* in BRADBURY, M. (ed.) (1970).

VISWANATHAN, G. (1988) 'The beginnings of English literary study in British India', *Oxford Literary Review*, vol.9.

WILLIAMS, R. (1983) *Keywords*, Fontana.

WOODROFFE, J. (1919) *Is India Civilised? essays on Indian culture*, Ganesh.

WOOLF, V. (1966) 'The Novels of E.M. Forster' in *Collected Essays, vol.1*, Chatto and Windus.

## Acknowledgements

Grateful acknowledgement is made to the following for permission to repoduce material in this book:

Davie, D. (1972) *Collected Poems 1950–70*, Routledge and Kegan Paul, © Donald Davie; Forster, E.M. (1989) *A Passage to India*, Penguin, reproduced by kind permission of The Provost and Scholars of King's College, Cambridge; Stallybrass, O. (1978) *The Manuscripts of 'A Passage to India'*, Edward Arnold, reproduced by kind permission of The Provost and Scholars of King's College, Cambridge; extracts from *Collected Poems* by Philip Larkin, reprinted by permission of Faber and Faber Ltd; extracts from *Selected Poems 1957–1981* by Ted Hughes, reprinted by permission of Faber and Faber Ltd/Harper and Row Inc.; extract from *The Hawk in the Rain* by Ted Hughes, reprinted by permission of Faber and Faber Ltd/Harper and Row Inc.; extract from *Spring Tide and Neap Tide* by Sorley MacLean, reprinted by permission of Canongate Press; extracts from 'First Men in Mercury' in *Poems of Thirty Years* by Edwin Morgan, reprinted by permission of Carcanet Press Ltd; extract from 'Unrelated Incidents' in *Intimate Voices 1965–1983* by Tom Leonard, reprinted by permission of Tom Leonard; 'Dead Language' from *Selected Poems* by Bobrowski and Bienek, translated by Matthew and Ruth Mead, reprinted by permission of Matthew Mead/Deutsche Verlags-Anstalt.

**Block 1 Introduction**
**Block 2 The Impact of Modernism**
**Block 3 'Englishness'**
**Block 4 Literature and Ideology**
**Block 5 End of Empire**
**Block 6 New Writings in English**
**Block 7 Language and Gender**
**Block 8 Literature and History**

Cover illustration: Imperial Assembly of India at Delhi; the ViceRegal procession passing the Clock Tower and Delhi Institute, 1877. Mansell Collection.